My Experiments With Unleashing People Power

My Experiments With Unleashing People Power

K K Sinha

BLOOMSBURY

LONDON • NEW DELHI • NEW YORK • SYDNEY

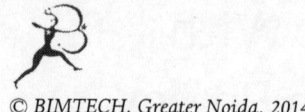

© *BIMTECH, Greater Noida, 2014*

First Published, 2014

BLOOMSBURY PUBLISHING INDIA PVT. LTD.
London   New Delhi   New York   Sydney

ISBN: 978-93-82951-48-3

10 9 8 7 6 5 4 3 2

Published by Bloomsbury Publishing India Pvt. Ltd.
Vishrut Building, DDA Complex, Building No. 3
Pocket C-6 & 7, Vasant Kunj
New Delhi 110 070

Laser Typeset by FORTUNE GRAPHICS
WZ-911/2, Shankarlal Street, Ring Road, Naraina, New Delhi

Printed at Replika Press Pvt. Ltd.

Dedicated to
my daughter Suvira Shyamlee
who has always been an inspiration

Contents

Foreword

MY EXPERIMENTS WITH UNLEASHING PEOPLE POWER is a very good documentation of the details, analyses and experiential wisdom of truths as seen by a practitioner of HR.

The title *Professor* may create the impression that this book was written by an academic. But, the fact is that Professor K K Sinha got his hands dirty in the rough and tumble of the challenging arena of people management for as long as forty plus years before donning the professorial hat. The authenticity of the large number of observations in the book is grounded in the fact that the writer has walked all those miles, before he decided to talk about it.

The first fifteen years of K K Sinha's career were spent in the blazing inferno of the extremely militant trade unionism of the late sixties and early seventies, which marked the industrial relations scenario in India as a whole, and more violently in places where he worked. He has also worked in war-torn Iraq. This baptism by fire stood him in good stead when he negotiated the employee relations terrain in NTPC, after joining the company in the mid-eighties.

This book is largely based upon his experiences at NTPC, where he rose from the middle level to the level of Director (HR) and remained there for nearly eight years. NTPC provided him the scale and the variety to test out his experiments.

Professor Sinha has done a great amount of work in his long tenure as Director (HR) at NTPC and today, we are reaping the benefits of the foundation laid by him in receiving awards for *Best Employer* and *Best Place to Work For* consecutively year after year. He is, therefore, ideally placed to document his merited rise at NTPC from a middle level executive to the highest position in the HR as Director (HR).

This has made his first-hand learning experience very rich and varied. It is also a matter of great pride for me that Professor Sinha grew up in the same part of the world as I did, and was instrumental in earning his professional stripes in Ranchi, where I also went for my degree in engineering.

I am glad that in his new avatar as a professor, he has decided to pen it all down in the form of this book. I am sure that his inputs for his pupils must be very different compared to those of full-time academicians who have never worked in the field.

This reminds of an interesting quote from George Bernard Shaw's '*Man and Superman*', one of his famous plays,

Those who can, do; those who can't, teach.

But here is a book written by a teacher who has done it all.

I am sure that this book will prove very useful to those who want to understand HR in the Indian context, and want to equip themselves better to deal with the challenges being faced by the economy and industry in today's hyper-competitive, highly uncertain and globally linked management world.

New Delhi
January, 2014

Dr. Arup Roy Choudhury
Chairman and Managing Director
NTPC Ltd.

Foreword

I AM HAPPY to read parts of the book, *"My Experiments with Unleashing People Power"* by K K Sinha. I am glad to see that he has fulfilled a desire that I always had. I believe a large part of our theory in HR is built upon the practice of it by good HR leaders and mentors like K K Sinha. When we introduced the HR function in L&T in the mid seventies, we only formulated what should be done and a lot of principles. It is only in implementing very sincerely that the HR function has been built in L&T and other places. In the late eighties and nineties it was corporations like NTPC, IOC, SAIL that have shown the way of what is possible, and how much the public sector can contribute to the theoretical and practical approach of HR.

Knowing NTPC, as an organisation and also K K Sinha, I am happy that through this book he is bringing forth for the public something that is less known to them.

It was under his leadership that the first ever known competency mapping was introduced at the top levels in the late nineties in NTPC. A scientific approach to manage HRD at top levels was initiated by K K Sinha at NTPC by preparing a competency directory for all GMs and EDs. This was promptly followed by a good attempt to use the 360 degree feedback and assessment centres for appointments to senior and top levels. Though some of these initiatives did not succeed the way they should have, he did not give up. When something did not work at the senior or top levels, he quickly followed it up by trying the same at the junior levels. Senior managers and superintendent levels were chosen and ADCs and the 360 degree feedback was tried out. These were done very successfully. A large number of internal trainers and assessors for ADCs were developed. Simultaneously, Performance Management System (PMS) was revised. All other HR systems were examined, renewed or revamped periodically.

It was K K Sinha's leadership that was responsible for NTPC to think ahead in terms of talent management and create many leaders in its own way at NTPC. I had the pleasure and privilege of being associated with some of these experiments.

I am glad to see this contribution from K K Sinha. This book will make various aspects clear, such as:

- A lot is happening in PSUs in India.
- There are good leaders in the public sector and they are less talked about as they don't share their work and experiences easily.
- Leaders like K K Sinha are doing a lot in PSUs both in terms of practice and contributions towards theoretical aspects.
- Innovations in HR are possible with determined leaders like K K Sinha.
- When experiments are attempted, a lot of people develop, progress and emerge as leaders, and many have done so while working with Mr. Sinha at NTPC.

I am sure this book will make great reading for all managers, management students and faculty members. This is an important addition to our HR literature. I congratulate K K Sinha for sharing his experiments with all of us.

Dr. T.V. Rao
Ex-Professor HR, IIM – Ahmedabad &
Chairman, TV Rao Learning Systems Pvt. Ltd.

Messages

While I was Chairman of the Public Enterprises Selection Board I have had the privilege of working with K K Sinha who was then Director (Human Resources) at the National Thermal Power Corporaton in evolving human resource development process and practices in our Public Sector Undertakings. His willingness to innovate was indeed refreshing and I greatly benefitted from my interaction with him.

Mr. T.K.A. Nair
Advisor to Prime Minister

HR Policies of NTPC evolved, from the scratch, over a period, in its formative years (late seventies and early eighties). Subsequently these policies kept on getting refined and perfected with creativity and innovation in human resources development, to emerge as benchmarks, worthy of emulation. Sinha's contribution was remarkable both during the early phase of formative years and more pronounced during later years. Obviously, this book, therefore, presents the strategy, the rationale and the nuances of NTPC's HR Policies and Practices, with demonstrated outcomes, in most authentic manner.

Mr. R.V. Shahi
Former Power Secretary, Govt of India

K K Sinha's last 10 years with NTPC at the helm of affairs was a crucial period for making contributions, transforming the HR and the organization itself. A good number of experiments and innovative initiatives taken by him had indeed enthused the people, raising their commitment to contribute their best at a critical juncture, when the entire power sector, as well as the economy itself was going through a massive change. It was a remarkable professional move, leading a large multi-unit PSU to rank in the top three of the Best Employers in the country.

Padmashree Dr. Pritam Singh
Director General,
International Management Institute, Delhi

I am happy to learn that K.K. has undertaken to write his NTPC learnings where all of us together built one of the finest institutions in the power sector, which the World Bank had described as a performing organization.... Personally I had always valued KK's advice in all personnel matters, more when I had taken over as CMD in 1988 and we visited all the projects and held Open Houses with all employees and he took over the job of capturing and dealing all personal matters of each employee. We built up a team with an open system of communication. Our HR systems produced leaders in the power sector of the country, in which KK's contribution of honing these individuals has been outstanding.

Mr. P.S. Bami
Retd. Chairman and Managing Director
NTPC Ltd.

Experience is always a great teacher. Reflecting on one's own experience is an even more enriching mode of learning. Most professionals either do not have the skill or courage or time to reflect on their long professional journey. That is where Prof. K K Sinha is different from the rest and stands out for his professional commitment even after 45 years of a meaningful career in the Human Resources profession. He has not only been innovative throughout his professional career, but made innovation look simple even within a supposedly constrained environment of a giant public sector. Simplicity has always been a hallmark of Prof. Sinha. I am sure he has put it to best use in gleaning out all the learnings from everything he has done in his professional career. I hope those HR professionals who value their self-development will greatly benefit from this new gift from Prof. Sinha. I wish his endeavour all success.

Dr. Santrupt B. Misra
CEO, Carbon Black Business & Director, Group H.R.
Aditya Birla Group

NTPC is currently acknowledged as the Golden Maharatna PSU for its world class efficiency in power generation and its financial prowess among all PSUs in India. It would have not been possible without all-round transformations in HR Practices and employees' empowerment initiated by Prof. K K Sinha during his tenure as the Director (HR). He is one of the few HR professionals in India who 'imagined' about the future need of leaders in power sector and implemented succession planning, leadership development and coaching. His experience will be very useful for all those who are seeking answers to the burgeoning problem of leadership deficit in Indian Inc.

Dr. H. Chaturvedi
Director
Birla Institute of Management Technology

Lucidly written narrative based on author's practical experiences of unleashing people power in a very large business enterprise by simple but innovative human resource practices. A must read for all those who have responsibility to lead their organizations through these uncertain times.

Dr. Arvind N. Agrawal
President, Corporate Development & Human Resources
RPG Enterprises

A perfect human being, a thorough professional and an excellent teacher – Professor K K Sinha's maiden publication "My Experiments with Unleashing People Power" is surely a must read for the budding HR professionals.

Dr. A.K. Balyan
MD & CEO, Petronet LNG Ltd.

K K Sinha's experiences and learnings, the 'distilled wisdom' in the arena of Human Resources Management is indeed a delight to all those who have known him as a path breaking, sensitive and humane professional.... I have always seen him as one who travels light with no mental baggage and it is this approach of his, that is required to face the challenges of the turbulent business world which exists today, wherein, he may get the benefit of history but not be burdened by it.

Mr. Rajeev Bhadauria
Director, Group HR
Jindal Steel and Power Ltd.

It is imperative that one generation of experts pass on the baton of knowledge to the next. This is best done through experience sharing and disseminating insights. Prof. K K Sinha's book is one such baton. I commend his effort to distill his rich experience of 45 years and put them together in a format that is both reader friendly as well as highly insightful. Prof Sinha has a unique blend of experience in public sector, private sector and academia and Gurus like him have lot to share not only for next generation of HR professionals but also for seasoned ones. I feel treatise like what Prof Sinha has put together will be of immense value to all of us who are students of Human Resources.

Dr. Aquil Busrai
Chief Executive Officer
Aquil Busrai Consulting

K K Sinha has put together his rich experiences in an extraordinary book that will be beneficial for the learnings of the current and future professionals. This is a noble thought to consolidate the everyday learnings and present it to the world for everyone's benefits. K K Sinha has an incredible track record as an HR Leader and a great learner and teacher of Human Behaviour.

Mr. Rajan Dutta
President – Corporate HR
Reliance Communications Ltd.

My friend K K Sinha has dedicated his life's work to studying how people's power can help in the business growth. KK has combined his unique perspective and ringside view as a senior HR professional with his extraordinary ability to cut through complicity and identified the core people's principles and practices that leaders can immediately put into action in their own organization. A trained moral philosopher, KK has built a highly successful people's organization wherever he has engaged, especially at NTPC, where he could demonstrate his unleashing people's power by making NTPC one of the top five Best Employers, consecutively for three years, an unique achievement for a public sector undertaking. He is perhaps one of the rarest few who has the blend of industry (private and public) and academia track record and sharing of his experience would be of great value to many students of people management....

Mr. P. Dwaraknath
Ex-Director –HR
GSK and MAX India Ltd.

The field of human resources continues to increase in importance yet we're still learning how to help companies master this area. Kishore's contributions to the field has helped to advance both the science and art of talent management. I look forward to reading more about the experiments and thoughts in this area. All my best wishes.

Mr. Marc Effron
President, The Talent Strategy Group &
Author: One Page Talent Management

K K Sinha is a pioneer in the field of human resource development in the country and is credited with several ground-breaking HR initiatives and processes that have made NTPC a truly global force to reckon with. He was instrumental in making NTPC emerge as an employer of first choice in the country, breaking the myth that a PSU cannot be a great place to work for. Under his aegis, HR truly became a strategic partner and driver for growth, propelling NTPC to reach zeniths of excellence.

Mr. U.P. Pani
Director (HR), NTPC Ltd.

Kishore had the good fortune of working in both the public as well as private sectors and that too in very large and successful corporations like NTPC, India's largest power company and RIL, India's largest private Sector Corporation. He served them at very senior levels from where he could get a full view of these corporations. Now he is giving back to the society by associating with the Academics in a good institution like BIMTECH. This provides him with an excellent combination of the corporate as well as the Academic worlds. I am sure in his long journey in the corporate world, several HR professionals and business leaders are personally coached and mentored by him.

His experiences in various facets of the HR and the business world is of tremendous value. The variety, depth and quality of his work life will serve as excellent learning material for the HR professionals.

Mr. Vivek Paranjpe
Strategic HR Advisor, Reliance Industries Ltd.

I have been lucky to have known KKS since 1977, continuously learn and gain from you. Most friends share with me that you KKS stand for unending Kindness, reservoir of Knowledge and inimitable Simplicity.

He has the rare distinction of working in both public and private sectors of corporate and the Academia, covering all facets of HRM enabling Competency, Motivation and Culture at every place you worked.

His ability to reach out to people, skill to simplify complex situations and add value even in adversity are worth emulating. I am sure, the book will capture the tip of the iceberg of treasure of learnings and be of value to all.

Mr. G.P. Rao
Chief-HR & MS
Recron Malaysia Sdn Bhd

K K Sinha has been a highly respected, self achiever and role model for the HR community in the country. It is extremely important to share the "wealth of experience and career learnings" as I feel it helps co professionals – both young and grown up to have a good perspective of the professional challenges and possible learning in such situations. The excellent and long career he had in the Human Resources profession is by itself a great example for young HR professionals to emulate as best as they can. And as he is sharing his experiences and learnings in a book, it will be a tremendous source of learning for the HR fraternity and also for other business managers too... I also feel that his career over these long years in both Public Sector and Private Sector Corporates of high repute will be all the more encompassing a wholesome view of the critical role of Human Resources.

Mr. S.Y. Siddiqui
Chief Operating Officer
Administration-HR, Finance, IT & COSL
Maruti Suzuki India Ltd.

I deeply appreciate the initiative taken by K K Sinha in bringing out a book, to share his knowledge and NTPC experience after almost four and a half decades work in the profession. I am sure, this will be an asset for the future generations of HR practitioners.

Mr. R.P. Singh
Director (HR & Legal)
Indian Farmers Fertiliser Co-operative Ltd.
New Delhi

I have known KK Sinha for over two decades, as a person as well as a professional. A humble person, always ready to learn and experiment, a person who has always created new benchmarks and then further raised the bar. It has always been a pleasure to meet him, as I have always learnt from him. The book, I am sure, will be an invaluable document, for students and practitioners and will be considered a must read for them.

Dr. Yasho V. Verma
CEO, ONIDA
MIRC Electronics Ltd.

Prof. Sinha is the epitome of dignity and poise. He has lead HR for a complex and large company like NTPC and had implemented several initiatives that has put NTPC in a league of companies where HR is adding significant value to business. His book will be of immense value to Gen Y aspirants who are looking for a career in HR. I am sure each of the experience and episodes that he captures in his book will have the practical real life flavor of dealing with rainbows of behavior and situations that one can deal with only if one has a holistic perspective.

Mr. Yogi Sriram
Sr. Vice President – Corporate HR
Larsen & Toubro Ltd.

Preface

GLOBALISATION OF BUSINESS has highlighted the intensity of business competitiveness to an all time high. The new economy characterised by the predominance of service firms, the Internet revolution, global competition, etc., has placed greater reliance on intangible assets for success. In this context, human capital has become the key component for survival and success. Unleashing people power in an organisation thus becomes imperative to achieve business success in the present business environment. As a result, people management has assumed a new dimension bringing the HR function to the fore.

The function of human resource has been evolving with times as reflected in the change in the nature of roles from being supportive and an administrative function to being a strategic function. The identity of the function has also been changing from "Personnel, Labour Welfare and Industrial Relations" to "Human Resource Development" to now getting titles such as "Human Capital Management", "Talent Management/Development", etc., reflecting the shifting focus and priorities.

In over four decades of my experience in people function, I have had the good fortune to see the growth of the people function through different stages, that too in a period of mega and radical changes taking place in the 1970s and then in the 1990s, and also in the economy as a whole in India. We had to keep learning, planning and then again learning. This became a very dynamic process causing tremendous acceleration in speed of changes, consequently demanding comprehensive transformation, particularly in HR and its people processes.

This book primarily dwells upon this experience with regard to a leading company of India, NTPC Ltd. and also on some of my experiments with unleashing the vast potential of people in an organisation, during challenging times, creating a vibrant and winning organisation,

Though I have chosen the title of my book as *"My Experiments with Unleashing People Power"*, I must admit that the ideas and perspectives of a large number of my colleagues and professionals from NTPC Ltd. and also from other organisations have gone into shaping my ideas about building people power and delivering results through them. The knowledge that came to create scores of innovative initiatives and experiments, came from my team, my leaders, unions, books by thinkers in the field of contemporary HR, some other organisations with whom we benchmarked or institutions of different kinds, and perhaps many more, who directly or indirectly, contributed immensely to my learning. The only thing I did was to always keep an open mind, explore, and always be inviting and generally tolerant towards mistakes, while unleashing a culture for experimenting all over the organisation. These experiments generally from the mid-nineties at NTPC and some others at other organisations, went on to find a place in various facets of NTPC's HR, and perhaps created a benchmark for others, particularly in the power sector, and also in other erstwhile economy businesses.

However, I have chosen to write very briefly about my personal journey, an odyssey of the making of an individual into a learning organisation, through a meandering and rough lifetime.

I have divided the book into four sections. Beyond this odyssey and connected to it, are four parts of the book, holding hands with each other in an intimacy of relationship, seamlessly repeating some at times for the genuine purpose of providing a rhythm of the song of learning, woven in and around the HR model created and used by us, that had been so circular, for the purpose of causing a natural and seamless overlap, that is dynamic, self-repeating, and in a self renewal movement. Obviously, this model has potential to survive, and therefore, the impact and process of renewals can survive, but for long in its inertia, if not lost till infinity, howsoever short. These have been laid out in the narrative, a treatise on our simple and ordinary looking experiments on human resources, kindling and unleashing the people power, that have been delivered.

Part I covers the changing business imperatives which have brought HR to the centre-stage and the common success factors, which provide the context for formulating and implementing HR strategies. **Part II** deals with the growth of people function over the years, particularly in India. **Part III** discusses certain contemporary people management themes narrating my experiences with each of them in the course of my work, as well as interaction with management experts and academicians. The concluding **Part IV** covers briefly, my assessment of the function in the days to come along-with expectations from HR practitioners in terms of their competencies.

As India is all set to become an economic superpower as predicted by a number of studies at the global level, the need for total development of the country's large pool of manpower in the corporate sector has become pertinent. It is rightly said that "A nation is as strong as its people!" Indians' are amazing, possess unfathomable strength and they can deliver, if honestly empowered, unleashed, and also supported by value development inputs, with a better quality of national polity, so significant in a large democracy like ours.

Through these pages, an attempt has been made to demonstrate of practices in a leading business organisation, to delineate the outline of such a blueprint with simple little initiatives for the organisations for unleashing people power, and understand how HR practitioners can leverage the capabilities of human assets to create business excellence, thereby contributing to the growth and prosperity of the nation.

K K Sinha

Acknowledgements

I NEVER THOUGHT that I would ever be able to write a book!

In 2005, when I was leaving NTPC, Indranil and Kanhaiyaji gave me this idea, and also structured some of the major steps taken by us during my eight years as Director on the Board of NTPC. Going from NTPC to Reliance Energy, Reliance Infocom and Reliance Industries, was a learning experience that I had never imagined. The scale, the world there and the fast pace, all of this left me with no time at all and the idea of writing anything vanished into oblivion. When I was at Jindals, the same pattern continued. There was so much to do and no time, at all! I would tell myself, "May be when I join a Business School–BIMTECH". It was some excuse or the other, and more than two years passed. It was Dr. Chaturvedi, our Director at BIMTECH, who kept on pushing me repeatedly as to why I was not penning down my experiences. He has been a motivator. And then once I was discussing with Suvira, my daughter and subsequently also during some of the telephone calls, she simply used to say, "Please put it down Papa as it may become obsolete, by the time it comes out."

The challenge was before me when I decided to sit down, but time always eluded me. I have been trying to pen down my thoughts and sometimes I have been very specific and personal, but later started finding a flow, a rhythm.

I would put down a few pages after my Santoor session in the morning. My feeble memory became a major handicap. While I had feelings, all recorded perfectly in my mind, the facts got jumbled up. I came out with some of these feelings, only a few pebbles of learnings and experiments. Some of them in today's context or even in the process of development, or mostly in brick and mortar industry may sound obsolete, and old, but they were all innovations and experiments, I recall, that delivered success.

I am immensely indebted to most of my friends who helped me compile this book. It does not seem very easy for me to acknowledge, each one, who contributed to this book from the beginning, or even as the ideas started coming in, shared with me but, I remembered to acknowledge all those who were partners in my quest for knowledge, and taught me all the time. This essentially gets mentioned next, in my odyssey, which is not a biography as such, but a treatise that speaks about the making of a lifelong learner and is useful and respectful through big and small initiatives, though sounding mundane, but impactful. This was possible only with the support of many of the NTPC senior colleagues, who so affectionately led me and guided me, my numerous peers and board colleagues who supported me, and the dearest are my team members who worked fervently and innovatively with me. I do not wish to make this list very small by attempting to mention a few only in my acknowledgements, here. But I can't forget to express my deep sense of indebtedness and gratitude to all of them.

An immense learning and guidance came my way, as I kept practicing HR, from M.R.R. Nair, P.S. Bami, Rajendra Singh, R.V. Shahi, C.P. Jain and Pran Nath, and also the Dronas and Eklavyas like Dr. Udai Pareek, and Dr. T.V. Rao, who had been my gurus every step of the way in my professional life and I would always feel deeply indebted, professionally and personally, to these teachers in my life. The support of my colleagues, and Directors on the Board has been immense particularly like B.N. Ojha, Narsimharamulu, Chandan Roy, R.S. Sharma, Shankarlingam, R.D. Gupta, A.K. Singhal and many more, and it was exciting to note and enjoy their deep love and support for people, which enabled me to seek ideas, consent and execution.

Much more learning used to flow from the few and famous professionals coming on the Board with me as colleague Directors like Dr. Pradeep Khandwala, Dr. Deepak Parikh, and Nobel Laureate Dr. R.K. Pachauri. They were always supportive on people development and very encouraging. Knowledge and learning descended incessantly. It was indeed a matter of great pride to be learning from them.

Immense training and learning also came from all my professional colleagues I served with in various organisations, and all the trade unions, their central leaders like Passey, Pandhe, Y.D., Gaya Singh, Reddy, Agghi, M.N. Jha, Debroy and all the great men in our executive and supervisory associations of NTPC, who always lent their love and support, made way and also stood by me for my experiments in the organisation and in my life. Their immense honest listening, understanding, and support from innumerable team members from NEFI, during the eventful last 10/12 years, were particularly memorable and a huge enabler in building relationships and a very supportive environment.

I recall incessant help and support from Indranil, Kanhaiya, Sunil Trivedi, Dinesh Aggarwal, Neeraj and above all from my HRD heroes Nagakumar and Ashok Swarup who always built me as my reverse mentors indeed. I cannot however, forget the keen support of all business unit/station heads and all the line teams with all their passion, and my business HR heads and total team HR all over, for so willingly and with so much excitement furthering HR for the NTPC family.

I, in the process of writing this book, have obviously taken a lot of inputs from NTPC and feel very grateful to the organisation and colleagues there, for providing relevant materials and some facts and figures to refer herein. I, in all humility, testify that the references made with regard to NTPC on all the pages of the book have also been based on my own memory and information, as I have been very intimately associated with this organisation in various capacities starting from Chief Personnel Manager to Director (HR), and am equally responsible for these references.

I am also indebted to the current Chairman and Managing Director of NTPC, Dr. Arup Roy Choudhury for his support and encouragement as I shared this project and for him readily agreeing to give a foreword to my humble creation. So has been the ready support flowing from U.P. Pani, the young, sensitive and very energetic Director (HR) there now, for which I shall remain grateful. I would like to extend my sincere gratitude to Prof. Manujata and Dr. Rahul Singh, my colleagues in BIMTECH, for extending their support in editing and publishing. I am also very grateful to Suresh Gopal of Bloomsbury India, who has been ever supportive and so persuasive for completing the book for release and on top of it and also asking for a couple of more, on which I have been working. Jyoti Mehrotra of Bloomsbury India has helped in editing the book and I am

Acknowledgements | xxvii

immensely grateful to her tremendous support in caring and improving the presentation, yet retaining simplicity, providing informal and colloquial style.

I have always felt hugely indebted to my wife, Chitra, who has always been extremely supportive and protective, and who has guided me in various aspects of my life and profession. I have always felt she could have done much better and been more successful as an HR Professional, than I have been.

I am also immensely grateful for all the intellectual support extended by my daughter Suvira, whose incessant showering of wisdom has always acted as valuable as rain, whenever I needed.

K K Sinha

My Learnings...The Odyssey

HOW THINGS EVOLVED and this journey taught me the first lesson that HR needs to be continuously transforming itself, and perhaps faster than the speed of the changing times itself.

I was born on 8th October 1945, at my maternal home in Dumka, Santhal Pargana, Bihar (now Jharkhand). My Father's family was based in Bishunpur, a village near the Himalayan river Lakhandei, which witnessed regular floods and where a respectable yield was mostly a dream. My Father was the only living child, with his siblings having fallen prey to an infamous plague catastrophe. He was a commerce graduate, and like the youth of that period, did not hold on to a job for long. He jumped into the struggle of independence that culminated in the Quit India movement, with the British Police often on the lookout for such record holders! There was obviously a dirth of jobs during the British rule, and my father was faced with the challenge to support a large family! Then came our independence in 1947 and it appeared, for a while, that things would change for the better. But the economic struggle continued as the main resource was whatever farming my father could manage on the land often struck by floods or drought. Upright and brave, Father finally got a job with the Bank of Bihar in 1950 and was appointed as a Manager in various branches of Siwan (Chapra), Laheria Sarai (Darbhanga), etc., over the years. A well known and imposing personality known for his strong values and principles, he left his mark wherever he operated, be it the society, the public he served or his own family. My family comprised seven siblings, me being sixth in the order. Having studied in the village till middle school, I shifted to Ranchi, a town, which was then a centre for good education. Father envisioned his children to pursue good education and gathered all of us, one by one, and guided us towards a better future based on learning.

In the village school, the Gandhi pattern of learning, known as the "multipurpose school", was followed, where learning was profound, liberating and multidimensional. We had the first four classes within the confines of classrooms, reading the text, Math, History, Geography, General Science, Hindi, and Sanskrit (no English), and the remaining half of the day was spent in learning thread making, cloth weaving, carpet weaving, cultivation, carpentry and a little bit of plumbing. There were no electrical workshops in school as there was no electricity in the village, which I understood much later. So, these 6–7 initial years in the village school perhaps helped us attain learning and skills that could give, if not an avocation, at least confidence that one could be self reliant in the process of survival. The biggest achievement during this period was perhaps, the realisation of the depth of conviction in human values that guided, as an ever robust lighthouse, to reach the very destination. I still recall the commitment, sincerity and dedication of our teachers in school, who would drive, encourage and want us to become like Gandhi, Nehru and Patel.

Every morning at four, all children were made to assemble under a huge tree in the middle of the village and sing songs and prayers in the so called Prabhat Pheri, moving from alley to alley, tola to tola, and house to house, waking up people with morning messages! I recall when Panchet Lama and Pandit Nehru were to come to Nalanda, most students of the school walked all the way to Nalanda (the Historical University campus) to get a glimpse… shouting nationalist slogans and singing patriotic songs all the way from the village! I also remember a call for shramdaan, inviting students to go on a month long camp to Farakka in West Bengal, where a huge earthen barrage was being constructed over river Ganga. Perhaps thousands, or maybe even lakhs of school and college students from all over the country came in rotation for Shramdaan. How excited and inspired everyone felt, working together, for a purpose, a vision for the country! It was a junoon. Nothing seemed difficult and definitely not at all impossible. Later, when I was passing over the Farakka Barrage while working in NTPC in the 1980s, it did not look as mega size as we had seen then, but made me extremely proud and happy to see and feel great about our little contributions towards the construction of the barrage!

During that period, Father was posted to the Ranchi Branch, which was not as rural as some earlier locations. He decided to get the family over from the village. In Ranchi, which was considered to be a very good education hub, he got me admitted to a Jesuit's Mission school, St. John's, with some difficulty (English was a total challenge then) but which eventually gave a boost to my further education. I finished school with a first division, did intermediate from St. Xavier's College, and enrolled into the undergraduate course of Patna University to do my Economics (Honours) and then Post graduate in Labour and Social Welfare. As decided earlier, I was determined to do IR, Labour or Social Welfare.

I recall father while in Ranchi called all four brothers once, to confer on some family matter. I was still in second year in college, not perhaps capable of independent thinking ... "I want all of you to be educated with the best I can provide, but a decision needs to be taken now whether any of us would want to go back to the village for rest of their life to look after our parental property or would want to pick up jobs and live in the Town (Shahar)". I recall the eldest of us was already in service and the second was destined to be a professor in College. We all opted to be shaharies and a major decision was taken by the family to dispose off everything in the village and build a house in Ranchi to settle down permanently.

While I was still in school at Ranchi in 1959, the youngest of our three sisters got married. The boy was working as a Personnel Officer in Tata's Colliery in West Bokaro. Visiting our sister during the summer vacation was indeed a treat then. The well maintained and well furnished accommodation, transport, and above all the respect…what else could one ask for! This was indeed luxury, coming from a middle class family with a large number of children, including relatives from the village, for whom our house was almost like a free hostel! There were perpetually 2–3 always stationed in the house, all brothers, who used to come to town to study. Some of them are still in touch, others we have lost contact with. My brother-in-law would often take me with him to the mine and washery areas, and I was amazed to see people depending on him so much for his help and support, and was amazed by the respect given to him. An aspiration started taking shape within that given a choice, this kind of a job or profession looked interesting for further avocation. And after doing Economics Honours, I opted to join the Department of Labour and Social Welfare for a degree from Patna University. However, the family was to witness harsh conditions, as immediately on completing the house after his superannuation, my father died of a cerebral hemorrhage and there were new challenges in the family. Two of the four brothers were still not settled. The older brothers then took over the responsibility of the family and helped their younger brothers to complete their education.

Like a few friends of mine, I wanted to do Labour Relations from XLRI, Jamshedpur, but the family could not afford the course as it was very expensive. I passed out with my post graduate degree in Labour and Social Welfare from the Patna University, getting the University Gold Medal. Due to some political struggle in the campus, including a police firing, the results were delayed by one year and were announced in 1969. This was the time of the great North Indian drought, which affected the economy immensely.

The economy was performing poorly in the mid-1960s. The growth of national income during this period had been slow. The commodity producing sector had been lagging behind as an industry, the basic and capital goods sectors had suffered and more importantly, the production of mass consumption goods had also lagged behind. The growth of non-farm employment was deplorable. There were higher rates of inflation. When I got the University Gold Medal, I cried, "I didn't know how I could get this". Having won the ILO Day Award in 1967 organised by IIPM-TISCO, I had become popular in my campus a year before passing out and was invited as a guest of the Tata's at XLRI, Jamshedpur. I still recall how Russi Mody, as chief guest, in his hilarious but serious message delivered to the students, spoke about the changes that were taking place in the Business world. He also narrated his story saying, that learning was his passion. He got admitted to Oxford and wanted to go to England, but his mother would not agree. However, after great effort he was able to persuade her to let him go. Russi Mody added that till the time of his departure, she kept on giving tips to him and once said that the people in England were very sensitive and had a lot of weakness for good etiquettes and culture, and ladies particularly, expected a lot of respect, courtesies and chivalry. Further, she advised him to remember to be courteous to the English Ladies, and demonstrate chivalry by putting off the cigar, removing the hat, and mischievously added that anything else he was able to take off depended on his luck! The auditorium resounded with laughter. The people present there – IR students from XLRI, Faculties, and the Personnel professionals of Jamshedpur itself – least realised that Russi was making a serious point for the future Personnel and IR candidates, though in a lighter tone with the usual Russi pun. Later, while congratulating me personally during Tea, he promised me a job after a year when I passed out with my Degree. I recall when I received the gold medal, I was very encouraged and wrote to him several times in the 6–8 months which I spent without a job, but... there was no reply. I started appreciating the 'Russi pun'.

Later, after almost eight months of receiving my results, I managed to acquire a job as Personnel Trainee, in a then small manufacturing unit Usha Martin Black (Wire Ropes), Ranchi. This gave me a good break in my career, good sustenance, a good profile and of course an excellent learning. I recall having been given a table in the small Time Office at the main gate, with four other people to share: three Time Keepers and the other Personnel Trainee, who was 6 months senior to me. My job was overseeing the Time Keepers, acting secretary to the Works Committee and Shop Committees, making a few recruitment and salary bills, and some Research Projects like absenteeism trends, causes and solutions, need assessment of welfare activities in neighbouring villages, etc. My colleague trainee was dealing in workmen leave, grievance handling, Trade Unions/Industrial relations and Disciplinary actions. The training was all on the Job! There were no classrooms, or any sort of orientation. While my colleague trainee (BN) was reporting to the Personnel Manager, Bakshi, I was virtually reporting to the Plant General Manager, Rana Pratap, and also the President, Brij Kishore Jhawar (popularly referred as Lali Babu in the Plant), who was a Promoter. The Plant had about 600 people and the relationship was close.

I recall that though the company was a known good pay master, once a wage negotiation with the Trade Unions had failed, and there was a lightning strike so well designed and organised, that before the workmen of shift 'A' could come out, the workmen of shift 'B' (around 200 of them), entered through the main Time Office, and before anyone of us could realise, a violent sabotage had begun inside the Plant. Executives were pushed by the leaders to go out and the workmen picked up wire rope pieces of approximately 3 feet long and thick, piled them up in hundreds (later it was revealed that these were quietly cut in preparation for days), and started hitting all machines, installations, laboratory, etc. This went on for 3–4 hours, till the police arrived late at night, in perhaps hundreds, with half a dozen buses and arrested/loaded them, searching for each one of them in the Plant. This went on for another 3–4 hours till all were traced, arrested and moved out. Next day the plant was a complete ruin. There was a total reign of terror. A dharna was done opposite the gate for long, followed by occasional attacks on commuting executives by bows and arrows. We, in the Time Office, were most vulnerable. We remained in the Plant campus for almost 90 days. As advised by a Kolkata Lawyer, Harlalka (I was assigned as his local assistant during the processes), the management, camping in the Plant for days, declared a lock out, pasting notices at the gates, sending notices to the homes of the workmen, and also had a large number of workmen terminated summarily. The agitations continued outside the gate for months. Then, following some violence at the gate, there was a Police firing in which a senior union leader died, injuring Policemen as well. Ultimately things came under control after a prolonged lockout, and the Plant was reopened, with repairs completed and the Plant re-commissioned. I remember these first 5–6 months were replete with experiences of training straight on the job and intense learning for me, not only in Time Management, and Establishment Management, Recruitment, etc., but practical dealing in the infamous Industrial Disputes Act, negotiation, bipartite committees, the disciplinary procedures, dismissals, grievance handling, dealing with law and order, and the list could go on! What I got to learn in the span of six months, I did not learn in 2 years of the Post graduate course in Labour and Social welfare/Personnel Management, as much ever!

And then there was a personal side, that later became a lifetime partnership pact for dealing with challenges. I met Chitra (my wife) when we were still in school. She was a stunning beauty and I fell for her ever giggling profile. We committed to marry when I was still studying and just couldn't wait after getting the Hindustan Steel job, and we tied the knot on 9th June, 1971. I provided a middle class living, which she always wanted to organize and better the things. She would be the one who would always adjust to my workaholic and social behaviours, sacrificing so much of energy, money and also her personal interests, including her own growth. So much so, that I always took her for granted! And then came for me an offer of an Asst. Personnel Officer in May 1970, from the then PSU leader, the Hindustan Steel Ltd. (HSL, that later becomes SAIL). About 15 of us were appointed by HSL. I recall, in a Selection Board comprising of 8–10 members from various Steel Plants/Units across the country, most of the questions and discussions were on what is going on in Usha Martin and what has been the learning. In fact, as I came to know later, this also became the reason of my posting to HSL's Coal washeries in the Dhanbad Coal mines areas, which faced perennial Industrial Relations and law and order problems and challenges! However, everyone in the family was very happy and proud that

I got a job in Hindustan Steel! I was immediately reminded of Russi's pun on things depending on luck for a Personnel and IR man.

Joining Hindustan Steel Ltd., that later became SAIL (Steel Authority of India Ltd.) was a matter of pride. It was equivalent to joining an elite firm in the Private sector. The Orientation cum short-term crash Training gave us the opportunity to travel to Durgapur, the base, apart from the other Steel Plants at Bhilai and Raurkela, and its Management Training Institute (MTI) at Ranchi. Those three months or so in Durgapur proved to be an occasion of immense learning once again. It was amazing to see agitations and processions almost every day. Every week, one or two cars seem to have caught fire in the Administrative Building. This was the time the government, tired of these agitations, later experimented by appointing a Trade Unionist, Bagaram Tulpule, as the General Manager of the Durgapur Steel Plant, thinking that this would work out and deliver peace. Lot many developments were taking place, not only in this prestigious, 15 year old Steel Plant, but several other factories in this, then so called "Industrial Ruhr of India" of the East. And one day we came to know that the Personnel Manager of perhaps MAMC (Mining and Allied Machinery Corpn.), then a Unit of HEC (Heavy Enineering Corporation) located in Durgapur, was literally pinned down on his office table with hundreds of alpins pricked on his body, and made to sign an agreement drafted by the union. The entire Durgapur region, rather the entire country, and anyone who would have read this story, would have reeled under shock. Later it was learnt that the management denied this agreement and got signed under duress. Hindustan Steels' training inputs were indeed rich and much different from what we went through during academics, just two years ago.

I recall 2–3 stints of training and orientation, organised and delivered by HSL's Management Training Institute (MTI), Ranchi. Mostly the cases, examples and stories of success and failure gave a true foundation indeed. I still recall the motivation and orientation given by K.T. Chandi (ICS), the then Chairman of HSL, who even stayed back after his session to have dinner with the young trainees. We were fortunate enough to receive orientation from leaders like R.P. Billimoria, A.K. Pal, J. Philip and many others, in some form or the other. An association with MTI always gave us additional sense of pride and also a feeling of camaraderie. Some of my batch mates, Sankarsan Acharaya and Gadadhar Upadhyaya who decided to stay on in the organisation, grew as Director HR and even CMD of schedule 'A' PSU.

My posting was finally announced in HSL's Dhanbad central office of Central Coal Washeries Organisation (CCWO), and my major task was the controlling of four of its coal washeries, which collectively sent washed coking coal to the steel plants. Central Coal Washeries Organisation (CCWO), Dhanbad, being a relatively smaller unit, gave me the opportunity of being a Personnel Officer with ample responsibilities, and less of Umbrella above. Having taken over a post with enormous responsibilities to shoulder, much of the time used to go in industrial relations alone, leaving very little time for personal relations! My bosses, I.B. Pandey [Later to become Director (Personnel) in Bharat Coking Coal (BCCL)], T.N. Srivastava, U.K. Choubey [Later to become Director (Personnel) in Coal India] and late S.N. Sahay [inducted into Hindustan Steels, with a repertoire of experience from the TATA's], all had so much to teach and train. This being a smaller unit of HSL, gave a vast variety of job responsibility and direct interaction with leaders in management, Unions and of course, a fair share of problems and challenges.

This, apart from intense establishment and industrial relations, gave me numerous opportunities in participating in training programme deliveries, relationship building and networking, in which I have generally been, as an introvert shy fellow, not so successful. It also gave me an elevated role position to represent my washery unit, CCWO, in inter-steel plant / unit personnel meetings, interacting with well respected, more confident and of course, better known administrators in the larger personnel fraternity of the Hindustan Steel family.

Thus, within two years of getting better grades, I got a fast track promotion, and from being the Personnel Officer and head of personnel of an entire washery unit, I was assigned a very challenging washery location at Santaldih in Purulia, (WB), which was located on the banks of the river Damodar. Becoming the head of personnel, though in a small washery unit, had given me a multiple role and responsibility exposure in personnel, industrial relations, administrations, township management, sports and welfare, legal including court cases, conciliations, tribunals, etc. And there were always so much of these! It was like going through the Coke oven, Blast Furnace, Steel Melting and Hot Rolling everyday!

I recall there had not been a single week, when there was no bomb explosion somewhere in our Santaldih township. This was also the prominent period of the United Front Government in West Bengal in 1967. I also remember this one particular night, while driving on our way back from Dhanbad to Santaldih after a union-management meeting in the CCWO, Dhanbad headquarter, after crossing the Maithon dam on that rainy night, we found the narrow road blocked felling some big branches of a tree. As we approached closer, and assuming that the branches would have fallen due to the strong monsoon winds, a bomb landed on the wind screen blowing it to splinters and injured the driver and the UTUC union leader sitting on the front seat. In the quickest response we all jumped out of the car and ran through the water-filled paddy field, in total darkness of monsoon night. I don't recall the distance we had run, ultimately to find some lantern lit hutments, inhabitants of which gave us shelter for the night and came back to see us off on the road in the morning, also to witness that everything of the car, except the body shell, was gone!

This was the time when the Government of India had inducted the Central Industrial Security Force (CISF) Act to develop a security force for its industries, the PSUs. The implementation or induction process was by giving options to existing security staff, a choice of joining the force with transferability clause, or lose lien, so that the new trained force could have been inducted. The union jumps in, existing guards don't opt for, nor vacate positions and there is chaos. We had to move the district court and ultimately evict them physically. Every day, every moment was an exploration, challenge, threat and a high speed bout of intense learning, as well!

In the meanwhile, suddenly a leading private company, Bata India, Kolkata gave me an opportunity for further growth. There was stiff competition for a position in Personnel, in their Patna (Mokamah) unit. I went through rounds after rounds of selection procedures, and it was finally Mr. Hammond (I recollect), an Australian in the final round, who made an offer of joining Bata India with good remunerations, good brand and different career path in the private sector. Chitra, who had just been in one year of our marriage, thought it was not a gift or opportunity to us, rather a possible threat of submerging back to the old environment in Patna, which would not have anything new to offer to our happiness or my career. She felt that any position in Bata but in a big city like Kolkata should certainly be my preferred choice, if it could be worked out! Chitra had proved to be my lucky star in a very short time. We committed to marry and I got the university gold, despite tons of blemishes to my record, we got married in mid 1971 and in just a year's time I got a fast track promotion, with independent charge, in a challenging unit. We decided and withdrew my resignation and expressed our regrets to Bata. Later, I named her my 'wish-luck' as whatever she would wish, brought happiness and prosperity. Life went on in the poverty ridden Santaldih for some more time.

In the meantime, Nationalisation of coalmines was in the offing, Coal India was to come and for coking coal, a separate company called Bharat Coking Coal Ltd. (BCCL) was born, which we were told, would also take over the four coal washeries of HSL and supply towards all the requirements of the steel plants. We both were somewhat apprehensive about going back to the coal industry, and the life which we had tasted well in these years at Dhanbad and Santaldih (in Purulia, a very poor district and an out and out leftist belt). While it was an excellent learning opportunity for me every day, we started wishing for an exit as we didn't wish to be taken over in a Coal Mine. Luckily, I got an option to go back to HSL. There was an opportunity in the Central Sales Organisation and Central Transport and Shipping Organisation of HSL in Kolkata, circulated by them. I pitched myself and was called for an interview. Kanungo and R.B. Patnaik interviewed me. I finally made it and landed in the Fairly Place office of HSL in the then Dalhousie Square (BBD Bagh). For me, coming from plants and mining business locations to a white-collared, urban, metro, modern, fashionable scenario was indeed an environment for transformation and paved a way for newer exposure and learning opportunities. This was in 1973 and the two years henceforth were once again quite eventful. Opportunity to deal with white-collared unions, enlightened and associated executive community, a fairly disturbed environment of the city of Kolkata, full of unrests, almost weekly bandhs and on top of it, nonstop load-shedding! I can't forget the early 1970s in West Bengal, then!

Suvira, our daughter, was born here and grew up in typical city difficulties and challenges. We would collect our ration on ration card, even baby food (milk), running from pillar to post. I remember how Bengali boys and girls of our office team would often and very sincerely run all over the city, including even their factory, to collect just a couple of tins of Glaxo's milk food! We would celebrate every little support rendered as our big achievements. Kolkata, after the turmoil of the late 1960s, would welcome non-Bengalis and couples as tenants, neighbours or para dwellers with open arms. On the slightest signal of difficulty, the neighbours, the para, would be all over your house bringing all the support that you would need, whether you knew them or not and the intensity or passion of every small or big festival, or such cultural occasions from grand poojas to Paila Baisakh or Jamai Shashthi, their emotions were embracing and very submerging. In Kolkata, we found ourselves at home with the culture. We had everything, except money, for a comfortable living. But working with Bengalis was indeed a great experience. Abundant love, care and support!

There, I recall, our interest in theatre grew so rapidly that we were all over Kolkata every week from Rabindra Sadan to Kala Mandir to the historic Star theatre to see modern famous plays like Mareech Samvad to Asami Hazir and uncountable of Gurudev's works! I still remember our trips to Shantiniketan, spending so much time in Gurudev's chosen home, our visits to several museums and of course the Vishwa Bharti. Despite the challenges, Chitra and I plunged deep into the cultural scene of Kolkata and Bengal, and relished every minute of it. In the office, after having been to towns like Ranchi, Patna, Dhanbad and the almost rural Santaldih, there were opportunities now in Central Sales Organisation to tour the different metropolitan cities and towns for work, serve and interact with also the administration in charge, directly with leaders like Wadud Khan, R.P. Billimoria, Hiten Bhaya, S.K. Daspatnaik, B.G. Gururaja Rao and many more. Then came the time when Steel Authority of India Ltd. (SAIL) was founded and established in 1975. It was a mega-integration through a holding company frame work. Lots of changes were taking place, that too very rapidly.

M.R.R. Nair came in after leaving Hindustan Steel, taking over as the Chief Personnel Manager and later General Manager (Personnel), Hindustan Steel Works Construction Ltd. (HSCL), a subsidiary of SAIL, to enable its organisation and consolidation. Nair was the first batch Personnel MT of HSL (1960), a brilliant, dynamic and aggressive HR leader who was to eventually be a very successful Director (Personnel) of SAIL and ultimately it's Chairman. In his plan, Nair wanted me to go to the Bokaro Steel Plant Unit, then the largest of HSCL and bubbling with problems and challenges. It was only five years past in my career, and I had seen so much, such wide range of responsibilities and also quick growth. I took the challenge, with a promotion again in 2 years! Russi's 'pun of luck' was always present, at the back of my mind. My immediate boss, Rama Krishnan was around twenty years my senior in age, a quiet and very pleasant personality. He was very experienced, cool and very empowering. He was indeed an excellent teacher to me and very close.

It was immense freedom and respect that I enjoyed at the Bokaro Steel City in spite of being junior in age, senior in position. A troubled location, 40–50 Unions, recognised unions ineffective with intra–union rivalries, lots of violence and political pressures – was the environment in which we used to operate. There was some agitation every day, some union meeting, and the most peculiar was dealing with numerous craft unions, welder's unions, fitter's union, Crane operators, winch operators, masons, carpenters, electricians, Argon Arc welders, charge hand unions, ITI trainees' union and so on! On top of it all, the engineers had an association and not only used to declare strikes and provoke agitation, but also used to adopt coercive methods including violence. They all had their demands, identities, and negotiating tactics developed, each often ready to stop work on the smallest pretext. There were many agitations and to mention at least one, it was once such an agitation in which the executives adopted a violent posture and had also a work-men's agitation, leading the General Manager and the Personnel Manager to remain on a car top for 7 hours, resulting in getting a 5 point agreement signed under duress. It started with a disorganised leaderless mass movement, but was later taken over by about 1000 young ITI trainees asking for jobs, while later the others rolled back in quickly. The agitation aggravated with police firing and one death, but this continued till substantially firm steps were taken in series. The union declared a Martyr's Day. Work came to a standstill. Armed CRP surrounded the campus for months. A juridical enquiry was ordered. We had to endure all this.

In June 1975, under certain economic and political considerations, the Government declared a National Emergency under the leadership of Mrs. Indira Gandhi, the then Prime Minister. There were focused agenda of change and transformation in the country with a twenty point economic programme and the actions were focused, specific target oriented and strictly monitored and reviewed at all levels of the Government hierarchy. Public Sector had an agenda given by the Government which were simply speaking of better discipline, commitment, higher productivity, quality of services and improving the overall performance. This target was huge but very relevant and led to a lot of improvement in the performance in the country. The environment became more disciplined, there was a huge reduction of wasteful practices, poor performance and indiscipline was not tolerated, and this also resulted into a number of terminations of employees who did not perform well and were not disciplined. Performance and deliveries improved and schedules of projects were adhered to and achieved. It was a different atmosphere, though many people felt that an unfair amount of coercion and pressure was exercised by the managements in Public Sector Undertakings, which provided good foundation and environment of better performance to the organisations. This lasted till March 1977, where after, substantial rolling back to past actions were undertaken by the changed central government led by the Janata Party, which amounted to a fair amount of confusion in relationships, especially industrial relations and overall industrial environment.

Nair, in HSCL, organised personnel and administration, its goals, policy manuals, system manuals, and enforced discipline with a firm hand and also slowly started his experiments in transforming the function, emphasizing and systematising the initial HRD format (Nair later formed and was a co-founder of the National HRD Network (NHRD) Network, to develop professionals with the changing HRD, to meet ongoing challenges and demand). Working 8 years with him at Bokaro, and later, directly at the HQ in Kolkata, was a great training and learning experience. He virtually became my chosen mentor and he kept contributing to my development happily, as long as he saw me placed in NTPC. On returning from Bokaro, when he was appointed as the Chairman, SAIL, we kept meeting occasionally at his residence in Asiad, as I also lived in the same neighbourhood. We lost touch for some time, when he moved on to SAIL in Delhi as its Director (Personnel), posting me to Iraq in a consortium company of HSCL. In those days, a posting to the Middle East was very much prized and sought after. Chitra and I were happy and proud, but this also suddenly resulted in another radical change, and presented a new learning ground for me. As head of Personnel with international exposure, in the tenth year of career, this was usually not available to many!

I was looking at HSCL's international business at that time, which was primarily growing in Libya and Iraq. I had amassed a lot of exposure of a new work-world between these two, and also developed bench-marking relations with EPI, EIL, IRCON, etc., who were operating in the Middle East, and had earned a very good profile and name. We were very lucky to get this posting. It was an opportunity to work abroad, learn in a cross-cultural environment and earn some money as well which was so rare at home. We made a very happy family!

Going to Iraq on a posting in 1980 suddenly became very challenging. When I was moving with my family with bag and baggage to Delhi, while boarding the flight, I read in the news papers that the first war between Iraq and Iran, regarding the dispute of waters of 'Shat al Arab', had broken out and all flights to Baghdad were cancelled. My wife Chitra took it bravely. I dropped her and our children to her mother's place, at our hometown and moved on to report to PCP HQ at Chandigarh. Based there at Chandigarh, in a short time I had to move a lot. To recruit manpower, I camped in rural Karnataka, Rajasthan, also Amritsar and Patiala's remote rural areas. H.S. Mejie used to advise me saying that I better start learning Kannada and the rustic Punjabi dialects, and get familiar with their culture as I was going to spend the next couple of years with them, at close quarters! I was travelling for almost 3 months, till the passage via Kuwait began and so we moved. Though it appeared challenging at the time, and many at home advised against going to the war infested Iraq, we apparently didn't have alternatives and decided to move on. I was in the second batch and the also the eleventh person to report to our camp at Basra. This was exciting! Kuwait Airport was very attractive but entry into Basra in buses, crossing the Safwan borders, was giving enough indications of the tough challenges that we were to encounter. Batches of officers and construction workers started arriving. The prefab factory was erected and construction work started in 2 of the 3 sites. We were getting the prefab factory from Denmark, all structures and materials from Kuwait, cars from Japan and so on. In a war struck country under national emergency, everything, whether immigration of people, customs clearances, currency repatriation, etc., and even procuring a ration card for provisions, were all tough processes and extremely difficult jobs. On top of it, under the Government orders there, we were to construct trenches as specified, around caravans and camps for employees and some families, to take shelter during the daily bombings.

I still recall how bravely Chitra managed an entry with two little kids of ages seven 7 and 5 years, taking about three days from Delhi to Basra, via Kuwait and the Safwan Borders! There were no means of communication like telephones, mobiles or even telexes working, in those days. The only way was through the use of the 'diplomatic bag', which would also arrive via Kuwait Airport and the Indian Consulate, and would normally take a minimum of 5–7 days. I got a message from D.C. Sahu and Bhatnagar bhai sahab that my family had left Delhi for Kuwait and hence should be received. I informed the staff at my Kuwait office and waited at the Safwan border's crossing, at the no man's land, between Kuwait and Iraq. They didn't arrive on the scheduled date, or the next day and finally reached the Safwan on the third day in the evening, in a bus. For all these three days, I was standing at the border checking all buses and taxis that were crossing the border. I couldn't leave the border and go back to the camp at Basra, didn't get any proper food for almost 3 days. And I did not have any means of having a message conveyed to me either from Delhi or the Kuwait office, and was also aware of the rough treatment meted out to passengers, particularly women, at the Kuwait Airport by the local officials. My words fail in expressing the agony and anxiety that I experienced. Spending all this time with the Iraqi Immigration Officers was extremely strenuous. Perhaps having me around for 3 days and nights on the borders, they later became somewhat supportive. It was a great relief to see Chitra and the children, all cuddled up in a heap in the bus, with swollen legs, dried lips and anxiety-laden faces. It was a great reunion! We kept thanking the almighty profusely as we drove in our van to the Basra camp!

The condition of the camp and things around us were quite scary. Many people coming to our camp from Chandigarh, or later Jhunjhunu, went through nervous breakdowns and we would have intense counseling sessions, and confidence building sessions with them. I eventually had the opportunity of constructing 2 Gurudwaras, 1 in Maqual, Basra and 1 at Umqasr, as most of the workers were from rural Punjab. On being posted there, I had to seriously learn to speak colloquial Punjabi and read Gurmukhi, and also speak Arabic, fairly well. It was fun, but so facilitating. Operating in offices of DGs from different ministries became easy and friendly because of the familiarity with the language. My interpreter was an Arab retired English teacher and made learning Arabic very easy for me. While working with some Danes, who had come with the other partner of the consortium, Larson and Neilson, it was fun but challenging again. They used to be very demanding. Then came the Jhunjhunu batches of Rajasthani labour and their integration needed a lot of caution and care. There was another site of PCP at Diwania which was also entrusted to me.

There was neither any official training given to us nor any of the usual conferences or seminars were conducted to manage the typical issues of cross-cultural diversity. We built our rapport with clients, the local Arabs, the Indian communities, the Consulate and Embassy, but the fact remained that we were under the typical stringency of the national emergency. Our advantage, generally felt, was the fact that we were Indians, and the Iraqis then had lot of respect and trust for Indians, particularly in the central Iraq region including Baghdad, Diwania, Najaf, and the south of Basra and around. Further, challenges came as Iraq was the only Middle East Arab country where bars, belly dancers and brothels were all available and so, regulating Indian single workmen, was a tricky and tough job. We would generally repatriate 90 per cent of salary, but even the remaining 10 per cent was perhaps good enough to take the tough Sikhs out of the camp to have fun. We generated a lot of goodwill, camaraderie and relationship with our workmen to enforce that they refrain from drinking. Though executives would be allowed in their camps, I had to turn a complete teetotaler, to set examples, before I enforced anything.

The worst was on a New Year's Eve; when in our Company in an accident, we lost 5 lives, including that of 2 ladies and a child. I know how difficult it was to send the two dead bodies via Kuwait during the emergency and much more in performing the last rites of the remaining three, whose relatives opted not to transport the bodies to India. In Islamic countries burning dead bodies, we were told, could create commotion, and so we were, though allowed by the Govt., because of our goodwill and relationship, asked to go deep into the desert under Military and Police protection.

I recall many such times, when there used to be discontent and agitation simmering because of tough situations like not much of contact with families, restricted movements, camp regulations, illiteracy amongst workmen from rural backgrounds, tough working conditions, e.g. temperature shooting as high as 50–52 degrees Celsius and on top of it regular bombings in the Iraqi Port area (who were our clients), and our camps, offices and sites were in these kind of war zones, where there used to be news of casualties all the time.

In just about two years there were lot of learning opportunities, plenty of tests and trials and we had all solutions developed on job, whether counseling skills, diversity management, welfare of people, managing industrial relations in an alien land, managing customs in emergent conditions where, mostly we depended on imports, managing govt. networking successfully. However, there were some trusted camp commanders appointed by the promoters, practices of some of them were so objectionable which I knew could cause serious trouble for the organisation. I used to share this frankly with the promoter MD, whenever he would come over on official tours from Kuwait or India. But I knew the practices would be operational with their consent or knowledge and decided not to interfere, rather withdraw myself. So I resigned after two years in Iraq, opted for repatriation back to Kolkata, though much against the wishes of the promoter MD who was very fond of me, perhaps because of my integrity and forthrightness.

Further, my wife intensely wanted to negotiate a posting in their London business, which I was very reluctant about. We collected our bonus, shopped for a couple of days in Kuwait and Dubai, and finally returned to Kolkata, sometime in 1983. We had a lot of respect in the promoter's family and also all the employees and enjoyed the tough and challenging times. Mejis' were wonderful people and treated my family as their own with a lot of respect and affection. Further, the Iraqis were wonderful people, too.

Everyone we dealt with, were gems, strong but shy, very cultured people. With excellent social and food habits, the Iraqis were jovial, social and hospitable, though somewhat little reserved due to the country's political scenario. They were very caring and respecting, particularly towards us Indians. I recall old Abu Khalid, the Mutarzuma (interpreter), fearless and very social, would occasionally invite me and my family to his home to dine. I would ask him if he was unafraid to invite foreigners to his house in these times of emergency, knowing well that the intelligence wing could cook up stories. He and his wife would say, "My house is your house, your family is my family, where is the alien?" The lunch parties thrown for us at his house used to be indeed exhilarating. The large and well spread dastarkhan with all the food in one huge plate (parat) with Khalida Bee's pilao, misallam, khaboos, liham lazeez, ending with halwa and dilibi, where was the diversity? Umm! That used to be great! I also recall Sayeed Maki and Basil, who were tough and demanding clients, but very appreciating and respecting. Maki had a weakness for Indian boutiques and Basil for Mercedes cars, but their integrity and values were unparallel. I also recall several occasions of going to DGs of Govt. departments and the RBI Governor's office in Baghdad. For entry, one would have to pass through three to four levels of security checks. Whenever I would be going to the Reserve Bank to resolve some currency repatriation issues, the guards at security would look at me and ask Inta hanood? Aiwa, I would reply and he would not make me open my briefcase, frisk me or even see my passport. They would pat my shoulders and push, saying, Roh, Roh (go, go). I don't know how this used to happen! There were many such instances I experienced there and used to always thank the behaviour of our Indian ancestors and the association built over decades by those Indians who were brought in by the British Army during World War I and even later, in the short 40 years of the British Colonial rule of Iraq, and those who were later abandoned there. This group of Indians had to perforce stay behind for life, get married to Iraqi girls, and settle there. These Indians then, mostly 'Hajjis' of 70–80 years or more were perhaps the builders of this Hanood image in Iraq, of which we were beneficiaries! Ours and the Iraqi emotionality, and part of the culture we were aware of, however, appeared very similar and this was a great advantage that enabled us to make easy in-roads.

When I landed back in Kolkata, things were changed. It was absolutely obvious that I was not welcome in the Headquarter. Lot of changes had taken place – a new MD had come, shook the company and had left; the environment and culture had shockingly transformed; my promotions were delayed and I was about to be posted to a unit in Bokaro again, and not Kolkata, which I desperately desired to build my onward plans. But Ghatak, a technical general manager, looking after P&A understood and helped. However, within 6 months, I soon got an offer from a new upcoming power PSU, NTPC, which was constructing 4 power stations at Singrauli, Korba, Ramagundam and Farakka. I got a posting as the Chief Personnel Manager at its Korba Super Thermal Station. It was a loss of almost three years for me, as the level was parallel but I had made up my mind to leave HSCL. This was a welcome change after serving SAIL and its subsidiary companies for around 14–15 years. When I look back at the journey of these 15 years of my initial career in retrospect, I find it to be generally very mobile and extremely enriching in terms of roles, responsibilities, location, growth, and above all immense learning with greater depth of values, high degree of humility and, sincere and passionate love and support for people in their development and growth. Building relationships had become a habit and also the key to success. We learnt being very sensitive and hugely people oriented, but also learnt taking tough decisions and challenges. I secretly learnt that Unions generally liked you to be honest and knew when and how to accept their members' mistakes, provided you have won their trust with unflinching credibility!

Coming to NTPC, an offer with loss of money and time was not depriving, rather rejuvenating, as I desperately wanted to come out of my old job. R.V. Shahi, the then GM (P&A) [later he went on to become Director (Operations) NTPC, CEO, BSES and also Secretary Power, Govt. of India], a wonderful leader and a super teacher, also from SAIL background, compensated much to me in pay fixation and even in loss of time. Shahi's analytic ability had no parallel and his ability to mentor and develop subordinates was very methodical and indeed par excellence. I'd always give credit for my development to my 3 Mentors: M.R.R. Nair, R.V. Shahi and Rajendra Singh. May be, I had choices in the learning menu, and I could make it a point to choose the best that they had, and had to offer.

While M.R.R. Nair demonstrated huge confidence, was people oriented but was always riding speed and was aggressive, R.V. Shahi was basically endowed with excellent cognitive skills, systematic approach, was candid and forthright, and being an excellent coach and teacher, he was very supportive and helpful, always ready to hold your hand; and Rajendra Singh was very trusting and immensely empowering, building values through demonstrating them, and in the process assisted me in building substantial confidence in myself.

Coming from the steel family of SAIL to NTPC, nearly a two decade junior PSU, and trying to make a beginning, was a threat as well as an opportunity. I moved on to Korba (now Chhattisgarh). My then boss, Jagannath Sharan, in HSCL, who had history of serving in the coal industry, while releasing me for NTPC, Korba, remarked during my farewell, "I know his story all along and now at least from a virtual fire belt, he moves to a peaceful belt, i.e. Madhya Pradesh...Let peace be his gain in this change. Amen!" I had changed eight eventful and challenging locations in these 15 years – Dhanbad, Santaldih, Kolkata, Bokaro, Kolkata again, Chandigarh, Basra, Diwania, Kolkata for the third time and then Korba! Before moving to Korba, I had explored the schooling facilities there and judging by what I found there, decided to leave little Suvira in the boarding house of La Martinere, her school in Kolkata. There were challenges but we went on with this decision as she was getting into the sixth standard had earned this coveted admission there with her own efforts.

Korba was a good community of NTPC with the first stage of the project being already commissioned and second stage erection in full swing; its Permanent Township was also nearing completion. In this 8 location journey, while my belief in humility and sense of values and straight-forwardness in dealing with people were reconfirmed, going through continuous and repeated violent and threatening IR situations had generally done away with my fears. I could plunge in and operate, with ease, and succeed perhaps in most disturbing circumstances. A very good learning experience came my way during this period, which I consider to be one third of my career life, preparing me for the remaining 25–30 years of my career.

But no matter how Jagannath Sharan would have predicted peace and serenity of Madhya Pradesh, I didn't have any exceptional or different luck there. As the Chief Personnel Manager, I got involved in building a good society and family of NTPC at Korba, of course with the complete support

My Learnings...The Odyssey | **19**

of the people. I started believing that things had changed and that it was indeed going to be peaceful. Then suddenly in one year's time it seemed to be over... in the latest edition of a literary magazine published by our Korba Public Relations Department, there appeared a story, written by an outsider associated with the Bhilai Steel Plant. A rumor spread that there had been a statement in the article casting slurs on the Chhattisgarh women. As the rumor spread outside Township into the town, some local leaders from the local political group also jumped into the fray. People, who had been holding some grudge on NTPC's General Manager, politicised it, generating a mob hysteria, demanding termination or at least suspension of 3 officers of NTPC, who were on the Magazine Editorial Board, and thus responsible for the commotion. Our unions unfortunately, supported the outsiders. All Executives, feeling harassed and agitated, threatened to form an Association and shut down the plant if any suspensions were administered. To make the situation worse, the General Manager, partly under pressure of the HQ, wanted to carry on with the suspension of the three Executives, irrespective of Executives' simmering agitation. I requested for two days from my GM and ran around the whole town, neighbouring villages, homes of MP and MLA, and of course met with, at our end, our Trade Union Leaders and also the Executives. I was also keeping in touch with my HR HQ.

I recall returning home past midnight, driving my jeep late in the night after my trips to the village, the MP, MLA and the State Admn., and finding 40–50 agitating but anxious Executives (I recall Anil Terway, Shishir Tamotia and many such great guys) sitting in my lawn or standing at the gate, waiting, but gradually developing appreciation and confidence in my efforts and also extending their support to my mission. I recollect telling them openly what I was trying to do, and that I would want them to bear with me, stating firmly that we must succeed. What I didn't share though, when I returned home again very late the second night, was the fact that the local politicians and the MP and MLAs were continuing to maintain unnecessarily hard stands, because of political views and were putting undue pressure on NTPC to bend and retreat from their decision. On the internal front too, the two Trade Unions of our workmen had been taking politically motivated stands, and being supported by the external political group from Korba, the Unions were taking out wild processions within the Township, brick batting the buildings, market places and threatening the families of the three employees with dire consequences in their absence. Next morning, as my time stipulated grace period drew to an end, I was called by the General Manager who said that he can't further hold pressure coming from politicians and State Administration and that I must issue the suspension orders forthwith, else the Plant could be set on fire and he won't be able to take the responsibility. Though he was a wonderful Officer and an excellent leader, but may be due to some external pressure or compulsion, he was unable to appreciate the intensity of the counter pressure being exerted by the Executives internally, which might have had a very bad impact on the organisation relationship in the long run. For me, either way NTPC would have got a severe blow.

I came back to my office, pondered for a while, and took a few quick decisions. I made my first call to the Delhi HQ, the second to Chitra at home, and the final one to the hideout of the three officers. Having finally made up my mind, I dictated two sets of letters to my PS – one transfer (to their place of choice) with suspension letters for the 3 officers (with a design and provision that they will be released to go to new places where the suspension letter shall stand withdrawn). The second letter dictated was my own resignation letter. I put them in envelopes marked to the General Manager and had them delivered to him, took my Jeep and drove to my quarter. I had not realised that my NTPC story would be so short and so insignificant! When I reached my quarter, I saw Chitra and the girls (Suvira was home on a vacation) greeting me with a smile as always. The little girls didn't understand the implication of a resignation. But Chitra did and came in support saying that things would be just fine and soon. In the house, in an hour's time, about hundred executives had assembled and all demanded me to withdraw my resignation. But I was determined that under the difficult circumstances, the efforts and action taken by me were the most appropriate. Next day, I boarded the flight to Delhi to meet the GM (P&A) HQ. But I first met my past employer of Basra/Iraq, who immediately offered me a job in Basra again, for ID 500, a fair and respectable treatment! The best was when I started narrating why I resigned NTPC job, Mejie was just not ready to listen! He just asked me to pack my bags and come to Delhi in two weeks' time, ready for departure. I also met Baljekar, who was, on retirement from the position of MD, HSCL, working for BIW. He immediately offered me a post at Bhilai.

I also went on to meet M.R.R. Nair who almost shouted at me and scolded me, as he often would when I'd err, and asked me not to think of going for either PCP, Iraq or BIW in Bhilai. He advised that I must remain in NTPC itself. He also called up Shahi and discussed my position. This was yet another point in my career when I found multiple supports coming from all

21

My Learnings....The Odyssey |

directions with options, in times of all kinds of depression and indecision. I rebuilt the value of demonstrating concern, empathy and support that we need to give in life to those in need. It taught me humility and the value of holding hands and extending support in times of crisis. Everyone taught me this... Mejie, Baljekar, Nair, Shahi, with whatever best they had to offer! When I finally met my P&A General Manager, R.V. Shahi, he remarked that he would need someone in the Delhi office and would be happy to transfer me to HQ if I should withdraw my resignation. I returned to Korba, shared the entire developments with Chitra. After much deliberation, we decided to move to the NTPC Corporate Office in Delhi and I withdrew my resignation. This was 1985....

At this point of time, I was feeling very low and somewhat depressed and drained out. Having faced so many situations in my career till date, never had I felt so helpless. Hindwan, a friend, arranged for a flat in Kalkaji. I had requested him to find one very near to our NTPC Office, as I was not feeling quite comfortable in this new city. I had always wanted to stay close to my Office and was generally lucky to have found accommodation very close to my earlier offices. In the Delhi office of NTPC, I was to report to B.P. Thakur, whose first reaction on meeting me was, "You are our hero indeed!" This sudden display of appreciation, though startling, was welcomed like the first shower of the monsoon on parched lands and I was relieved to some extent. After a few days, while I was settling down in my office, Renu Rajpal from Power Management Institute softly knocked on my door. Soft spoken and humble, Renu introduced herself and expressed her view on the much talked about incident. She said that she had heard about the whole incident and wanted to prepare a case study on this episode. She spent the next couple of days querying about the sequence of events and subsequent actions. I don't recollect if she could write a case or not, but she definitely made me feel very great and it helped me to regain my courage and confidence. I can't forget her favours!

When I came to the Nehru Place HQ of NTPC, I realised that a considerable number of changes had taken place in the administration in a few years time. A.K. Shah, CMD, and R.D. Gupta, Director (Personnel), were on the verge of retirement, and M.L. Shishoo was to become CMD, and later Rajendra Singh (Late) was to join as Director (Personnel). NTPC was already having enough employees' grievances, dissatisfaction, mistrust, and lack of communication. As a consequence, all round agitation from Trade Unions and Supervisory Associations erupted frequently, many of them becoming violent, inflicting threats and injuries to the Executive community, who in turn expected that the Management should protect the Executives by acting against rampant indiscipline and cases of violence. I could recall incessant agitation in Korba, including long drawn workmen and Supervisor's strikes, threats and manhandling of executives. Still more challenging was the position in Farakka, with repeated instances of work stoppages, agitations against Executives and the Organisation. Shahi's understanding on the industrial relations was extremely good and focused. He used to give a brief, for instance urging us to be more people oriented, attend to their welfare, encourage and determine their perks, better Quality of Work Life, and at the same time deal with cases of indiscipline and strikes with a firm hand of the Organisation. This fitted my IR Model as well and I was adept in dealing with these situations. We began taking action even on radical trade union leaders, or their unreasonable issues, of which there were quite a few, with firmness, and started ensuring and enforcing the principle of 'No work, No pay' in all instances of work stoppages and agitations. I recall taking this position in Farakka, enforcing the "No work, No pay" policy there on account of a unreasonable strike in the Equipment Zone for 9 days, perhaps for the first time in NTPC!

I also recall a relay hunger strike carried on by one Union in Korba for 30 days with only 3–4 workmen sitting on the strike each day. They could not gather much support on issues that were instigated by politically inclined leaders and raised with vested interest. In due course, the workmen lifted their tents as a sign of the end of the relay hunger strike, a failure report of conciliation was issued and an adjudication eventually started. However, immediately after the relay hunger strike, we deducted a punitive amount of 3–4 days of the wages of each workman sitting on the hunger strike. Later, the labour court issued an order that the relay hunger strike was a strike in ID Act and was illegal in a public utility service. As the order was in contravention of the necessary provisions of the Act, hence the deductions of wages by the employer were legal and justified, much to the disappointment of the Union leaders. By this time the Union had lost support and as they did not get any relief from court on the issue of wage deduction, their membership count reduced drastically.

Gradually, the message was becoming clear to the lot of workmen, but there were cases when the organisation had to relent. On top of it there were uncertainties dealing with Personnel issues dispassionately and uniformly. Indiscipline of Trade Unions was tolerated by central leaders and also at times by the Organisation, causing similar or more intense repercussions amongst the Executives. There were various power pockets of dealing with groups of employees and situations, further leading to mistrust and acceleration of the deteriorating scenario. The Executives, apart from sporadic retaliations to protect themselves, started creating formal Associations of Executives one after another in the Plant/Projects and later got together to form the Federation of Executives (NEFI). During the management of M.L. Shishoo, there were hardly any reasonable briefs that would be given to handle different situations, and though the briefs given by Shahi to handle situations were firmly established in the organisation and had long term perspectives, they were later over-ruled by Shishoo, in view of his lack of trust on his team. Unlike Shahi, he was not people friendly; he had made himself unavailable to even his very senior Team and at the same time often tried to micro manage situations based on the information and advice of very selective people. There were changes in the HR department not only at the Corporate but unit levels also. However, strategies needed focus and direction which had been lacking in the organisation for a long time. The all round agitations kept on mounting and by then the Executives had become fairly vocal and aggressive. In the meantime, Shishoo brought an HR General Manager, virtually at the level next to the Director (Personnel). Shahi ultimately was to be moved to an alternate role and position. This obviously weakened the Management's plan to restore good relations and also establish discipline as the new guards needed time to understand the situation and further develop their own strategies.

In the meantime, in the year 1997, NTPC gave me an opportunity to undergo training at Templeton College, Oxford, under the Colombo Plan. I was to participate in the Advanced Personnel Management Programme which was for a duration of 3 months. It was indeed an unforgettable experience with sharing the same platform with great teachers and acquiring an in depth view of the working of the British Industries, old and new. 'The Iron Lady' Margaret Thatcher's tough handling of the Coal Industry and other strikes, and the Privatisation of uncountable businesses and industries, was indeed remarkable and awe-inspiring!

I recall our interaction with a British Trade Union Leader when he narrated the woes of the sale of a series of businesses like Port, Shipping, and even Water supply in cities, which had been so far done by Municipal organisations. When inquired as to why the single Trade Union, which had a majority in the country, could not hold any stand against such decisions when these were incorrect or unacceptable, the answer was pretty unusual for us. "We dare not, as Maggi would run her horses on us!" At that instant, I recalled several strikes in India – the Railway strikes, the Textile strikes, the Coal agitations, the Jukta Front time of strikes, and one could go on! Where was our Government's concern in improving production and productivity, stopping immense loss of man days and putting an end to so much of unabated violence? This really brought to the forefront the stark difference between the two systems of administration.

These Foreign Trainings, rare and very competitive, were wonderful opportunities for exposure, and proved to be great sources of learning. A person travelling to Europe or America, even then, was someone to be seen with, someone to be very proud of, and someone to be sent off by almost a crowd of friends and relations! We were able to explore a fair part of Britain and also Europe. Watching the fierce but decent debates on volatile issues like privatisation in the House of Lords, and some other debates in the House of Commons, was an exhilarating and educating experience in itself. Chitra was with me for some time and we were able to save even in that expensive country. We thoroughly enjoyed our stay in England, indulging in plenty of trips and shopping, and had fun filled moments there. In fact, one of the most amazing thing we experienced there was the use of the office desktop personal computers in colleges! This was another first for us!

P.S. Bami took over as CMD in June 1988. He had a major advantage of his positive image and a very long association with NTPC since its formative days. He was not only liked, but was very well respected by all the sections of employees. Despite being at such a designation, he was very approachable. When he took over, the Executive agitation was escalating. Though there were senior HR Leaders at the Corporate, he'd call me and ask for inputs and suggestions, which restored my faith in myself. I recall that once I requested him to take steps like making direct communication with his executives down the line in all Units/Projects. I was amazed at the promptness he showed in accepting this suggestion and along with Venkat, Gualti, Chander and I, organised trips to most of the Plants, addressing masses of Executives, and listening to them. He was referred to by an affectionately coined name as our 'Bhishma Pitamah'. His policy of open communication lay a strong foundation of a good relationship that was going to be nurtured in the times to come. Executives had been showing total lack of trust in us, the HR department, and indication that gave us a very strong message for change so that NTPC could start working towards building of a new culture that could create and sustain the great Organisation.

Bami's tenure of around 4 years was tough and beset with mixed developments and experiences. NTPC's projects were progressing well, operations were excellent, but receivables were low because of the peculiar jam of poor responses from the different State Governments who were our primary customers.

In 1992 a terrible misfortune fell on my family as we lost our younger daughter, who was just 14 years. We were not able to face the truth and slipped into a long and dark time hole of oblivion. My wife was a total wreck and I kept suffering a deep guilt complex and had gone virtually insane, blaming my work engagements like the Unchahar take-over which had resulted in a sort of exile in Lucknow hotels for months. Work had definitely eaten into my family life. It was a great career success story but on the family front, we suffered an irreparable loss. My elder daughter passed out of school and got an admission in the B.Arch course in Ballabh Vidya Nagar, Anand, in Gujarat. While she was preparing to move to her hostel in a University Village, I suddenly got a job in Baroda, IPCL (on lien) as its Corporate HR. It gave us an opportunity to be closer to our elder child and also provide a change of environment to the family. But this was to last for only a short while. Though a very good Organisation, IPCL was already facing an imminent problem of losing a monopolist position, with cheaper, well packaged and easily available imports to the business in India. IPCL was not seeing the writing on the wall, nor was it exercising the required care and control. In the meantime, my daughter, who was studying at Vidya Nagar, procured an admission in Delhi's TVB School of Habitat Studies in the coming session. Once again, with the desire to be close to our daughter, we made the decision to leave Baroda and come back to NTPC, Delhi. NTPC, in my absence of little less than a year, had grown distant from me and on my return I had to wait for months for a suitable job portfolio. S.M.C. Pillai was the then Director (Personnel) and G.K. Agarwal was AGM-HRD. My position was occupied by D.G.K. Rao. I did not get even a room for 5–6 months!

In the meantime, The Government of India (the Manmohan – Narasimha Rao duo) took gigantic steps and that too very significant ones, for the transformation of the economy, unleashing LPG. So far, the power sector had mostly been under the Government domain and thus, the doors of the mighty sector were opened up, suddenly pulling NTPC in the midst of a whirlwind, encircling it with newer challenges. While NTPC was already facing its own share of problems of mistrust and agitations, this change in the sector and economy seemed to add fuel to fire. With the arrival of the so called 'Fast Track' Companies like Enron, Cogentrix, AES, Power Gen, Siemens, ABB, Alstom, etc., there were also a large number of Indian Independent Power (IPP) Producers who queued up to try their luck in the Power Sector, that had suddenly been thrown open for them. Many things were happening around at the same time, but I recall two very impactful developments on NTPC's position, making it further challenging: one was that this change resulted in the reduction of NTPCs probabilities of attaining new Projects; rather there were instances where projects already sanctioned to NTPC went out to others, including the Fast Track Companies. In the past, NTPC was used to growth which also gave an opportunity to its people to grow along. Successful executions and celebrations had become a part of life, habit and culture. Hence, this change was a huge blow for the family of NTPC. Frustrations mounted, as growth stopped almost suddenly. On top of it all, the Fast Track and other IPPs started building their Teams of Power Engineers and NTPC became a very good poaching ground for excellent and ready talent. Money was flowing and was very lucrative for the talented personnel, who had the opportunity to find both, career growth, along with very good financial reward, a front where NTPC was lacking immensely. Quite a handful of Executives left NTPC causing lot of anxiety and apprehension in the minds of people. Many Executives at the visible levels of GM, ED and even few Directors left, spreading a feeling as if the ship was going to sink. Further, there were groups, rumors, and unfounded news of sale of some units, escalating the fear in the minds of people, resulting into distrust, apprehensions and further agitations. Executives attrition increased by 5–6 times.

This was the time Rajendra Singh took over the position of CMD in mid 1992 and NTPC appointed S.M.C. Pillai as Director (Personnel) near the end of 1992, and Ashok Trehan, as 1994 drew to a close. Both were entrusted with some additional charges of Operations or Projects. We kept busy mostly in the typical transactional activities of the HR department of NTPC, reacting to agitations, doing promotions, transfers, etc. A vacancy for the position of Director (Personnel) was created as Trehan opted to become Director (Technical). I was a General Manager and was not eligible as per the NTPC rules to be a candidate. PESB appointed Pran Nath of SAIL as Director (Personnel) in mid 1995. By appointing Pran Nath as Director

(Personnel) a silent transformation, of course for the betterment, seemed to have begun in NTPC. An honest, forthright, excellent HR professional, Pran Nath was a development and learning oriented HR executive. He initiated lot of changes in HR and in the Organisation. I used to admire his straight forwardness as well as his adherence to his principles. The 2 years of intensive learning under his leadership were very rejuvenating for me. In fact, he ensured the successful installation of some of the new and powerful initiatives which would be primarily needed to be sustained by his successor in order to create a good culture in NTPC. He was very protective of talent and had tremendous respect for people. This was the period of positive HRs resurrection in NTPC after a long interval. Our learning had been initiated; HRs abilities and strategies to creating an environment of learning, unleashing creativity at all levels and developing a strong leadership pipeline, started sincerely. I became an Executive Director and looked forward to assess myself as well as my HR Team in a new light, and to improve our learning abilities. There was so much to see, read, research, analyze and learn about in the entire process of taking NTPC forward. We knew the potential and capabilities available and wanted these to have a multiplying effect for creating a culture of ownership, openness, innovation and renewals.

I knew I was empanelled for the post of Director (Personnel) in NTPC. I recall I was extremely nervous when the date of the PSEB interview was fixed. I caught hold of Sunil Trivedi to teach me, coach me, and prepare me. What ensued was a compact and elaborate, intensive and as well as at times very extensive, learning process. We discussed leaders, leadership, Business and Business leaders, Economics and Economy, Reforms and LPG, the Power Sector in the world and India, Finance and Accounts in general and that of NTPC, models and cases of relations and laws, Rehabilitation and corporate social responsibility, and so on. It was indeed very intense. We would spend hours every evening, burning the mid-night oil, as I wanted to acquire knowledge in every related area. I wanted to prepare as the best and was certain that these efforts would surely have contributions. Sunil was a wonderful teacher, in addition to being a very well read, knowledgeable and sensitive human being. I could truly realise how learning in all forms and from all directions could always strengthen people.

In NTPC there was a need to 'HRise' both the HR and line. Pran Nath superannuated in two years as I took over as Director (Personnel) in 1997. I was very clear that the HR Department and through its channels, the entire Organisation needed to learn how to enthuse, develop and bet on people. The first plan for me therefore, was to create a blue print to ensure a general environment of trust and ownership, discipline and mutual respect, and learning and creativity. We targeted on 'HRising' the few hundreds in Team HR with their development and also at the same time giving them a vision and road map to march towards creating a value based culture of performance, respect and celebrations. We started the same move of 'HRising' the line, and initially including the entire leadership, whether Directors, EDs, General Managers, Functional Heads, etc. Intensive mechanism of communication and extensive training, primarily focused to creating the desired culture, was unleashed.

On becoming the Director (Personnel) of the PSU, I had somehow picked up a reputation in some of the Bhavans of being a person who would not agree or compromise on wrongful pressures, going against the interests of employees of the organisation, or against the basic core values. I had barely started my journey of transformation in NTPC when I encountered fairly strong differences with a Minister, when I held on to my stand of not accepting a certain proposition which was not fair to the organisation and its people. I had felt that instead of dragging the matter further, it may be better to move and give up my position tendering a resignation to the Company. As a reaction to my move, there was lot of furor in the Organisation and the media, who started reporting lot of stories. As I recall, instead of being available to the media to clear the air, Chitra and I decided to move out of Delhi immediately for a week, to an anonymous destination leaving no contact details. When we returned after a week, things in the media had cooled off substantially. This went on for some time, and finally I was requested by the Minister, CMD, and also by most of the employees through their associations, to withdraw the resignation, which I did, perhaps after 2 months or so. On the withdrawal of my resignation, I declined the job I had got with a very major Group in the meantime. This increased the respect towards me, not only from the media and executives within the organisation, but a very large number of professionals outside as well.

We used very open, honest and transparent processes in the PSU. We started several introspective surveys and laid bare, what the employees felt and found in the Organisation, in the process receiving their expectations of the changes they would want and also supported sustainably the ideas and proposal of the employees.

My 8 years as Director in the Board of NTPC were toiling but very satisfying. It was a blend of both pain and pleasure. It was a journey, at times, in wilderness, and at others a movement with the masses. The great teams of line and HR, the employees and their representative Unions and Associations, all worked together towards a common goal, as if they had all been waiting for change... and the change was gradual as well as radical at times; a non-surgical change, that emitted so much pleasure and happiness that even the pain of some surgical ones became bearable... with a vision of a cleaner and brighter dawn. People and raters started assessing and talking very high of the Organisation. Everyone in the Organisation took the responsibility of consolidating the desired capabilities and building up of the performance and celebration culture in the Organisation.

HR started similar strategic moves while laying out the general action plans, involving people to bring out the desired difference in all related areas like IR, Rehabilitation & Resettlement, Safety, etc. We started the process of creating capabilities and excitement in the team HR, who were to be the major players. An excellent team for HR, led by Naga Kumar and Ashok, supported by some genius youngsters, was unleashed all over. They were selected on the basis of their aptitude, capacity to think and the ability of creating something new ceaselessly. Indranil, Kanchana and later Kanhaiya, brilliantly earned the staff support and the responsibility of developing and reverse mentoring me! We had frequent Heads of HR meetings with all Unit HRs, with clear instructions of bringing 1 or 2 of their young team members. I started articulating the HR Vision and comprehensible time bound action plan for actualising the Vision, Values and the initiatives in the building blocks. They were asked to make presentations of plans and achievements and above all, the new initiatives that they have been taking to strengthen the actualisation plan. We also made groups of HR girls and boys and exposed hundreds of them to intensive HR training in leading Institutions like XLRI, TISS, IIM (Lucknow), MDI, etc. We also invited HRs of leading Organisations who had been doing good work in their field, e.g. Talent Management, Leadership Development, PMS, including Private companies like HUL, Johnson & Johnsons, GKW, LG, JK, Maruti, Infosys, Reliance, and PSUs like SAIL, BHEL, IOC, etc. We also organised to take our HR team in batches to visit some of the corporate on their premises and interact with their HR on different practices, for instance BHEL, WIPRO, Satyam, Infosys, Maruti, HUL, GE, etc. We also exposed some of the Team HRs to the process of Benchmarking and present interesting Projects of a set of leading corporate to analyze their existing practices and develop recommendations for implementations. We were learning from success stories, best practices, excellent benchmark, etc. We wanted to learn and experiment continuously. Sometimes we seemed to be in a hurry, while at others instances we would chew with a lot of time in hand, soaking in all that we could!

We used to distribute interesting Leadership, General Management and People Management books and their summaries to HR people and also others to create a continuous learning habit and provide professional confidence. A continuous attempt was made to involve Team HR at all levels and all Units in their Training Centre, Mentoring activities, Professional circles, Talent Competitions (NOCET), etc. I made it a point to call the last 2–3 batches of HR Trainees and ask them to suggest what new could be done and what needed to be done to sustain the earlier initiatives. I recall Satya, an Executive Trainee, suggest during one such rendezvous, to bring out a new Professional Magazine, which could also invite contributions of executives. That's how Horizon was born, and Disha, even now, regularly forwards its issues to me through mail, adding years to my life! We had unleashed all Unit and Regional HRs to consult people at their end and bring out new initiatives to support and intensify all 4 HR building blocks; and also share with the corporate HRD and other Units and Regions, to enrich everyone with the developments in various fields. We would share extensively copies or summaries of all Feedback Surveys, their recommendations, reports of Benchmarking exercises, reports of Best Practices in HR in several successful companies, openly with all Regions, all Units and even all Associations and employees' representatives. Everyone came together on our journey for change, everyone started thinking change, imaging, relating, contributing and welcoming change. Every initiative, of whatever size and shape, coming from whatever level, Unit or process, added substantial value and a spark of energy and colour. Everybody in HR, everywhere, was energised, excited and had become innovative. 1 or 2 small Units even made a fortnightly HR bulletin to share the events of the Unit.

I started visiting Plants more frequently and regularly, usually alone or accompanied by the CMD or other colleagues, started articulating in formal as well as informal meetings or cultural meets. Frequent opportunities of visits of the Power Minister, or organising some VIP visits occasionally, including the Prime Minister's visit, were also seen as occasions of learning and improving ourselves. I would visit the Plant or Unit twice or thrice for the same, supervising the arrangements for such activities. This became a practice with the families, and children of schools seriously involved in this exciting movement. I knew I had by then, a ready, confident, sensitised and enthusiastic team to deliver the mission developed.

With time, however, my reading had become slow. Yet, there was so much to be read and absorbed to keep myself and the teams learning energy flowing at a good speed. To keep abreast with the surroundings, I engaged the services of a coach for learning the skill of rapid reading and needed several sittings to develop the skill! Sunita at PMI helped me with this element and also helped me in improving my computer skills. I realised that I also needed to develop my skills of counseling to deal with senior leadership team members, colleagues, and particularly in the process of rebuilding commitment to tackle the fast increasing executive turnover. ASCI helped me readily and gave me one-on-one lessons, developing a fair degree of counseling skill in me as well.

I also attended a number of strategic training programmes at leading Business Schools all over the world like the Michigan Business School, Harvard Business School and others, either for training or deliveries. Many memorable incidents marked the occasions, for instance while attending the International Conference of Best Employers gatherings at Scotsdale, USA, or addressing students in Wellington University, Cornell Business School, Martin Hautus Business School, New Zealand, etc. One very educating learning occasion that I recall, was in Michigan Business School, in the year 2000, where Dave Ulurich and Wyne Brockbank were Programme Directors. There was so much new to be learnt from these great trainers and the several trainee colleagues representing leading International businesses from world. I recall that in Michigan, we had an opportunity to listen to Dave Ulrich, who was our Programme Director, many times, and as a bonus, we were fortunate to be addressed by C.K. Prahlad. Their talks were so much enlightening. There was so much to learn from them and so much to experiment on the basis of their research, their suggestions and advises, specifically meant for HR professionals, world over. I was very proud to be a part of such presentations.

Indranil was updated in reading and used to push books and journals like HBR, selected articles of importance and ensured that I read them too.

The two books that influenced me greatly those days were The Living Company by Arie de Geus, and The Fifth Discipline by Peter Serge. We used to emulate or at times even copy great learnings and experiments elsewhere without any inhibition. The concept of learning organisation came in both The Living Company and The Fifth Discipline. And I found the cogent theory base in our HR movement, the core for our HR Vision, which C.K. Prahlad once so forcefully presented in our Michigan interactions.

We developed action plans based on a list of identified initiatives for all the four focus points of the HR Vision: "A family of committed and world class professionals… ultimately leading to make a Learning Organisation, which is flexible in up building capabilities regularly." From here we firmly learnt and erected the four HR Building Blocks to support the making of the learning Organisation, envisioned by my Team HR. I had heard both Dr. Udai Pareek and Dr. T.V. Rao, whom I always considered as the founders of the modern HRD in India, talk of such Building Blocks. I knew that I had intellectual support which would work with me to fulfill the Vision.

We also wanted the Team HR to swell with pride and self respect, unleashing the feeling of consistent ownership and natural energy in the team to deliver any challenging goal assigned. We went to the Board and then to the government with a convincing proposal to change the conventional 'P&A' to the forward looking, sensitive and people development oriented 'HR'. Ours was one of the few PSUs to have gone forward in adopting this transition, and that too for a very valid purpose. Over of period of time, P&A had developed a negative connotation, which could be tackled with this transition, to a large extent. This was welcomed by the employees all over and we energised HR with this new recognition.

There was so much innovation, learning and so much experiment that revolutionised not only the HR, but virtually pushed the entire Organisation towards a movement with a true slogan of 'People First' and sometimes 'People before PLF'. Bit by bit, volume by volume, I learnt from so many participants of the Team. Sunil taught me macro business positions and strategies, making me understand the nuances and used to be very regular in his classes—one person I recall holding my hand while I was building my general knowledge and alignment. Rajendran and Sudhakar, I recall, taught me industrial relations, the courage, confidence and art of being open, transparent and forthright in dealing with people and their institutions. I knew there were instances when, while dealing in industrial relations, I would vacillate, but Rajendran and Sudhakar would hold me by the cuff and even shake me to confirm the right position and stand! Sanjeev was a policy and compensation strategist, and also excellent in his marketing abilities and could sell an idea to internal customers very convincingly; Mazumder, whom I used to always affectionately refer to as Dada, always gave me emotional support and examples of patience and endurance. And there were many more who incessantly and silently supported and taught me all the time. And there were everyday learnings from everyone that perhaps gave me energy, knowledge and a vision to take on a huge organisation which had the inherent potential of being the greatest. There was so much of positive energy and support flowing from the line, the wonderful Engineers, the spine and brain of the organisation, that our movement became very brisk and with so much synergy, accelerating the Learning and Development process. They were all the transformational leaders who considered and delivered oneness and ownership as the basic elements of the emerging culture, irrespective of their being at the level of a Director, ED, GM or new trainees or even executive associations! I learnt true empowerment from Rajendra Singh. While I was, at times, very critical of him in certain aspects and would also infuriate him due to certain fixations of mine, he was magnanimous and perhaps used to enjoy my frequent stubbornness in view of his inherent trust in me.

And then there was Chitra, my wife, partner and a sincere friend, who would always show the way and stand like a solid rock behind me, supporting me on issues whether on file or in Board, so that I could convert many of my visions and actions into reality.

In 2005, when I was leaving the Organisation, almost every location in NTPC wanted me to visit them once. We were amazed to see the emotions and deep affection demonstrated by everyone at Stations, Projects, Regions and Corporate. I, like a sentimental fool, would often mismanage the tears that used to roll out many times. I had been moving across these locations throughout my career and it was same everywhere, but leaving NTPC in 2005 was a heart breaking experience. Even now when I look back, I always realise that the richest account that I have is the emotional account, full of affections of thousands… in which they keep depositing even now, while I am gone and long retired.

I recall, after around 8 months of my release from NTPC and also leaving Reliance Energy in Mumbai, my daughter's marriage alliance suddenly got settled and we decided to conduct the ceremonies from our incomplete house in Greater Noida, Uttar Pradesh, which then was almost a deserted place. We were exploring our jobs involved, in view of the 7 days time given by the couple to perform the marriage, as both would travel from USA and return in a week! We could not get a hotel or any other marriage venue at such a short notice and settled down to make the arrangements in Stellar Gymkhana in Greater Noida, fearing that most of the guests may not come to a distant and a remote place. I visited the Stellar Campus for an inspection and they were showing me the rooms and lawn where I suddenly saw about 8–10 of my ex-NTPC colleagues sitting around a table. I enquired if they had any special occasion and were celebrating over lunch to come all the way to the Club? In reply to my query, they kept smiling, but then one of them shared that they were discussing a checklist for arrangements of my daughter's marriage. There was Ajit, Pranav, Amarnath, Ajit Ojha, Pradeep Pandey, Hassija, Hakam and others, who, without telling me (I had left NTPC by then had taken over the charge and the responsibility of organising everything! I shed tears of relief. Chitra and I were amazed . . . this could happen only in a family.

And there were also some, who for some reasons known to them alone, did not like me or the actions I took on them! I learnt to endure and tolerate so much, but wanted to adopt transparency and being forthright, which perhaps aggravated their anger and hatred against me. But with the hope that they'd understand the integrity of the purpose that made me move differently, and would forgive me . . . I always moved on.

And there was so much to learn from many more in life; and also so much more from each one that I have mentioned here very briefly. But I had to be frugal with a conscious mind that what I wanted to write here was a treatise of my learnings and my team's experiments, and not any kind of an exhaustive biography. Neither did I deserve to be written about, nor I wanted to be written about, except for the purpose of showing my intense and sincere gratitude for the learnings I received, without incurring any cost, from a host of people who built in me whatever I have, from perhaps something I never had.

I still feel, I am definitely incomplete and the journey is still on, like that of the half golden Mongoose of Mahabharatha, who kept hopping from Yajna to Yajna with the insatiable desire to find that something more, something more pious than Yudhisthir's post victory MahaYajna, that could change the other half of his body also into gold, and indeed complete this ever incomplete journey.

PART I

HUMAN RESOURCE IMPERATIVES FOR GLOBAL COMPETITIVENESS

1

Challenges Of Changing Business Environment

"Now! Now! cried the Queen. "Faster! Faster", and they went so fast that at last they seemed to skim through the air, hardly touching the ground with their feet, till suddenly, just as Alice was getting quite exhausted, they stopped and she found herself sitting on the ground, breathless and giddy.

The Queen propped herself up against a tree, and said kindly "You may rest a little now."

Alice looked round her in great surprise. "Why I do believe we've been under this tree the whole time? Everything is just as it was!"

"Of course it is", said the Queen "What would you have it?"

"Well, in our country", said Alice, still panting a little, "You'd generally get to somewhere else if you ran very fast for a long time, as we've been doing!"

"A slow sort of country!" said the Queen, "Now here you see, **it takes all the running you can do, to keep in the same place.** If you want to get somewhere else, you must run at least twice as fast as that!"

– *Through the Looking-Glass* and what Alice found there,
by **Lewis Carroll**[1]

THOUGH LEWIS CARROLL was a humble boatman on Isis in Oxford, telling stories only to entertain tourists, he does have the timeless wisdom which is available only to the 'unschooled' minds. The lines from his famous book, *Through the Looking Glass*, captures a 'truth' that describes the situation of our times. In today's dynamic business environment, even to continue their existence, individuals as well as business organisations need to continually be on the run. Competition has truly become global in nature. Sweeping changes have fundamentally altered the business landscape and the rules for competing. All companies, irrespective of size, nature of industry and geographical locations, are impacted by these sweeping changes.

Further, the pace at which change has been taking place has been increasing at a rapidly accelerating rate. The agricultural way of life lasted some 5000 years; the Industrial Revolution and factory system for about 250 years; the Information and communication revolution has completely altered business and society in a short span of around 50 years. Nobody had ever thought that so much transformation would happen so fast. In 1895, Lord Kelvin, the great British physicist and the then president of the Royal Society quoted: "Heavier-than-air flying machines are impossible". Within a decade, in the year 1903, the Wright brothers took off from Kitty Hawk. Within a century, NASA proposed to send a manned Mission to Mars. I am often reminded of the Crystal Ball gazer or economic sorcerer Alvin Toffler and particularly his *The Third Wave* (Bantam Books, U.S., 1980). His prophesies seemed wild but mostly coming true. Toffler had predicted that there would be assault on the nation which would include the rise of non-national powerful entities and that knowledge and information would be the primary determinants of power. This goes to prove that changes, though not permanent, have been taking place at a mindboggling speed. The Business arena, like all spheres, has also been changing rapidly and radically. Important business realities amongst the numerous existing ones, that influence the companies in the present economy, include:

GLOBALISATION

While studying Economics as a Graduate student during 1964–66 in Patna and listening occasionally to Prof. Gorakh Nath Sinha talking of the world becoming one economic unit, scarcely did we realise that this could be the reality for our own country as well, that too within a short span of our life time.

Looking around, we find that the entire world has become one market leading to economic interdependence, global operations, global workforce, global regulations and intensified competition. Companies no longer compete with the local competitors only in terms of products, quality, costs, durability, speed, etc., but with the global players as well.

A global organisation does not mean doing business abroad, setting up an overseas customer base or exporting and importing technology or expertise from other countries only. Today when the economy is getting integrated, the companies, while doing business from their country of origin have to do global sourcing of resources including capital, technology, raw material, human resource, and also establish their performance level to be at par with the best in the world. It implies that globalisation is all about having a global mindset and global approach in all business activities.

Further, today the competition can spring up from any corner. As Thomas Friedman puts it in his book, *The World is Flat*, doing business instantaneously with billions of other people across the world has been made possible by the lowering of trade and political barriers and by the introduction and implementation of exponential technological advancements. Globalisation 3.0, as he calls it, is driven not by large corporations or giant trade organisations like the World Bank but also by individuals right from desktop freelancers, and innovative start-ups all over the world.

The companies have to compete at global level for not only products and services but talent as well. This has seen an increase in the management of an organisation's people and resources, and meeting the challenges of working with multiple cultures, dealing with varied economic and political conditions, working across multiple time zones, operating in varied business environment and thinking globally to name a few.

MERGERS AND ACQUISITIONS

Mergers, Acquisitions, Takeovers, Joint Ventures, Alliances, etc., have become a routine fact of corporate life. Companies have been adopting the approach of growth by way of mergers and takeovers as an alternative to organic growth. Especially in Indian context, mergers and acquisitions have been taking place on a much larger scale in the recent past.

The challenge posed by these mergers and alliances are tremendous, particularly in terms of people integration. In fact, a number of mergers could not achieve desired benefits owing to issues related to people and cultural assimilation. Thus, an elaborate HR strategy is required for successfully meeting the HR challenges in case of mergers and takeovers such as manpower placement, retention of key talent, cultural integration, communication plan, etc.

India started realising the imperative changes in the global economy as well as in its domestic front and decided to open up in the early 1990s, and introduced the liberalisation, privatisation and globalisation of the economy. Out of the nine sectors opened up by Government, foreign trade, agricultural and rural development, and exports came under the priority list of the policy-makers, while it was the power sector that became the guinea pig of the government's experiments with the changes brought about in the economic policies. I recall being in NTPC those days, and remember how shaken we were when we saw that in no time, almost all big international power players made their entries in India, eager to explore the opportunities the sub-continent had in store for them, e.g. Enron, Cogentrix, National Power, AES, etc. They snatched from us not only the prospective projects but also the most valuable resources, which were invaluable in these times of change, i.e. the talent. While revamping and realigning its HR to the changing times, we, at NTPC, found it challenging to retain our human resources and keeping them abreast with the changing times, as well as to prepare the people's mindset to deal with these new requirements arising out of the prevailing commitments towards economic globalisation.

According to the business strategy which suited the need of the changing times, NTPC went on to acquiring sick and old power stations in the country, one after the other, which enabled it to improve its accounts by liquidating some of its outstandings to meet its requirement of expansion, and at the same time providing the required challenge to its man power by giving them the opportunity to turn around the sick and underperforming power stations into profit making ventures. We were successful and I wish we could have had, as suggested several times, a division or a subsidiary for turning around sick stations, as a business strategy.

RAPID TECHNOLOGICAL CHANGES

Rapid technological changes including the Internet revolution have been taking place, redefining the organisations and the way we work. Improved technology has made the world smaller, enabling businesses to move money, information and ideas around the globe faster than ever before. It is regularly shaping new markets, new forms of competition, new ways to work, new nature of employment contracts, etc. Technology, among other things, is allowing the creation and availability of huge databases to enable faster decision making and also swift communication. With information being available anywhere with the click of a mouse, it allows the flexibility to the people to work in virtual teams and even move their jobs from the workplace to the comfort of their home, thus changing the way the people interact and relate to each other.

SENSITIVE CUSTOMERS

"The customer is king; the customer is always right...", has been one of the oldest and most important adages in business. In the aftermath of the World War, the economy was characterised by huge shortages and the consumers hardly had any choice. This scenario persisted for quite some time. This was the era when the producer was the king and would rule over the market economy. But now the customer has staged a comeback in a big way and the corporate world has woken up to this important factor. Customers, with a little help from the available technological information, are getting more educated, more informed and sensitive to price, value, quality, brand, services, etc., and take no time to switch to another brand/company as they have more choices available in the market owing to the presence of a large number of players in any market segment. Further, the aggressive competition amongst companies for attracting and retaining customers is continually raising the customer's level of expectation, thereby 'raising the bar'. What is perceived as customer delight becomes an essential aspect for meeting customer satisfaction in no matter of time.

CHANGING NATURE OF WORK AND WORKFORCE

The nature of work and the workforce has changed dramatically. The old social contract at work characterised by security, longetivity of the job, the fact that the male member was the breadwinner, etc., have given way to a new social contract which has resulted in an increased insecurity amongst the work force, a variable job duration, women coming out to work in the same numbers as the men, etc. The new employment relationship has replaced the long-term relationship and loyalty, that were important features of yesteryears, by employability, which emphasizes on the capabilities and competencies of the employees, i.e. their aptitude, attitude and behaviour towards their work and environment.

The workforce profile is also marked by a characteristic change with an increase in white collar employees, the number of women employees, introduction of varied types of jobs like permanent, part-timers, temporary workforce, and consultants. The concept of part-time employees, contractors and consultants, which was earlier limited to unskilled, semi-skilled and skilled employees, has been extended to even senior executives. There has been an increased diversity at the workplace where people from varied cultural, educational and regional backgrounds, etc., get together. The new generation of workforce entering the workplace is techno savvy. Technology has been part of their lives, whether it's video games, computers, internet or cell phones. They love to work hard and are extremely competitive.

An era of talent war had commenced. Never before had India ever experienced such a rampant, I would call, manpower piracy, with growth in the new economy businesses that needed radical talent instead of developing talent within the Organisations as was the usual practice in the old economy businesses, which were mostly academy organisations. Talent was developed according to the needs of the organisation, moulding and preparing the workforce as per their abilities and aptitude. But with time and changing organisational needs, there was a greater realisation for preparing and developing human resources and thus began a large scale practice of talent development, particularly with functional and skill inputs, through organised Training and Development where expenditure of capital and time was considered as an important component of investment. The manpower piracy, which occurred with different organisations luring talented and trained manpower, resulted in an unrealistic rise in compensation levels, unreasonable negotiations that did not have any logical relation with the existing cost of living and particularly the rate of inflation. New theories and new practices had started evolving. Public sector organisations, which had been typically academy organisations and mostly followed the principles of the old economy businesses, reeled under the pressure of the regulated process of manpower movement across the PSUs. As a result, they started losing talent at a much faster rate in view of changing practices, new emerging cultures in market, and growing alternative job opportunities and options with lucrative compensations. NTPC was no exception. And with new IPPs and Fast track multinational Power giants coming in the wake of changing regulatory systems, the rate of exits in NTPC increased manifold.

2

Critical Success Factors

"During the past fifty years, the world of business has shifted from one dominated by capital to one dominated by knowledge. Knowledge has displaced capital as the scarce production factor – the key to corporate success."

– Arie De Geus in *The Living Company*[2]

IN THE PRESENT turbulent environment, even the factors of competitiveness are fast changing. It's no longer factors like technology or capital that would put a company on a higher platform in terms of success but multiple factors, mostly intangible in nature, which now determine an organisation's competitiveness. Such intangible factors would include knowledge, brand image, customer responsiveness, ability to learn and adapt to new environment, speed, etc.

There have been a large number of studies to pinpoint the success factors of companies which have emerged as leaders in their respective fields. I have especially marked three studies that are quite influential and useful and have received a lot of respect and acceptability by both the academic as well as the corporate community. The first of these studies included the one conducted by the Royal Dutch/Shell executives headed by Arie De Geus, which was published in the book *The Living Company*. According to Arie De Geus, living companies which survived for more than 100 years are characterised by their strong commitment to *People, Values, Learning* and *Innovation*.

The second study was conducted between 1988 and 1994 by James Collins and Jerry Porras, the Professors of Stanford University, in which they interviewed 700 CEOs of US companies to find out which were the most admired companies. The findings published in *Built to Last* contained 18 visionary companies.

The third such study was conducted by Jim Collins and his team between 1965 and 1995. Based on research of about more than 1400 companies listed in Fortune 500, Jim Collins and his team identified 11 companies which made a leap from 'Good' to 'Great' in a span of 30 years. He concluded that all these companies had certain common characteristics which he clubbed under 7 concepts (Level 5 leadership; First who, Then What; Confront the Brutal facts; Hedgehog Concept; Culture of Discipline; Tecnology Accelators; and The Flywheel).

After the review of such findings and my own experience, I have identified the following major factors which are the common ingredients for the success story of any organisation in the present business environment, impacted by challenges as enlisted in the previous chapter:

SUSTAINED CAPABILITY TO CHANGE

Various challenges emerging from global competition, mergers, technological changes or any other factor – internal or external to the organisation, make it imperative that the organisation has an inherent capability to change. Such capability implies the sensitivity of the organisation to the environment and its capacity to change and adapt to new situations. It would entails, amongst other things, the creation of a learning organisation where there is continuous upgrading of capabilities at individual as well as the organisational level.

With the advent of the 1990s, the NTPC as an organisation was still oblivious to the fact that there could be disturbing radical changes on the horizon. Suddenly the sector, which was confined to State and Central Undertakings or Departments, opened up for business, changing the entire perspective and bringing in substantial number of threats which were so far unknown or rather kept at bay. LPG opened up the rest of the sectors and reformed the rules of business, extensively covering all the sectors rapidly. The workforce at NTPC were used to the peace of a sustained business environment and had not seen so much of change in the course of their services which demanded radical and quick transformation as a typical living company which went through various times of turmoil, but remained winners even for 100 or 200 years or more. According to Charles Darwin, neither the strongest nor the most intellectual, but only those would survive who are adaptable to change.

I need not delve upon this critical factor of change, as this is the most researched and written about truth in the world.

CUSTOMER FIRST

The most important success factor in the present environment is to create an organisation which is customer focused at all times, an organisation where the customer is the first and foremost priority. Customer orientation is essential not only for the service based companies but all organisations, irrespective of their nature of business. Such focus would entail faster decision making, thrust on maintaining quality, innovation, supportive employee attitude, etc. All these factors would require the building and supporting of a conducive organisation structure and environment that makes the organisation customer responsive. Many organisations have been taking a structured approach towards their managing customers through initiatives like Customer Relationship Management (CRM) using technology and people to gain an insight into the needs and behaviour of their customers and provide quality services to them. In fact, the most vital part in accomplishing the customer focus is having satisfied and committed employees. Only if your employees are satisfied, can you think of satisfying the customers.

The large scale comprehensive reforms unleashed by the Government of India, changed the profile of the power sector drastically where the consumers were now to become very significant milestones. All organisational policy making would revolve around how to bring the customers closer, and hence NTPC needed to reform its commercial policies, practices and behaviours.

COST COMPETITIVENESS

Though capital has become easily available to support and drive good ideas and ventures, the increasing demand of shareholders and pressure on profit margins make it imperative for companies to be the cost leader. To achieve this, it needs to have cost competitiveness in every aspect of its business process through strategic sourcing, innovative pricing strategies, inventory control, deployment of technology, etc. Further, cost consciousness and austerity needs to be made a part of every individual in the organisation.

The prerogative of the power sector to demand its price irrespective of its cost was taken away and the organisations needed, perforce, to learn being cost competitive in view of the ever changing tariff structure and mechanism. This needed a greater sense of ownership to be instilled in every employee involved in the organisation.

SPEED

In today's era of rapidly changing scenarios of the business the speed and pace of doing work is everything. The survival and growth of any company depends on how quickly it senses the opportunity or threat and responds to it to their advantages. The companies, irrespective of size, nature of business, etc., must have a high speed in decision making, acquiring technologies, capturing markets, introducing products/services, etc. To instill such speed in the fabric of the organisation, supportive structure and systems need to be in place including decentralised decision making, high level of empowerment, team based and flatter organisational structure, etc.

INNOVATION

Another important success factor today is innovation and creativity. Companies need to continually bring innovation in every aspect of business including products, delivery of services, etc. Employees at all levels need to think creatively and be inventive. Innovation should not be limited to only select individuals or specific department such as Research and Development, but it has to be the responsibility of all individuals in the organisation. Towards achieving this end, a number of efforts grew as Critical Success Factor (CSF), such as knowledge management, freedom of experimentation, creating a culture of risk taking, etc.

Corporate social responsibility (CSR), which was being practiced till recently by many corporate houses as a charitable measure, is fast becoming an important part of the overall business strategy. Companies are realising that they must have a positive social image to penetrate and establish themselves in any market. If they contribute towards betterment of the community and the society where they are operating, they not only create goodwill for themselves but also contribute meaningfully to the development of society, having an indirect impact on their bottom-line. In a nutshell, they have to be good corporate citizens, contributing to the community in which they operate and to society at large.

NTPC, then operating in the midst of uncertain policy and vision on CSR, was to put substantial emphasis on this aspect which had provided a substantial lead to other players in the sector.

PEOPLE

All the current business realities mentioned above, emphasise the fact that the human aspect of business ought to be better harnessed to achieve sustainable success. Hence, out of all the success factors enumerated above, people happen to be the most differentiating and the most important factor as the onus of driving the other success factors lies on the shoulders of this factor alone. The importance of people is clearly evident from the words of the business leader, **Alfred Sloan** of General Motors:

> "Take away my money; take away my factories, warehouses and land. But leave my people, and in five years I will have it all back."

In fact, a number of empirical studies, too point towards the criticality of people in the success of great companies. In the study published in the management bestseller *Good to Great*, the author, Jim Collins, talked about the principle of 'First Who, then What', which clearly emphasised the importance of People factor, which he further qualified as 'Right People' where he emphasised that people were not important because they were assets but were important because they were right for a job.

So the writing on the wall is very clear that:

Only your people can give your firm the sustainable competitive advantage.

If the greatest factor for competitiveness in organisations is the people, I believe, the human resource function has the greatest opportunity and ability to help the business achieve excellence. Udai, the late Dr Udai Pareek, while addressing an all Director (HR) meet in the power sector CPSUs, emphasised the very fact of capitalising this factor, and considered this as an opportunity for HR professionals to show their mettle.

So far, we, in personnel function, were primarily involved in personnel establishment, operation related and transactional activities. Welfare and industrial relation activities were our primary focus and training and development activities were well organised. I would say NTPC, under Hazarika and Shahi, had organised its personal policies, systems and processes very well. They were pragmatic and pretty proactive and strategic. Both carried forward a vision that was primarily aimed make this new and upcoming PSU the best, and the best they created undoubtedly. They strategically built a new organisation, avoiding all pitfalls, and brought in great learnings and experiences from SAIL, BHEL, Electricity Boards, etc., to the best use. This was a remarkable achievement. We indeed had great visionaries and executioners as our HRs founders. Above all, industrial relation was a major challenge and a challenging task to handle systematically, creating an environment to crystallise systems and a strong work culture. Shahi had a wonderful team of capable personnel in this new organisation. Experts and very capable people like B.P. Thakur, A.I. Bunet, Ch. R. Rao, O.P. Sharma, R.A. Sharma, S.K. Naula, R.N. Ramji, and many more, contributed their respective skills and aspirations, and helped achieve the organisational goals. They all grew in the organisation and went on to become Directors, even Chairman and Managing Directors of leading PSUs. It was an immaculately laid down structure and culture of a 15 years old, but very rapidly growing organisation, that was ready to usher in new changing times with an economy that had been left exposed based on the grand LPG mantra. It had to face a spate of changes, all sudden and full of tsunami like surprise, force and speed! The need of the hour was not only to realign the vision, mission and values, but also to quickly upgrade the role of very efficient transaction, and to simultaneously adopt quick transformational roles and plans to drive the organisation to a new era emerging in the country.

PART II

HUMAN RESOURCE FUNCTION

3

Human Resource Function:
Over The Years

During one of my school vacations, I received an invitation from one of my close relatives to spend my holidays with them. I packed my luggage and headed to a place situated in the industrial belt of present day Jharkhand. During those days we hardly had the privilege of telephones, and even letters would take weeks to reach. So, I was a true Atithi (i.e. guest, implying coming without prior information), having promptly accepted the invitation but reaching unannounced. As the office of my relative was near to the Bus station in the remote mining area, I first reached the office with my baggage. He took me around his office and we arrived at a cash counter where people were queuing up to collect their weekly pay envelopes.

We witnessed an argument between a worker and the cash clerk. My relative kept listening quietly and then intervened, asking the clerk to pay as the worker claimed, stating that the worker was right.

We further moved on. On reaching the plant I saw a good number of people smiling at him and wishing him fondly. Some even came forward to talk to him. I could see the people flocking around him with respect and following him, seeking magic solutions to something or the other.

THE PERSON WAS my brother-in-law, married to my third sister, who was posted as the Welfare Officer in one of the coal fields of Tata Steel, a leading private sector Company in 1960. I was quite fascinated by the sight which not only exuded a sense of authority and power, but also a feeling to make an impact on so many lives by solving problems and caring for people. In fact, this was the incident which later acted as the prime motivator for me to take up Personnel/Human Resources as a profession. Though the incident mentioned is neither aimed to glorify or belittle the job, my idea is just to convey the status and the sense of power being enjoyed by the profession in the era of the 1950s and 1960s when it was responsible to help people and create a positive workforce, and the evolution it has made since then in the Indian context.

In India, the people function can be viewed as having evolved through three broad phases:

- Labour Welfare and Industrial Relations (IR)
- Personnel Management
- Human Resource Management/Development

In the Industrial Relations and Labour Welfare phase, the function of Human resource primarily addressed the issue of industrial peace. The Industrial relations function was born in response to the Trade Union movements in the 1920s and 1930s. The era was characterised by mass production, factory system, and repetitive jobs. The focus in this phase was on building good labour relations and maintaining industrial harmony that was the ideal situation as well as the most essential feature, so much sought after by everyone in the profession. This was taken as the key to all success.

In the Personnel phase, it focused on the issue of stability. The emphasis of the function was on the correct administration of entitlements such as benefits, perks, and social securities like pensions. The concepts of human relations, as highlighted through Hawthorne experiments at Western Electric by Elton Mayo, theories of industrial psychology by Hugo Minsterberg, and the famous Maslow's Hierarchy of needs theory, influenced the practices of the function. The attention was paid on workplace motivation and satisfaction besides compensation and welfare orientation. This phase grew with the learning and practices of the earlier phase of industrial relations.

The progress to Human Resource Management gathered momentum around the early 1980s. In this phase, the focus was to address the greater issues of growth and development of people, recognising people as the most valuable resource in organisational performance. Confrontation and negotiations were getting replaced by trust and cooperation. The embryo of movement of the function towards the developmental aspect of HR function may be considered to have been laid when a separate dedicated department called Human Resource Development was set up in Larsen & Toubro Ltd (L&T) in 1975 on the recommendation of professors from IIM Ahmedabad, Dr. Udai Pareek and Dr. T.V. Rao, whom I always considered the founders of Indian HRD.

I believe some confusion still exists about the exact role and structure of Human Resource Development in many organisations. In NTPC, it was viewed as an integral part of overall HRM and gave clarity to the roles of various sub-groups of HR by renaming the Personnel and Administration function to Human Resources. Various sub-groups were created within the HR as HR-Employee Development, HR-Employee Benefits, HR- Employee Services, HR-Employee Relations, HR-Employee Welfare, etc., reflecting the nature of role and orientation of people working in these groups. The new nomenclature was coined to update and realign the organisation's employees and particularly Team HR, to the changing times and needs of recreating HR as transformational leaders in the organisation.

The emphasis on recognition and growth of HR as a profession is being done in a number of ways. A number of professional bodies in the area of HR, such as National HRD Network, Academy of HRD, and National Institute of Personnel Management (NIPM), have come up and are doing quality work in promoting the profession. Besides teaching HR in most of the management institutes in the country, there are institutes offering exclusive courses in HR such as XLRI, Jamshedpur; Tata Institute of Social Sciences (TISS), Mumbai; Department of Labour and Social Welfare, Patna University; Xavier Institute of Social Service (XISS), Ranchi; Symbiosis, Pune; Utkal University, etc. Further, full time specific courses on HR had been started in the recent past by leading institutes such as MDI, Gurgaon; IMI, Delhi; IMT Ghaziabad; Delhi School of Economics, etc. In industries too, there has been an increasing trend in all kinds of organisation to entrust the management of their human asset with people having formal qualification in Human Resource/Personnel Management.

Till the 1980s, any graduate was eligible for appointment as Personnel officer in NTPC. However, since 1992, the entry as Personnel Officers was restricted only to management qualified professionals. Though HR has yet not got the professional status that is enjoyed by professions like Engineering, Medicine, Chartered Accountancy, etc., and it is talked about contemptuously by many that the function is still being handled by people with varied qualifications and backgrounds such as social work, labour welfare, psychology, etc. I understand this state of affairs also exists with other management functions like marketing and finance to a large extent, where people from diverse backgrounds are working parallel with those having management qualifications. I don't think it would do much harm to the function as long as the Executives are endowed by the characteristics of strong people orientation. Rather, I believe, it adds variety and newer perspectives to the profession, bringing in ideas of improvement from varied backgrounds. In fact, later in NTPC, we used to invite and induct performing line people in HR, as this was considered to be a very useful strategy to not only meet the shortages with ready right people in HR but also give it a new perspective where the line starts identifying them as one of them and not different. This had, in fact, brought in very people sensitive line with field experience in HR, allowing it a newer and closer personality.

It can be seen, thus, that the HR function has evolved over the years keeping abreast with the needs of the business. However, of late, the function has been facing a lot of pressure from various quarters regarding its value addition to business, its linkage with the business and at times even a question mark is put on its relevance and existence. HR Professionals have been tirelessly attempting to establish a direct correlation between people and the success of business, attempting to convincingly develop various scorecards and dashboards to measure HR's deliverables and impact on Business, ultimately trying to prove that HR function's expertise and contributions are something that cannot be separated from a business in order to deliver organisational success, growth and excellence. Once Prof Udai Pareek, the eminent management thinker and father of the Indian HRD movement, on being invited in the late 1990s to address the Directors and other Senior HR Officials of Power Sector Central PSUs on the Power HR Forum, remarked that the future of HR function can be viewed as both gloomy as well as exciting in the present context. That morning in Jaipur always remained a memorable one in my professional learning indeed.

Udai said *gloomy* because:

(i) The Specialist role that HR has been performing was getting outsourced to Super-specialists, i.e. consultants and specialised HR service firms who are supposed to deliver those services more efficiently and also more economically.

(ii) A large number of routine works of HR were getting computerised and automated. Various packages and programmes having employee self service features were being made available by the IT firms taking care of many operational routine functions of HR such as attendance, leave management, LTC, advances, compensation, manpower management, MIS, etc.

(iii) Line Managers were increasingly acquiring general management qualifications and were getting equipped to handle many of the basic HR issues themselves.

(iv) Managing Industrial Relations, the mainstay of HR function in the old economy, was gradually losing prominence, as new economy organisations had emerged having non-unionised workforce.

In view of these happenings Udai had remarked that there would hardly be much left for HR Professionals to do.

However, he said, that the future would bring exciting opportunities for HR professionals as well, if the profession truly focused and appreciated the people focus in organisations, which could transform the threatening gloom into very exciting times for the profession.

Exciting, according to him, because:

Only human asset/the intellectual capital could provide an organisation the sustainable competitive edge which was essentially needed in these rapidly changing times. A number of case studies and empirical researches had proven that a direct correlation existed between business success and the quality of the human resource. This implied that HR function was going to be the key business function in the years to come.

One of the greatest entrepreneurs of the current times, Dhiru Bhai Ambani used to always say that we bet on people. Everything else in business, be it an excellent business model, strategies, technology, R&D, finances, delivery and execution, followed automatically.

To have an idea about the emerging concerns of HR function in the present business, I also looked at themes discussed in HR seminars/workshops at some of the prominent professional bodies and business schools including, National HRD Network, All India Management Association, etc. Some of the common HR themes in all these conferences included the following:

- Talent Acquisition and Management
- HR Branding
- Employer Branding
- Leadership Building
- Managing Transformation
- Managing global workforce
- Innovations in HR
- HR as a Strategic Business Partner... and so on.

These workshops and discussions gave opportunities to grow our awareness on the new HR, and our learning concerning the fast emerging HR concepts, trends and practices, enriched us continuously to keep redesigning and adapting contemporary techniques in our transformational journey in NTPC.

For developing the HR Agenda for the future, we would link it with current and prospective state of business strategy. It was essential, in the rapidly changing times, that we would identify and assess the gaps in business environment and strategy, the organisational capabilities available, viz., the requisite talent with reference to the future environment and strategy; and supplement the HR practices today, viz., the HR Practices that would be required for actualising the future business strategies and organisational capabilities that have already been identified.

HR TRANSFORMATION

To understand the climate and culture, a study was carried out by The Power Management Institute (PMI) of the NTPC. They used various instruments administered through questionnaires, interviews and the IIM Ahmedabad report. The motives/orientation studied were the same as mentioned above. The study indicated that amongst the prevalent motives in NTPC, dependency, control and affiliation were the most dominant ones.

Thus, the organisational climate of NTPC could be interpreted by studying a combination of the following motives:

(a) *Control–Dependency:* A bureaucratic and rigid hierarchy dominated the organisation. As the approval of the higher level office was required before any action was taken, decisions were usually delayed. The mindset of the employees was such that they thought it was more important to follow rules and regulations than to achieve results. The senior employees protected their subordinates who did not make any procedural mistakes.

(b) *Dependency – Control:* The organisation had clear cut channels of communication and was controlled by a few people who ultimately made all the decisions.

(c) *Control – Affiliation:* The organisation was hierarchical but placed more emphasis on good relations among employees than on results. Informal groups based on relationships were seen as important.

(d) *Affiliation – Control:* Although the organisation was concerned with maintaining good relations among members, its form was bureaucratic.

(e) *Dependency – Affiliation:* The top management controlled the organisation and promoted their own 'in – group' members, who were extremely loyal to these managers.

(f) *Affiliation – Dependency:* The organisation valued the maintenance of friendly relation among members and one or two people were making most of the decisions. Employees were rewarded on the basis of their proximity to top persons.

A survey was done by PMI (Renu Rajpal was always making the difference) in July 1989 on organisational culture and values in NTPC, focused on four sets of value orientations which influenced all categories of organisational activity.

(i) *Power orientation:* Defined as strong centralised power, demanding conforming behaviour of subordinates.

(ii) *Role orientation:* Power which was legitimised by the role (still with few people) being played, with strong emphasis being laid on hierarchy and status. With this orientation, predictability and stability were given more respect than the competence of the employees.

(iii) *Task orientation:* Authority which was legitimised on the basis of knowledge and competence. This orientation emphasised the achievement of super-ordinate goals.

(iv) *People orientation:* Decision based on concerns for individual needs and the goals. Development of human resource was a valued goal in this orientation.

The study indicated that although the desire of the employees in the company was to have a high degree of task-orientation and people-orientation, the existing culture, however, found these to be very low in practice, with the most dominant dimensions being power-orientation and role-orientation. Thus, there was a vast difference between the desired and the observed course of action.

The same study also looked into the HRD climate. The average score of HRD climate in Indian organisations had been pegged at 54% by Dr. T.V. Rao, which indicated a 'considerable scope for improvement'. The acceptable level of HRD climate is a score of 60%. The HRD climate survey of NTPC indicated a score of 53.7% which was just touching Dr. Rao's average (The HRD Missionary). According to the study, the dimensions which were rated low were:

(i) *Investment of time and resources* – Only 44% found their superiors investing adequate time and resources for the development of the employees.
(ii) *Consultation* – Merely 44% felt that the seniors consulted the subordinates when important decisions about them were taken.
(iii) *Openness* – Only 41% felt they could be free and frank with most people.
(iv) *Conflict management* – 43% felt that the differences were recognised but remained unresolved.
(v) *Help* – Only 48% felt that ample help was provided to the employees for acquiring competence in doing the job.

The following dimensions were given high score by the senior management:

— Superiors friendly and easy to approach (96.5%)
— Most people help and cooperate (60%)
— Superiors took care to listen (59%)
— Freedom to express problems with superiors (56%)

The study was found to have contradictory results and showed that though on the surface, relationship between people was 'friendly and cooperative', the concern for the development of people did not meet the employee's expectations. It had also been found that the involvement of subordinates in decisions concerning them and their influence in decision making was generally low. The most frequently scored item against this dimension was that the 'Superiors generally dominate discussions', or 'Subordinates are fearful to express their view'. It was also indicated that while differences and conflicts were present, these were seldom expressed and therefore, not resolved or worked through. Both these aspects would adversely affect a climate of openness and trust which was one of the pre-requisites for human resources development and team work.

The above studies helped in understanding the context of the organisation in the 1980s and the beginning of the 1990s. Based on introspection, a future strategy was devised to address the issues of organisation climate. Thus, the decade of the 1990s saw various HRD interventions being introduced in the organisation to effectively change the climate of the company. Some of the interventions worth mentioning were: attitudinal training programmes for mindset change; building openness and transparency through communication matrix; mentoring; re-launch of Quality Circles; development centres; new policies like job rotation; transfer; computer loan; etc., as well as review of existing policies. Two major initiatives launched during this period were framing of the Vision and Values of the organisation and e-enablement of HR systems through Peoplesoft.

I recall, when I started speaking to Dr. Baldev Sharma and Dr. Sodhi for *Bodh I* (we gave this name to the first organisation climate survey) and began sharing the idea with Unions, various Associations and even the line leaders at all levels, everyone was skeptical, and there was a flurry of questions … we have been telling you…, why this?' And we went on explaining to each and everyone that we needed more detailed, focused and specific inputs to bring about effective changes in the organisation. The best was the response of NTPC Executive Federation of India (NFFI) and also later National Bipartite Committee (NBC). We started making open and transparent presentation of the findings of the study by Sri Ram Centre (SRC), and compiled their suggestions and queries to create our agenda for further action. Everyone was surprised but committed a lot of support, and we garnered much appreciation and ownership in the process. Whenever we encountered some challenges in the implementation of the changes, a few of them would extend a helping hand, enabling us to accomplish our goals. The general appreciation and mood was to partner the work of transformation that we had undertaken.

To assess the impact of the initiatives, a comprehensive climate study was conducted in the year 2001 through Sri Ram Centre for HR and IR (SRC). This study called *Bodh*, studied the organisational climate across 22 dimensions clubbed into 6 major components, viz., Perception towards work/organisation, Corporate Policy, Employee salary and benefits/

facilities, development of employees, Managerial practices and Industrial Relations. A total of 57% of the employees across the organisation participated in the series of tests that were conducted.

The findings in dimensions like lateral trust (66%), commitment (70.7%), job satisfaction (67%), job content (60%), interpersonal relations (62.3%), etc., were high, thereby implying that the employees of the organisation were much more satisfied on these dimensions than they were in the early 1990s. Areas of concern had now shifted towards career advancement (48%), communication (55%), performance appraisal (45%) and rewards (53%). The movement of the organisational climate towards task-orientation and people- orientation was evident from the earlier power and role-orientation. The overall satisfaction score of *Bodh* 2001, derived as a percentage, was at 61%, which showed a considerable movement from the earlier measured score of 53%.

The *Bodh II* survey was carried out in 2004 to assess the climate after the action plans of *Bodh I* had been implemented. During these 3 years, a number of new activities were taken up including revamping of the Performance Appraisal system, introduction of non-monetary rewards and recognition schemes, implementation of the HR balanced scorecard, strengthening of the communication system, etc. The *Bodh II* survey covered responses from 65% employees across the organisation.

TABLE 1: Summary of Executive Parameters

Executives		
High Ranking	*Medium Ranking*	*Low Ranking**
1. Safety and security 2. Monetary benefit 3. Org. commitment 4. Job satisfaction 5. Lateral trust	1. Training and education 2. Vision, mission and values 3. Interpersonal relations 4. Executive management relations 5. Job contents 6. Welfare facilities 7. Delegation of authority 8. Quality management 9. Objectivity and rationality 10. Participative management 11. Communication system	1. Recog. and appreciation 2. Organisational culture 3. Industrial relation 4. Scope for advance 5. Performance appraisal

The overall satisfaction scores in the organisational climate as assessed in *Bodh II* had considerably increased, indicating that the employees were more satisfied in comparison to 2001. Dimensions like job satisfaction (72%), commitment (76.3%), job content (66.3%), lateral trust (65.3%) and interpersonal relations (68.3%) continued to be high. The scores on dimensions like career advancement (54%), performance appraisal (65.3%), communication (62%), etc., had also shown that the satisfaction levels were increasing. The overall satisfaction score of *Bodh II* derived as a percentage

TABLE 2: Summary of Non-executive Paramaters

Non-executives		
High Ranking	*Medium Ranking*	*Low Ranking**
1. Job satisfaction 2. Org. commitment 3. Lateral trust 4. Safety and security 5. Interpersonal relations	1. Organisational culture 2. Job contents 3. Quality management 4. Vision, mission and values 5. Non-executive management relations	1. Recog. and appreciation 2. Object and rationality 3. Welfare facilities 4. Monetary benefits 5. Participative management 6. Communication system 7. Training and education 8. Industrial relation 9. Perf. appraisal 10. Scope for adv.

TABLE 3: Comparative Findings of *Bodh I* and *Bodh II*

Areas of Assessments and Concern Emerging from Climate Surveys – Bodh I and Bodh II	*Bodh I*		*Bodh II*	
	Ex.	*N.Ex*	*Ex.*	*N.Ex*
Grievance Handling	1.29	1.57	1.55	1.57
Scope for advancement	1.44	1.36	1.74	1.62
Participative Management	1.70	1.60	1.80	1.64
Performance Appraisal	1.35	1.42	1.71	1.81
Recognition and Appreciation	1.59	1.65	1.87	1.85
Organisation culture	1.58	1.97	1.86	2.02
Objectivity and Rationality	1.73	1.65	1.93	1.79
Welfare measure	1.75	1.63	2.08	2.02
Monetary benefits	2.20	1.63	2.34	2.00
Communication System	1.65	1.59	1.90	1.86
Training and Education	1.93	1.59	2.03	1.96
Subordinate Development	–	–	1.63	1.57
Work-Life Balance	–	–	1.68	2.07

was 64.68%. This score crossed the threshold level of Dr. T.V. Rao of 60% (Ref. The HRD Missionary).[2]

The major issues of concern which emerged from *Bodh II* were again career advancement and performance appraisal. Apart from these two, work, life balance and subordinate development were also rated low. A detailed action plan to address these issues was made and was implemented. Based on this feedback, a new Career Development System was created and was introduced for the benefit of the employees. Issues regarding the new performance management system were deliberated and the policy was revised to take care of the concerns of the employees. Similarly, guidelines on work life balance and subordinate development were initiated and circulated for implementation.

The changes brought about in the climate of the organisation in the last 10 years had been done in a systematic and planned manner, with a very well thought out strategy. This strategy had been implemented with vigour and with the contribution of all the employees of the organisation. NTPC, as an organisation, was moving from power and role-orientation towards task and people-orientation. The climate of the organisation was moving progressively towards achievement, with affiliation still being strong amongst all the players.

I attach some of the significant chapters of the Sri Ram Centre's *Bodh I* Report containing the significant findings along with the recommendations from where we honestly developed our action plan in phases, examining the areas of immediate concern and marking the ones for future action.

I have also referred in Table 3 some of the findings and strengths of *Bodh II*, in the people of NTPC and its climate, showing substantial improvements over the previous assessments done by *Bodh I*.

A summary of high ranking, medium and low ranking parameters, as found by the study, is also given in Tables 1 and 2.

LOOKING AHEAD

In the mid 1990s, NTPC management had already started planning for its second Corporate Plan for the upcoming 15 years, i.e. for the period

1997–2012. I recall there were certain eminent people who had extended their support for the development of the plan, like Dr. Pradeep Khandwala of IIM, Ahmedabad, who also became a board member later, and Dr. M B Athreya, an independent Consultant of eminence. Our internal team primarily comprised of Anil Ahuja and Sunil Trivedi, two very hard working executives, who were at the pinnacle of their analytical thinking and insights. The corporate plan document for the period 1997–2012 was named '**Looking Ahead**'. I can distinctly recall that despite challenges and limitations, as team HR, we had been successful in providing a fairly rich content and a commitment to deliver during the plan period. Excerpts of the Plan are quoted below:

"Having committed and stated in the Corporate Plan, these challenges always remained in my focus, as a solid way forward. We also knew, as Team HR, that these had to be delivered all over – in Stations, in Projects, in Regions and in Corporate, not only to transform HR, but had to be delivered to primarily transform NTPC as an Organisation, in order to sustain its winner's persona which had been the result of the efforts of every person associated with the Organisation.

GOALS

- To develop a learning Organisation having knowledge-based competitive edge.
- To create a culture of team building, empowerment and accountability to convert the knowledge into productive action with speed, creativity and flexibility.

STRATEGIES

Integration of HRM

Human Resource Management (HRM) is the responsibility of all Managers. All managers are to be sensitised and equipped to look into the aspects of career planning, on-the-job-trailing, motivation, re-training, rewards, communication needs, etc. The Personnel Division will provide the professional back-up, tools, techniques, supplements and facilities.

Institutionalisation of Values and Ethics

The key element of the HRM strategy will be planning and implementation of concrete and continuous programmes by the HRM Group to ensure the internalisation and institutionalisation of the corporate values by each and every employee across the horizontal as well as vertical boundaries. Periodic value-audits will be carried out by an external agency to assess the prevalent corporate values and the nature and extent of their congruence and divergence from the desired values, so as to enable the Company to chalk out appropriate HRM interventions. Values which do not fit in with the holistic scheme of things may well be deleted from the list of corporate values. But the values that are retained MUST be institutionalised and internalised. The primary responsibility for this will be with the Personnel Division, while the entire organisation, at every level, shall be involved in the process.

With ever-increasing global thrust on corporate governance and ethics, NTPC would usher in a culture which is conducive to effectiveness and brings about congruence between the vision, mission and objectives of the Company with its values, ethics and culture. This will supplement the values already adopted by the Company.

Organisation Culture

Our organisational effectiveness in the new environment depends upon a favourable organisational culture. The culture will be such as to encourage knowledge and competence, and development of people will be a highly valued goal. An atmosphere of trust will be generated through appropriate initiatives including those to be taken for inculcating respect for corporate values and ethics. Free flow of information, transparency in policies and actions, adoption of code of conduct, interventions through behavioural instruments, etc., will be given priority for institutionalising change in the culture of the Company.

Organisation Restructuring

Till August 1982, the corporation functioned with a two-tier structure: Corporate Centre and Plants. Keeping in view the growth projections of the Corporation, a new three-tier structure consisting of Corporate Centre, Regional Headquarters and Plants was implemented. In the mid 1980s, the Corporation was moving from a project organisation to an operating organisation. An organisation study done by IIM, Ahmedabad in 1989 recommended, among other things, moving towards a holding company, with Regional Subsidiary Companies model. Later, an internal committee (Rajendra Singh Committee) re-examined the issue and adopted the basic themes of decentralisation and integration through the Task Force concept.

Since 1991, with the enforcement of the liberalisation and globalisation policies of the Government of India, and under the pressures of market forces, the need for an appropriate organisational restructuring to align the Corporation with the new vision and objectives was felt. The Athreya Management Systems Report on Organisational Restructuring, 1995, also underlined this necessity.

The rapid-response requirements and commercial compulsions of the coming decades call for such restructuring. The corporation will thus initiate restructuring NTPC's plants as 'profit centres', harmonising current operations as well as project executions; regions as 'growth centres', and Corporate Centre as the 'policy centre'. This 'policy centre' would retain only broad policy making and strategic functions: long term planning functions, responsibility for research and development and core engineering, liaison with international bodies, overall monitoring of NTPC's performance, and overall development of NTPC's human resource and management systems.

A task force shall be established which will delineate the detailed contours of restructuring, incorporating all the acceptable recommendations of the previous studies leading to a new organisation structure. Distinct responsibility centres, cost centres and profit centres with evaluation criteria shall be created. A new study would also be taken up in due course of time. The change of the organisational structure, as mentioned above, shall be supplemented with new 'Delegation of Powers' and thrust on grooming of leadership and an empowering work culture.

Training

Training will be used as a crucial tool to create the right attitude and for the development of competence among the employees. The gap between the best global organisations and NTPC will be targeted to be bridged through training and retraining schemes, wherein learning and necessary unlearning will be concretely embedded. Training shall equip the people to deal with not only incremental changes but also episodic or quantum changes in terms of organisational restructuring, business process reengineering or diversification, etc.

Organisation Renewal Cell

An 'Organisation Renewal Cell' will be created to study and eliminate obsolete, obsolescent policies, practices, procedures, etc., in order to update the Organisation with new techniques.

Organisation Climate

Proper motivational climate through material (salaries, perks, employee welfare) and non-material (empowerment, participation, job enrichment, job rotation, career growth) motivators will be ensured on a continuous basis, through periodic upgrading or changes to motivate and retain talent. The welfare packages will be designed in a manner to portray the feeling that NTPC is a caring company.

Performance Appraisal System

The Performance Appraisal System will be reviewed periodically to accommodate or engineer changes. The 'Assessment Centre' concept for the assessment of potential within the organisation will be used for transition to the next decision making level and also for transition to higher category in the management system.

Job Rotation

Short-term and Long-term plans of job rotation will be developed, keeping in view organisational requirements and individual aptitudes. The detailed job rotation plans will be prepared by the Personnel Division of the organisation in consultation with the HODs.

Career and Succession Planning

The career and succession planning module will be developed for employees. In the first phase, the modules will be developed for employees up to three levels below the Board level. Depending on the feedback, all executives will be progressively covered.

Specialists Cadre

At the end of the first five-year-slice of the plan horizon, i.e. in the year 2002, the possibility of implementing 'specialist' and 'generalist' cadres will be looked into. If implemented, the generalists will be given job rotation, while specialists will be motivated with job enrichment programmes.

Periodic Assessment

Every year, the Corporate Personnel Division, will present its assessment of the strategic advances made in HRM and shall evolve appropriate monitoring and accountability mechanisms to make it a natural, smooth and continuous process integral to the philosophy of HRM.

Communication

Communication within the Company and with the outside world will be given greater thrust through inputs from behavioural experts, psychologists and sociologists. The image of the Company as a socially responsive organisation shall be established through appropriate media and publicity related initiatives and social-help interventions. By the year 2005, NTPC will achieve a distinct social personality in addition to its high profile corporate personality".

With our HR Plan prepared and in place, we started implementing the policies and strategies laid down in the Plan. In the process, Team HR, that was already inspired, motivated other professionals, drawing everybody's functional support and ownership in building the future HR of this great organisation, which was destined to turn into an organisation with a capacity of more than 40,000 MW by 2012.

As time progressed, we kept the process of development dynamic, making modest changes and improvements in the plan. During the course of implementation, we kept educating ourselves and as a result the plan was constantly renewed keeping in mind the dynamic nature of the workforce in the great organisation. The entire process was very exhilarating, primarily because we were able to involve not only hundreds of Team HR all over the stations and other locations, but also a host of line and other functional teams, to become active partners in this journey. We could introduce stimulating agendas and methods of HR to our Team throughout the Organisation. As a result of the cumulative efforts, everyone discovered, everyone developed and all enjoyed delivering to achieve and convert the latest agenda into reality. Perhaps the smiles of appreciation and approvals of thousands and the true respect for the Organisation were the best rewards they could get for their hard work, and Team HR was further reinforced and motivated to put their next foot forward.

In the meantime, we had entered the new millennium with hope and excitement, with the Government working fervently on the economic reforms and liberalisation process that they had initiated in the previous decade. There were a number of changes, however, still being made as the Government kept redrawing the contours of power industry in India and were continuing the process of policy development that had been undergoing successive modifications. Private participation, in the so far exclusive domain of the Government in power generation, transmission and distribution, brought in very basic changes in the power sector and at the same time ushered new and competitive challenges before NTPC. We were all required to live with these challenges, grow with the challenges and also remain winners as ever.

I recall the letter from the Ministry of Power, Government of India, advising NTPC to consider its restructuring to make a robust organisation primarily in the wake of the advice given by the Disinvestment Commission. This was a significant and important advice which gave us a host of opportunities to deal with related issues like HR transformation. Keeping this in mind I conveyed to the Chairman, the Board and eventually the Ministry of Power that there was an urgent need for revamping and transforming the entire HR profile of the organisation that would be able to deliver sustainable success to NTPC. This eventually led to the appointment of an international Consulting agency (M/s. A T Kearney) to look at the total gamut of business and its delivery in NTPC. We put the HR agenda in the terms of extensive reference, which was initially looked upon with amusement from a majority in the Organisation but later became the focal point of the Organisation's renewal initiatives.

NTPC had been a continuously winning Organisation from the beginning, but with the flux of time and the novel and rapid changes in the business environment brought in new threats and challenges, which its employees were required to meet bravely and capably.

We had also instituted extensive climate surveys as referred above, which were able to reach more than 65% to 70% employees, ushering hope and enthusiasm in the environment. What was significant was that through this process, the HR department was able to compile an extensive and very honest feedback from the employees on practically all aspects of people management, as well as business strategies.

We started building up our agenda for action, leading to HR transformation. We relied on theory as well as practices for this transformation. Dave Ulrich has mentioned in his works that theory without practice is just an irrelevant occurrence and leads to abstract thinking, and practice without theory is never sustainable. This always remained etched in our minds while we immensely learnt from both, the best of the theories and best practices, so that the changes that we were to introduce could be accepted and were sustainable. We were all open to noble thoughts, ideas and learning from all directions (*Aa kno bhadrah kritvo yantu Vishwatah…* Rig Veda).

However, we were also very conscious and convinced at all times that HR must begin from outside, which not only became a huge challenging task but also a big facilitator. We were convinced that unless we generate support and harmony at the peripherals or outside, the transformation that we wished to make, for a sustainable partnership with business, may not be feasible.

We also had a challenge to 'HRise' not only the Team HR but also to transform the mindset of the line managers and leaders throughout to deliver sustainable success, as HR transformation is not a standalone activity but is primarily concerned about creating business success that needs the support of everyone in the organisation, as well as from all its stakeholders, whether internal or external.

Provoked by the state of affairs, paucity of time available with Team HR, as well as the Line, we wanted to create a culture of leading with theories as well as practices, through success stories and all kinds of new initiatives, though NTPC had yet to become internet savvy then.

We involved a large number of line managers and leaders into the HR role, either directly or through some clandestine or camouflaged initiatives, whether in the peripheral issues of CSR or IR, Governance, or the core areas in the transformed HR structure of building competence, commitment, culture or system. A consciaous attempt was made to involve and include, in this journey across the high rising waves of challenges, all, or at least as many as possible, the enthusiasm of the Line managers, the brilliance of our NTPC Engineers, and this came so willingly and readily. It seemed as if they were all ready to be taken in on the journey of rebuilding a strong NTPC. It appeared as if we were all little school children and friends who were doing *Shramdaan*, collectively, at the then mighty Farakka Barrage with our little hands.

This also prompts me to share my experiences on some of the key concerns of HR functions prevalent in the current scenario, besides some basic people concerns which have been discussed in Part III of the book with delineation of practices in a large Power utility. Further, in order to develop a robust agenda and work towards realising it, we had taken into account, substantially, all surveys and feedback. When we engaged M/s. A T Kearney, we gave them a rich and detailed agenda canvas to address, as presented in the broad headings below, including our HR strategy, in the project *Disha*:

ORGANISATIONAL TRANSFORMATION EXERCISE

We embarked upon an Organisational Transformation (OTS) exercise with the objective of positioning NTPC as a premier and competitive power utility of international standards and to maximise the value of NTPC's equity. The consultancy for Organisation Transformation exercise named as 'Disha' project was provided by the leading global consultant M/s A T Kearney. The exercise encompassed the following areas:

(a) *Business Strategy:* To study the present role, size and business planning process of NTPC keeping in view the long term corporate plan; To study the existing systems of NTPC and suggest how the company can globalise.

(b) *Restructuring:* To identify the impact of growth plans, business environment and strategy on the structure of NTPC. Accordingly, study the alternatives for restructuring the organisation on the basis of fuel, geography, etc., and also to analyse the efficiency of the decision making process and the delegation of powers.

(c) *BPR and IT*: To study the key business processes, systems and procedures in the organisation and benchmark them with other leading companies; To study the state of computerisation and application of IT, and to suggest improvement areas and implement changes.

(d) *HR Strategy*: Identify HR imperatives and develop an HR strategy in light of current and future business strategies; Assess the organisation culture and conduct competency assessment.

As part of the above initiative, a 15 year Corporate Plan had been drawn, that contained strategies for NTPC in all its spheres of activities up to 2017. This document was summarised and disseminated to all employees as '*VISION 2017*'.

The Organisation Transformation exercise identified 14 major initiatives to be implemented in a short time frame covering the 4 areas mentioned above. In the HR strategy, the existing systems that were being revamped were Performance Management System, Career Development System, Training and Development, Reward System and Manpower Planning. The new initiatives that were scheduled to be introduced were Knowledge Management and Idea labs for enhancing the innovation and creativity of the employees.

The Diagnostic study was completed by June 2002, wherein the gaps/weaknesses of the existing systems and processes prevalent in NTPC were identified. The recommendations of the Disha team were enumerated and presented to the management in December 2002. The recommendations in the HR strategy area covered the following:

1. Performance Management System
2. Career Development System
3. Rewards and Incentive schemes
4. Knowledge Management System
5. Manpower Planning
6. Other HR areas like Idea Labs, Training and Development, etc.

The implementation of the recommendations commenced from September 2004, after the Board of Directors accepted all the recommendations spanning all the areas on 16th July, 2003.

In the first phase of implementation, work in 3 areas of HR were started, namely, Performance Management System, Knowledge Management and Rewards and Incentive Schemes. The other recommendations were taken up for implementation in a phased manner at a later stage.

PART III

UNLEASHING PEOPLE POWER THROUGH HUMAN RESOURCES

4

Aligning Human Resources With The Business

ONE OF THE most significant changes in HR Function in its journey from its origin to the present day has been its shift to what HR now stood by and encouraged – from being an administrative and support function to becoming Business partners. In fact, this theme had been at the core of discussion at any gathering, seminar, and conference of HR for the past couple of years. Rightly so, aligning HR with the Business had been my most important experiment within a large multi-location process organisation (in the typical brick and mortar cluster that was the product of the old economy) which would continue, given the dynamic nature and context of business.

NTPC Limited, a leading Public sector power utility of the country was set up by the Government of India in 1975, primarily to plan and promote India's thermal power sector and grow its capacity to meet huge shortages in the country. NTPC quickly grew as the largest power generating company in India.

While I was still there, the Company had a generating capacity of around 30,000 MW, with its net worth of Rs. 44,958 crore and a large number of power plants/offices. With a total manpower of about 25,000, it had a competitive Man: MW ratio as the benchmark in the country. The company had been primarily into thermal power generation but had diversified into hydro-electric generation, Power trading, Power distribution, Coal mining and plans to diversify into Nuclear power generation, LNG through Joint Venture/subsidiaries, etc., were in the development stages. It had been growing indeed!

The Company had been consistently rated amongst the Best Employers and Great Workplaces in India by renowned agencies including Hewitt Associates, Great Places to Work Institute, Mercer Consulting, etc. The company had followed the 'People First' approach. A competitive yet congenial environment was created where we learnt, experimented and practiced to leverage the potential of its employees to achieve its business objectives. In fact, NTPC takes immense pride in its highly committed and competent human resource.

In the first phase, we took steps to 'HRise' the large Team HR (almost around 450 then). We envisioned and inculcated a widespread feeling of commitment and excitement in them to work towards the fulfillment of the vision and a plan for change, nurturing their capabilities all the while. The challenge for the next phase was to 'HRise' the Line and all other functions as well as all the important Stakeholders, like unions and associations. The entire process of change was quiet, seamless and simultaneous at all levels. We unleashed a learning and enrichment fever through trainings; seminars; expos; conventions; sharing of books and summaries; research; engagement of consultants of repute; benchmarking and gathering best practices; joining professional institutions to see the developments taking place; inviting the best Corporates to share their practices and success stories . . . all to build on our own plans and mood for transformation.

Everyone directly involved with HR, whether in HRD, IR or Employee Services roles, were greatly appreciative of the new emerging vision and the crusade of transformation, which had garnered a lot of support and ownership from all sections of the Organisation. It was their instant belief and confidence in whatever we planned and executed, that they were motivated to do anything great and new. The *love and passion for people* and the enthusiasm to attain the set goals . . . it was indeed a delirium, almost trance like state that had enveloped the entire organisation. It reminded me of one of my favourite Pop songs by Jim Reeves. . .

> *For I'd walk a thousand miles,*
> *And swim the seven seas...*
> *I'd count the stars in the Milky Way*
> *And leaves upon a tree....,*
> *To see a twinkle in your eyes*
> *and a dimple when you smile...*

What a Team! What passions for People ! Everyone moved forward in a rhythm propelled with creativity and a harmony. How we mustered a strong relationship with all Unions, central leaders and above all our Executive Federation, during the wonderful journey that we had embarked upon together! It was as if all hearts were ready to be taken, and the only thing we needed to do was to demonstrate and extend honest trust and openness, with transparent intents of partnership. The empathy and reciprocity was just unimaginable. I don't recall any major agitation or complete strike during those wonderful eight years of emotional journey. What an Organisation – the entire Organisation moved with the same rhythm, the same understandings and towards a new challenging vision! One thing was clear – they all wanted to be different and also act differently. This was perhaps our greatest advantage.

NTPC has had a strong culture of performance and long term planning since its inception. In 1996, I became Executive Director and a year later, Director (Personnel) on the Board. During 1997–98, we had undertaken a major organisational transformational agenda and exercise along with M.B. Athreya and we came up with **Looking Ahead** as our corporate plan. Later, as the desire, tempo and acceptability grew, we also engaged an international consultant, A T Kearney, to partner with us in this journey. This decision was taken with reference of the Government's Disinvestment Commission's advice, for not disinvesting the Organisation but for looking at its working for improvements. This provided a good opportunity to revamp the People function and aligning it with the overall business strategy.

I recall one of my training programmes on advanced HR at the Michigan Business School, Ann Arbour. Great HR Consultants like Dave Ulrich and Brockbank were program Directors. I was aware of Prof. C K Prahlad from India, who had done lot of work on Business strategies, working at Michigan Business School. I secretly nurtured an intense desire to meet and interact with him, when fortunately we met him for a very brief interaction. He gave a shock treatment to all of us participants from different leading Organisations across the globe saying, HR had lost its way, its goal and that it no longer had a cogent theory. This retort by one of the big names remained in my thoughts even after coming back. I really wanted to clear the mist and haze, and looked for at least a cogent goal for our HR crusade in my organisation, NTPC, which would act as a light house for all of us, giving us a valuable and purposeful direction. I have always been a confirmed believer of continuous learning, and our HR journey in NTPC was one where we were always open to learning from all directions. We used books, research, trainings, conferences, roundtables, best practices manuals, bench making, knowledge creation, internal surveys, observations of leader in organisation, employees at large, new young juniors, the leader of associations and unions, etc., for amassing the derived knowledge that could be evaluated logically and intelligently and be implemented by the HR in building an Organisation, transforming continuously and incessantly.

In one of the HOP meetings, Nagakumar and Ashok Swarup organised a mini workshop with an agenda to debate and discuss the creating of a value actualisation plan and a new HR Vision. Later, we also had Dr. Sunil Unnyguptan, ex-ASCI, to help our Team HR align to the needs and direction of developing an HR vision. An HR Vision was developed involving the Team HR from all Stations and Regions, building around the HRM Goals laid down in Corporate Plan, which read:

> *To enable our people to be a family of committed world class professionals, and making NTPC a Learning Organisation.*

Every word was extensively debated by the Team HR and chosen to express their thinking and ultimate HR Vision. And I finally found a cogent goal for our HR...a *Learning Organisation.* With this resolution, a comprehensive human resource strategy was formulated which rested on four building blocks:

– *Building Competence* amongst employees primarily through providing training and various developmental opportunities and systems;
– *Building Commitment* towards the organisation's vision, values and goals;
– *Building Culture*, and an enabling environment which motivates employees to contribute their best to organisational goals and celebrate and rejoice all its achievements.
– *Building systems*, i.e. people process and systems such as Recruitment Performance Management, Reward, Communication, Benchmarking, Human Resource Management System, etc., and above all technology supported by IT and ERP.

Under each of the above four building blocks, a number of initiatives were taken, some of which would be discussed in the subsequent chapters under appropriate themes. I would especially like to discuss certain initiatives undertaken under the building block: Systems building including Outsourcing, implementation of Human Resource management system aimed to substantially deal with the so called periphery, and *free HR from very critical transactional roles* to enable it to concentrate more on value added services. Besides, a few initiatives such as Benchmarking in HR areas, Introspection studies, Surveys, etc., were conducted which gave us an idea about the critical needs, both individual and organisational, that needed to be addressed by HR.

OUTSOURCING

The objective was to outsource peripheral activities to optimise manpower strength and cost, as well as to enhance the quality of service delivery by HR. The services outsourced included running and maintenance of industrial canteens, guest houses, sanitation, horticultural works, etc. There had been many judicial cases against public sector organisations on absorption of contract labour, causing immense difficulties. NTPC also had judgment and tremendous trade union pressures for absorbing contract labour in canteens, township securities, cleaning, etc., and the consequent pressures and fear always forced HR to incessantly struggle for finding a way out of such situations. Work pertaining to these had created immense pressure on us that had resulted in the loss of a lot of HR time and energy. The period of 1980s and 1990s had been witness to numerous such scaring cases and judgements. And to top it all, the Organisation had to face reprimands and media flak that as the public sector we needed to be more welfare oriented! The idea was to get the best of specialised services involving the least cost and to ensure that the provisioning of such functions and specialist services do not absorb too much time of HR in this operation. The initiative also stemmed from a need to insulate the organisation from threats or hazards of absorption under the provision of contract labour laws and not putting the employer into uneconomic arrangements of providing these services, essentially through its regular departmental employees. At the same time, it was designed with the purpose of ensuring the basic benefits and securities like provident fund, insurance, compensations, etc., to such contract labour, which was the idea behind such regulatory legislations. As there were countless judgments for absorption of the workmen of contractors in such services, pioneering steps were taken in the various industrial sectors.

Therefore, we initiated the running of all industrial canteens and guest houses through a strategic partner, a Co-operative Society 'Indian Coffee House', the employees of which were members and shareholders, who were drawing structured compensations and benefits including PF and Pension. Of course, the society was not founded with an idea of exploiting these member employees for making profits. Similarly, all the cases of identifying and assigning all housekeeping jobs were assigned to 'Sulabh International'. We issued advices to all stations and the new system worked pretty well at various places.

Further, a Joint venture company with a leading private power company was also launched to handle all maintenance activities of the power plants and also to provide insulation against impacts of litigation from employees and Trade Unions of contracting agencies. We created 'Utility Power Teach' with Reliance Energy. They were, in their own rights, acting as Principal Employers, freeing the Organisation and its HR from a very heavy burden of typical transactional responsibilities, enabling greater focus to development and transformational roles. These were some of the wonderful experiments in the field of People Function providing better quality services which not only insulated NTPC from the vagaries of the laws through uneconomic absorptions, but at the same time also ensured better compensation and benefits to the workmen. The days were different, the practices were different and the legal cultures developed by judgements were very demanding. Our team learnt and enjoyed innovating and experimenting endlessly in these challenging environments.

HUMAN RESOURCE MANAGEMENT SYSTEM

PeopleSoft HRMS which was later named as 'Utkarsh' (meaning *excellence*) was initiated very early (NTPC was amongst the first few clients of PeopleSoft in India) to utilise the development in IT to enhance objectivity, speed and quality of HR service delivery. Many of the HR services including attendance, leave, children education reimbursement, LTC and several other employee services were intended to be taken care of through this initiative. This was also designed to deal with ease with the other HR functions like

Performance Management system, Training & development, etc., and that too by the on-line provision. Thus, HR took the lead in NTPC by putting in place a robust ERP, which was so much needed for growth and excellence considering the need of the times. I borrowed Ambreesh from Engineering, who was the crusader and a big support in this endeavour, and Barbareek, whom I had met at Rihand, joined us in inducting the technology.

MAKING HR ISSUES AN ORGANISATIONAL PRIORITY

To make HR issues a Business priority and to bring it to the attention of Business leaders, the key HR initiatives were introduced through apex management Forums like Executive Committees' meeting comprising of Executive Directors and Directors; Management Committee meeting comprising EDs, station representatives and GMs; Regional Management Committee comprising Business Unit Heads/GMs of the Region and; Site Management Committees comprising Departmental Heads at business unit level. It was made compulsory to give a specific time slot to discuss HR issues and agenda, update status and generate involvement and ownership in line as well as cross functional teams. This created and sustained the line's interest in HR, substantially enough to generate HR's impact on the Organisation. We silently transferred the ownership and responsibility centre of HR to the line along with our full support. This created the magical support and people trust in HR, which had already started gaining ground gradually as we also rolled out initiatives like Development centres, Mentors, Quality circles, professional circles, NOCET, Chanakya, etc., intensely involving a huge number of line managers at junior and middle level across the Organisation. They all felt excited and the best was that they were all committed. Our effort was to 'HRise' the line as a strategic partner, generating the most critically needed synergy, which was the next step to our effort to professionalise and inspire team HR in the organisation.

THRUST ON SURVEYS AND FEEDBACK

An essential requirement for bringing about development in HR is to have a correct picture of employee needs and expectations, directly from them. Towards fulfilling this requirement, we started a culture of introspection and feedback in HR. Organisation climate survey was conducted on a regular basis through an external agency in order to get an honest and sincere feedback. Besides, a number of snap surveys were conducted about various HR initiatives. Action plans were developed based on these gap analysis, feedback and suggestions, and were implemented carefully with involvement of line management and also of the opinion makers, like the unions and associations. Further, surveys were conducted to make impact assessment, which used to enable developing strategies for sustenance and continuous improvement. We were transparent and the assessment results, the good and not so good, were extensively shared with the Unions and Associations. On receiving these reports, we were often bombarded with common expressions like, "We told you... Didn't we tell you so?". Such responses were only assuring the acceptance of the new methods and required commitment and support. We would be inviting their suggestions for improvements, making them virtual partners in change. This generated a lot of interest, trust, and at the same time, ownership of employees and Associations/Unions in the change, as they realised that their expectations were being developed as agendas for action by the concerned authorities.

This was followed by similar and more focused feedback surveys in other areas of concerns like education, health, etc.

HR BENCHMARKING

In order to assess the level of various HR practices and understand the gap, we considered it appropriate to conduct plenty of benchmarking exercises. A number of benchmarking projects were taken in various areas of HR with leading private and public sector organisations as the benchmarking partners for the first time. This provided a good framework for improving upon the existing people practices of NTPC, in line with the best practices in the industry, eliciting greater employee satisfaction.

Just like conducting several feedback studies, we also had many Benchmarking partners and lot of research inputs of best practices to learn from. A large number of Benchmarking Partners were involved, which included several PSUs and excellent Private sector winning organisations, who willingly shared their rich people practices.

The following benchmarking projects were identified to learn and bring in the best of contemporary practices, being hailed by various organisations, for adoption in NTPC.

1. Promotion system – identify best practices and reduce process cycle time
2. Training evaluation model
3. Customer orientation in HR systems and processes
4. Leadership development
5. Executive trainee recruitment process
6. Reward and recognition – non monetary
7. Communication system
8. Creativity and innovation
9. Work life balance

Some of the Organisations We Partnered for Our Benchmarking Projects

   (i) Bharat Heavy Electricals Ltd. (BHEL)
  (ii) Steel Authority of India Ltd. (SAIL)
 (iii) Larsen & Toubro Ltd. (L&T)
 (iv) State Bank of India (SBI)
  (v) Godfrey Phillips India Ltd.
 (vi) Glaxo Smithkline
(vii) Tata Steel
(viii) Indian Oil Corporation Ltd. (IOC)
 (ix) Xavier Labour Relations Institute (XLRI)
  (x) Standard Chartered Bank
 (xi) ICICI
(xii) Titan Industries
(xiii) Wipro
(xiv) Aditya Birla group
 (xv) Infosys
(xvi) Oil & Natural Gas Corporation (ONGC)
(xvii) Gas Authority of India Ltd. (GAIL)
(xviii) Maruti
(xix) Indian Institute of Technology (IIT)
 (xx) All India Management Association (AIMA)
(xxi) Gillette
(xxii) GE-Capital
(xxiii) Hughes Software
(xxiv) NIIT
(xxv) Corporation Bank
(xxvi) Tata Consultancy Services (TCS)

(xxvii) Hero Honda

(xxviii) Sasken communications, etc.

Excellent Organisations, good friends – all were willing to partner and share. We had engaged a large number of good professionals for these projects, which were passionately learning regularly in during the development of the project as well in their implementation. It was amazing to see their excitement grow, their knowledge multiplied, and their professional network widened and grow immensely.

INTEGRATED MODEL FOR HR AS A STRATEGIC BUSINESS PARTNER

Subsequently, an integrated Model for HR as a Strategic Business Partner was developed to provide a framework for execution of HR plans. This model integrated a lot of learning that came to us in HR. This Model, based on the four Building Blocks of HR Strategy, i.e. Competence Building, Commitment Building, Culture Building and Systems Building, gave a closed loop mechanism for generating and implementing HR Initiatives, and also showed linkages and inter-dependencies on various factors in a holistic manner.

I had come across an article 'Intellectual Capital = Competence * Commitment' in Sloan Management Review 39(2) in 1998 by the HR Guru from Michigan Business School, Dave Ulrich, who spoke of Intellectual Capital as a product of competence, multiplied by commitment (Intellectual Capital = Competence × Commitment). This appeared very interesting, very correct and drew a lot of attention. This became a very valuable learning input for me.

Commitment and *competence* are embedded in how each employee thinks about and does his or her work, and in how a company organises to get work done. It is, according to the author, a firm's only appreciable asset. As the need for intellectual capital increases, companies must find ways to ensure that it develops and grows. There are five tools for increasing competence in a firm, site, business and plant: hire new talent from outside; invest in employee learning and training; hire consultants and form partnerships with suppliers, customers, and vendors to share knowledge, create new knowledge, and bring in new ways to work; remove employees who fail to change, learn, and adapt and; find ways to keep valuable workers. Companies also need to foster employees who are not only competent but committed. Employees with too many demands and not enough resources to cope with those demands, quickly burn out, become depressed, and lack commitment. A company can build commitment in three ways: First, *reduce demand on employees* by prioritising work, focusing only on critical activities, and streamlining work processes. Second, *increase resources* by giving employees control over their own work, establishing a vision for the company that creates excitement about work, compensating workers fairly, sharing information on the company's long-range strategy, and providing new technologies, among other things. Third, *turn demands into resources* by exploring how company policies may erode commitment, ensuring that new managers and workers are clear about expectations, understanding family commitments, and having employees participate in decision making.

I found the concept very focussed as well as very relevant and decided to use these two as solid building blocks to be prioritised and addressed by HR in NTPC. However, debating internally, I also added to these two building blocks of *competence* and *commitment*, two more, i.e. *culture building* and *systems building* in order to prioritise these two equally and also give the

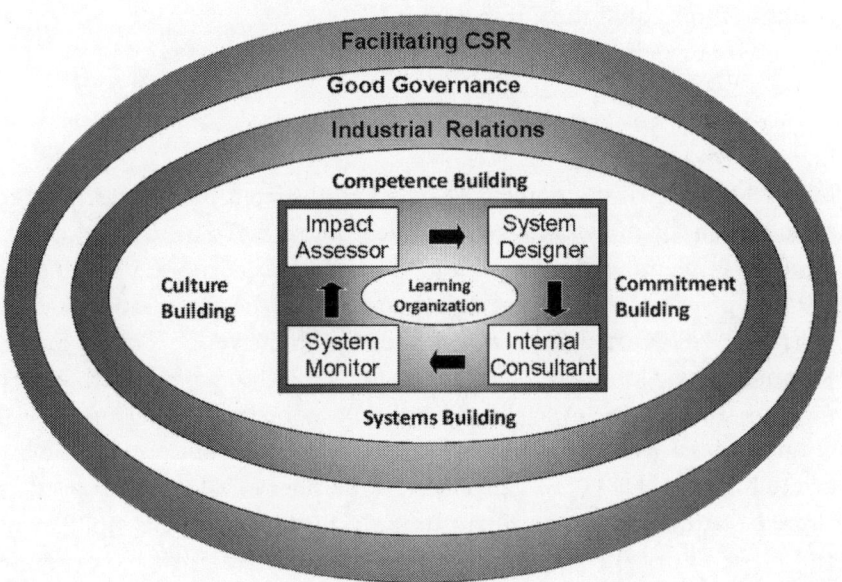

FIGURE 1: HR as Business Partner – A Model

four building blocks a robust structure and very strong footing virtually. Nagakumar, Ashok, Indranil and Kanhaiya carried these concepts forward, virtually acting as my think tanks, thus detailing it as per our requirement. This Model was robust and provided a sound conceptual backing for all HR initiatives taken in the Company, which is briefly described below in logical sequence. This gave a wide and very exhaustive coverage of HR issues required to be addressed comprehensively and leading the transformation of NTPC, creating a learning organisation. We also appreciated that such a transformational menu, if acted upon, would provide a robust foundation as well as a structure with processes that would be sustainable in the very long run.

The concept developed and evolved as we learnt and experienced. During the process we identified some factors that formed concentric circles around the building blocks and the core of the vision, effecting the overall performance and delivery. These, we identified as: *CSR*, *Good Governance* and *Industrial Relations*, which not only become the essential peripheries, but also provide the required support structure, the pride and harmony to the ever dynamic and changing HR, for a sustainably winning organisation.

I was convinced that no development was possible or even if attempted, would not be successful and effective unless peace and harmony were made available throughout the Organisation.

Facilitating CSR

In our HR model, the outermost circle represented the concern of the organisation for the society and outlined the role of HR to develop and facilitate implementation of all initiatives towards corporate citizenship. HR thus plays an important role in strengthening the organisation-society interface. NTPC had formulated a comprehensive Corporate Social Responsibility- Community Development (CSR-CD) policy, much before most of the PSUs or even the Government conceived, to take up social programmes in a more systematic manner and as a part of the responsibility of the Business. NTPC was also made a member of Global Compact – a United Nations initiative. This primarily focuses on social upliftment and plays a critical corporate role towards inclusive growth, corporate branding and generating harmony, that is so essential for development and growth.

Facilitating Good Governance

It involved two aspects of the organisation: Hard and Soft. 'Hard' aspect included designing the organisational architecture, delegation of power, etc., so as to allow for maximum speed in working, empowerment, innovation, etc. 'Soft' aspect included the Vision, Mission, Values and their actualisation, culture building, strengthening internal communication system, etc., so as to create an enabling environment for actualisation of individual as well as team potential with integrity and consequent dignity. HR assumed their importance in organisational transformation and chose to be a very active catalyst, primarily because it had evident contribution in creating a positive and supportive work culture, building a great organisation. This created an environment of peace, respect and high self esteem.

Sound Industrial Relations

Building sound employee relationship constituted the first concentric circle surrounding the four building blocks. Since it was not possible to have development and growth without industrial peace and harmony, efforts needed to be made to secure this in the first instance through establishing good industrial relationship, i.e. relationship with internal stakeholders, such as employees and unions/associations, as well as external customers. A number of participative forums had already been created at the various Unit, Region and Corporate levels for information sharing, consultation and finally joint decision making with the representatives of employees. This included systems such as National Bipartite Committee (NBC), Plant and Shop Councils, Safety Committee, Canteen Management Committee, Employees Welfare Associations, etc. These systems were made more active and participative, demanding much more supportive contributions. Interactions with Union/Association representatives through a new platform of 'Partners in Progress Workshops' provided periodic sharing and alignment of all levels of employee representatives to the Vision and Corporate plans, short term strategic plans requiring them to identify critical issues that needed to be addressed by employees and their representatives and develop action plans to actualise them. This significantly helped in creating a positive mindset of representatives of Executives Associations and Trade Unions, alleviating their concern for organisational issues and developing a deep sense of ownership, generating desired harmonious environment that are the essential ingredients for

Aligning Human Resources With The Business

the growth and development of people and the Organisation itself. As a consequence of these strategies, all our Union-Management interactions and meetings, structured or unstructured, transformed into a very healthy constitution and format based on transparency, mutual appreciations and understanding. We started working on exchanges of benefits and demands on almost all issues, based on a principle of *something for something*, which I had heard C Venketratnam (IMI) preaching in all IR Training interactions with us. This consolidated and strengthened the harmony in relationship, always making it very meaningful for the Organisation.

During the negotiations with various Employees' and Management Forums on NTPC like National Bipartite Committee (NBC), Supervisory Employees Joint Committee (SEJC) and NTPC Executives Federation of India (NEFI), over a period of time we started asking the employees' representatives, giving them the agenda for giving up some of the inefficient practices that could be eliminated to optimise resources and improving the cost and productivity. Some of the significant issues resolved mutually between Employees' Unions and NTPC Management representatives under the move for *Something for Something* are indicated in the Annexure C.

Learning Organisation

As per the Model, the ultimate goal of HR was to create a Learning Organisation, i.e. an organisation which is flexible, responsive and adaptive. The idea was to create an organisation, which was constantly increasing its capabilities at the individual and organisational level. A number of initiatives had been taken in the organisation towards increasing capabilities, including NOCET, Business Minds, Professional Circles, TQM, Integrated Knowledge Management system, planned interventions, constant training opportunities, long term educational opportunities giving new and higher degrees and diplomas that enabled career growth as well as providing an opportunity of holding a very respectable scroll in their hands, thus adding value to their capabilities. These added qualifications were like growing wings for taking a flight from the cliff of excellence that they had already delivered in NTPC. We made some of our programmes competitive and also partly contributory, which created greater value and appreciation for them. These brought in substantial energy and excitement amongst the employees for an all around learning. People felt ready to experiment, create and innovate.

Further, based on the four Building Blocks, the HR function started moving towards its ultimate and the cogent theory – a cogent goal – of the creation of a learning organisation, by performing different roles.

BUILDING BLOCKS OF HR

A few cases or initiatives are listed below for illustration, to generate an understanding of the initiated programmes. Some of them have also been detailed subsequently.

BUILDING COMPETENCE

- Effective Job Performance depends upon having an appropriate set of competencies.
- Competencies are basically functions of Knowledge, Attitude and Skills.
- Responsibility to identify right competencies, select the right people and build the required competencies, rests with HR.

In the total gamut of building Competencies we generally identified the following areas for improvements:

- Talent Induction
- Training and Development
- Leadership Development
- Performance Management
- Job Rotation
- Doing Competence Mapping, AC/DC
- Knowledge Sharing
- Long-term educational opportunities

BUILDING COMMITMENT

We used different methods with some new and old initiatives to build solid commitment amongst the employees.

- Using Dave Ulrich's 'VOI^{2}C^{2}E' Model for building commitment, shared in the training programme I attended in Michigan Business School, which he described in his book 'The HR Value Proposition' (Harvard Business Press, 2005), we elaborated and implemented various initiatives under each of the seven areas. It only allowed us to organise and structure our initiatives in all the identified areas Dave researched on.

Commitment Building through VOI²C²E

- *Vision* – provide employees with a compelling Vision
- *Opportunity* – Give employees opportunities to grow in the organisation and learn new skills.
- *Incentive* – Reward good performance.
- *Impact* – Give employees the opportunity to do meaningful and challenging work.
- *Communication* – Build culture that allows free flow of communication, both vertically and laterally.
- *Community* – Inculcate a sense of belongingness among employees (spread organisational pride).
- *Entrepreneurship* – Provide sufficient organisational space for employees to learn and grow.

This led us to revamp the following areas with initiatives picked up externally from either some Bench marking or best practices collections like:

- Rewards and Recognition
- Strong Social Security Net
- Mentoring
- Career Development System
- Strong Talent Induction (Management Trainee / Artisan trainee System, etc.)
- Comprehensive Training System (Minimum 07 days)
- Global Exposure
- Integrated Career Development System
- Developing Leaders at All Levels
- Glorified all Recognition
- Innovative benefits scheme
- Sparsh-caring culture
- Creating Strong Corporate Identity:
  – NTPC Song

- NTPC Flag
- Raising Day Celebrations
- NTPC Story

BUILDING CULTURE

We knew that only an enabling Culture will maximise the potential of Human Capital of an organisation.

Culture, which is 'the way things are done'. Hence, it is the established norm of the working and behaviour in an organisation. It is basically a reflection of organisational values. NTPC's Team HR worked consciously on a challenging agenda of culture building, which apparently seemed hazy and very abstract. Their commitment was of high order and they were enriched with a treasury of knowledge and experience from a number of organisations. They set up role models for each value for all others to emulate. This was a tough task but made easy because of the tremendous amenability and readiness exhibited by the masses and support extended by the seniors. By becoming role models themselves, the seniors had started enjoying the entire practice which helped in accelerating the process.

- Core Value Actualisation
- Open and transparent, and plenty of Communication (Communication Matrix)
- Participative Forums
- Creating Performance Culture
- Creating Culture of Celebration
- Culture of Discipline
- Risk taking/freedom to risk taking
- Partners in Progress
- Encouraging Space for Creativity
- Tolerance for Innovations
- Involving and Caring Family
- Adventures in Attitude and Team building

BUILDING SYSTEMS

In order to create a supportive culture to motivate people for better performance, HR needs to create suitable Organisational/HR systems.

These systems would include Performance management, CDS, KM, Rewards, etc., as well as organisational architecture and sufficient delegation.

- Flatter Organisational Structure
- IT enabled Systems
- Organisation introspection and Renewal
- ISO
- Benchmarking and Global Benchmarking,
- ERP, Peoplesoft Implementation (For better delivery of HR services)
- Disha : ORT : AT Kearney
- TQM tools such as 5S, QC, Business Excellence Model
- Performance Management System
- 360° / AC/
- Career Development System
- Simplification of policies / Single window
- HR Score card
- IT enabled KM system

Our agenda used to be 'rich and ever enriching'. Team HR was always renewing itself and also its agenda. The entire process was very dynamic. As part of HR, we were continuously monitoring the feedbacks and assessments, and busy designing simple HR systems, helping the line and the organisation to learn and also understand their impact, overseeing the working of the system and assessing the impact of the systems implemented, and finally, based on the assessment output, redesigning to meet the customers' needs. Thus, we kept the entire process very dynamic and self recreating for sustainable success.

We infused the required dynamism, adapting from the popular role format of HR, as below, taking in our process of continuous change and improvement:

(i) *Systems Designer* – We started designing HR systems and HR strategies for achieving the business goals and realising the business strategy. Our objective was to assess and articulate the needs, explicit or implicit, of the employees as well as the organisation and develop appropriate systems to fulfill those needs. The abundant feedback, inputs of different fora and lot of learning in various sectors enabled Team HR to conduct successful experiments.

(ii) *Internal Consultant* – Act as Internal consultant to Line Managers and equip them with people skills for effective implementation of HR systems in their departments/units. A number of such enabling systems were created, such as HR Ambassador, Training Coordinators, QC Facilitators, Mentors, Assessors from line, HR for Line Manager's workshops, Skill Training in handling PMS and related feedback and counseling, etc. This procedure seamlessly integrated the line to the HR roles. The Business Unit Heads were requested, to visit their Training Centres (EDCs) regularly and essentially. After talking to some of the batches of trainees on a regular basis, the Business Unit Heads, looking at its huge potentials, started enjoying the practice. We were also assessing and developing the learning needs of people, through Assessment/Development Centres, sometimes through 360, or Hogan, etc., and also share the results with the individuals and their Supervisors to work out their development route. Everyone's focus now was on the capability building of individuals and their teams.

(iii) *Systems Monitor* – As a systems monitor, the HR department constantly monitored whether HR processes and initiatives were being implemented as per the intended objectives. It was done through conducting constant reviews, Human Resource Information System, several HR audits, etc. We extensively used the quarterly reports of the Heads during HR Meetings for deciding, sharing and monitoring. In fact, we started to have regular meets for Regional Heads of HR for this purpose. These meets also served various purposes of empowering, engaging and elevating the Heads of Regional HRs, and initially, I would often take part to support the Regional HR Heads in the process.

(iv) *Impact Assessor* – In this role, HR measured the effectiveness of HR systems/processes, the value that was created and demonstrated how HR added value and helped the Organisation to achieve its goals through undertaking various introspection studies, feedback surveys such as Organisation Climate Surveys/*Bodh*, Best Employer Surveys, e-Darpan, Vidya, Swasthya, etc. These provided valuable inputs to HR and the Organisation to revisit all processes and systems that enabled us in updating and aligning them to the needs of the Organisation on a regular basis. Above all, these generated so much understanding, trust and confidence amongst the employees at all levels, silently building a well-bonded engagement.

This was used as a dynamic process to account for the expectations of employees and customers, changes in organisational requirements, changes in external environment, etc., and to continuously update the people systems. The successful implementation of these strategies resulted in institutionalising the capacity for change and enhancing HR delivery on a continuous basis. It eventually led to HR aligning with the business and delivering improved business results through people.

THE OUTCOME

It may be difficult to attribute the success of NTPC entirely to the contribution being made by HR function, given the difficulties in quantification of all the contributions of HR. However, the contribution of HR in NTPC had been quite perceptible from the high level of satisfaction of the key consumer of HR services, i.e. the employees of the company. Various indices of manpower productivity have been witnessing the improved upward trend over the years.

Some of the indices showing continuous rise in Productivity in 10 years, since 1999, are indicated in Annexure D.

Further, Table 3, displaying a comparative assessment of two Bodh Surveys through SRC, gives an insight of the impact of change driven by HR in NTPC.

We took these encouraging findings that were the result of the hard work put in by the entire organisation, for an agenda for action for ongoing improvements, and all such indications were never taken as a destination by HR, but a journey to be undertaken, perhaps without a pause.

On different occasions, the company had been consistently rated amongst the top ten or top five of the 'Best Employers', 'Best Companies to work for', 'Great places to work for in India'. It was also rated the best in the country for the excellent HR metrics by Mercer Consulting – Business Today survey, 2005. It was indeed astonishing for everyone in the industry to see a PSU entering the arena of the best, that also in top 3!! I still don't know how we got straight to the Top 3 faction! And hence, we made Team HR to appreciate what all they could do. However, we also emphasised that it was not a destination that had been reached, but a journey that is still on, and that we shall have to keep moving forward. Team HR made a closely knit team, comprised of great learners and passionate deliverers.

5

Managing Talent

IN THE PRESENT knowledge era, talent has become an important lever for propelling a business towards success, as a consequence of which talent management has become a key issue for HR professionals in organisations, irrespective of their magnitude. Before delving into the various ways to facilitate the talent, I would like to briefly discuss certain facts about the talent. Derived from various sources, Talent can be described as the innate ability, aptitude, or competence of an individual. It is a special ability that allows someone to do something well and includes untapped capabilities. Talent, I believe, is what Jim Collins has adequately put forward. According to him Talent means the *Right People* – People with right set of skills for your business requirement and the right attitude to do their tasks. Hence, we learnt and like his findings, also recognised the importance of People and acknowledged that it is not people that are your most important asset *but that the right people are.* These are the right people for whom you must fight for and strive to motivate, develop, grow and retain them.

However, with my experience, I consider that talent is not something limited to the top management or key leadership positions. To paraphrase Aristotle who said that we are identified and recognised in the world by our repeated deeds, and in this process of doing, excellence becomes a habit and is not confined to just a one time act. I too have the same opinion that talent is what we repeatedly do to develop expertise and achieve excellence. Therefore, it would imply two things. One, talent can and does exist at every level in the organisation. Secondly, it is something that can be nurtured or developed. Thus, it is essential that HR professionals and all managers develop their capability to identify the talent required for the success and help nurture it to the advantage of the organisation.

As per my experience and review of literature on the subject, I deduced that managing Talent in any organisation broadly involves the following aspects:

(a) *Attracting/Selecting Talent* – To identify, attract and select best talents;

(b) *Aligning Talent* – To align them to the company vision and goals;

(c) *Nurturing Talent* – To provide them opportunities for growth and development; and

(d) *Recognising Talent* – To recognise the contribution of the people.

Right from its inception, NTPC had laid a lot of emphasis on attracting and developing talent to drive its business goals and had been taking a systematic approach towards this.

ATTRACTING AND SELECTING TALENT

EXECUTIVE TRAINEE SCHEME

The process of talent acquisition in any organisation generally follows either the 'build' or the 'buy' strategy. After its inception in 1975, NTPC had to initially resort to the 'buy' strategy but eventually a decision was taken to go for the 'build' strategy for the long run. In fact, the building of a talent pool definitely pays in the long term, though a company has to resort to other options too in this age of high attrition. Hence, the Executive Trainee (ET) scheme was conceptualised by NTPC in the year 1977 to identify and select young professionals and groom them through comprehensive and innovative induction, orientation and other HRD practices, empowering to take up leadership roles. The ET scheme was introduced for recruitment in Engineering, Finance, Human Resource, and Chemistry Departments and became a regular annual form of investment in building up of a long term leadership pipeline.

The executives hired through the NTPC Executive Trainee scheme were put on one year training period, which comprised of the right mix of class room and on-the-job training to inculcate in them the right attitude, value systems and functional competencies. This process has helped NTPC in infusing the required approach and skills amongst the newly hired young

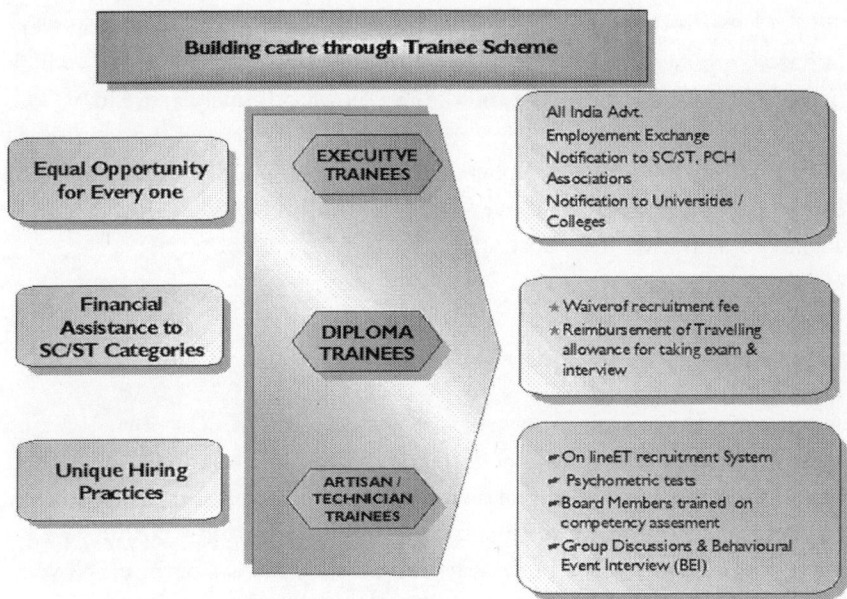

FIGURE 1: Talent Hiring: Executive Trainee Scheme

engineers and other professionals who join NTPC as freshers, having been placed straight from colleges and Institutions. Today, these batches have developed, grown and reached levels as high as that of the Board, and have accomplished this at a younger age as compared to earlier trends. These achievements come with a greater sense of ownership and belongingness, just like the 'right people' that Jim Collins described. Based on the current needs and experience we kept on improving and improvising the structure and introduced various other competency based selection methods. This process turned out to be the Treasure creator in NTPC... a Treasure that became a never ending one, having sowed a self creating and self developing seed in the Organisation.

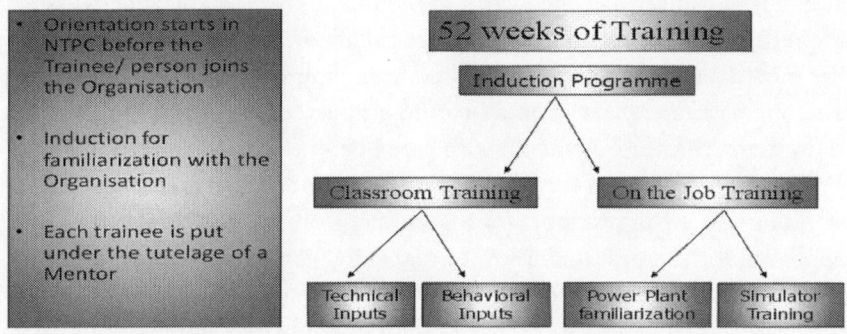

FIGURE 2: Orientation: Executive Trainee Scheme

Similar schemes of hiring talent at different levels of the organisation were initiated, e.g. Diploma trainees, Artisan/Technician Training, etc., which helped us to attain our goal of building a continuous talent cadre in NTPC. I recall Shahi proudly commenting that while our manpower was a small group within the units, our plan was to have a good Training Centre in every power station, how-so-ever small the station would be. It was indeed a solid contribution towards building of a strong talent pool.

COMPETITIVE COMPENSATION AND BENEFITS

A competitive compensation structure always remains an important factor for attracting talent. NTPC had created a composite compensation and benefit structure comprising of a competitive remuneration package, fairly big performance linked incentives with all other benefits, facilities and a strong social security net. This always remained attractive for the employees. Particularly at the Talent induction Level, NTPC's Cost to the Company (CTC) used to be almost double than the best of the comparable Private Sector organisations in the typical brick and mortar, or the process industry.

The strong social security net remained a key benefit component for employees in the public sector enterprises, including NTPC which had further been made appealing for its employees. Some of the social security schemes, besides those which were provided by statutory provisions, included the family economic rehabilitation scheme that extended the benefits to the spouse of deceased employees; death relief scheme in which a contributory sum was made by every employee; employee self-contributory pension scheme; voluntary employee benevolent fund; group insurance scheme; group personal accident insurance scheme; and to top it all the post Retirement Medical Scheme that allowed medical benefits for the retired employees and their spouse till life. In fact, this became one of the most critical benefits that resulted in retaining talent in NTPC, giving a strong assurance and support to the employees and their spouse after retirement, the period when health care becomes so essential to people. I am always conscious of the unfortunate fact that despite Narasimharamulu standing as a strong support for a good Pension Scheme, I failed to get it approved for the grand employees of NTPC. This has been perhaps the only shortfall in building of a great supportive family of NTPC, an aspect which was included in the HR Vision by me, but remained unattainable and a cause of grief to me.

EMPLOYER BRANDING

We were aware of the intense competition that had come in the so far quiet and secure power sector. Conscious efforts also needed to be made to position the company as a preferred employer. The branding of the company as an employer of choice is essential not only to attract the required talent but also to motivate the existing employees. This is, in fact, an amalgamation of multiple factors including overall corporate reputation, nature of industry, contribution to society, profile of leadership, people orientation, etc. Though NTPC has always put emphasis on the people aspect, it was also thought appropriate to enhance its image as a preferred employer. Towards achieving this objective, the company decided to participate in all leading best employer surveys being conducted in the country. This practice energised not only the HR department but also the people from other departments, engaging employees at all levels to make efforts to further improve the HR climate. After all the employees had travelled along the path of transformation of NTPC for a considerable period, I recall the first time we ever entered a rating by global consultants, Hewitts Associations, in 2003 – we found a place as high as among the top three! We unleashed a celebration that lasted for a week, illuminating all buildings in the Stations/Plants, Regions and Corporate, sending sweets packets with messages of acknowledgement to all the families who had always extended their support to NTPC, in their own quiet manner, in this march of excellence! Everyone knew they have achieved a great thing, acquired a proud personality! How united NTPC appeared, how glamorous the Organisation emerged and how proud all the employees and their families felt! To the HR department, this achievement also provided an opportunity to benchmark its practices with the other best in the country and bridge the existing gap. Later, the objective of making the company a preferred employer was added as an important part of the long term corporate plan of the company for the year 2017 and concerted efforts were always being made to achieve this goal.

CHALLENGING ASSIGNMENTS

NTPC takes pride in having a work culture that believed in demanding, supporting and recognising strong performance orientation. The thrill of erecting a huge power plant, costing thousands of crores, in a barren remote area, bearing all sorts of hardships and surpassing the previous completion time, always remains immense, having laboured as a team right since its inception. The culture of setting and meeting deadlines, targets, milestones, set during project erection had extended in all the spheres of the company's activities. In fact, when the company participated in the Best Employers survey for the first time in the year 2003, and was rated the third best employer in the country, the result analysis published in *Business Today*[4] praised the company with the remark that "it is the company with the heart of a public sector undertaking, but mind of a private enterprise!"

NTPC – POWER HR FORUM

NTPC had taken a lead role in the creation of a *Power HR Forum* comprising of HR representatives from 10 Power Utilities in the Central Power Sector under the Government of India like NTPC, NHPC, PowerGrid, NEEPCO, Bhakra Beas Management Board, Satluj Jal Vidyut Nigam Ltd., Rural Electrification Corp., Power Finance Corp. Ltd, Damodar Valley Corp. Ltd, THDC, etc. The Forum was set up with a Mission *"To aid in the development of Power Sector HR Professionals"*. The Forum set itself a Vision of *"Identifying the best practices in power sector PSU's, undertake HR policy research and advocacy and set benchmarks for others to emulate"*. The forum regularly worked towards sharing mutually useful information, best practices in the area of Human Resources, pooling of infrastructure, and also to join hands in developing common benefits for the employees of the members of the Power Sector companies. This became a very powerful initiative for creating a culture of useful networking, mutual sharing and learning, and establishing an all round synergy that excited all the participants to become a professional force working towards mutual benefits. The Power sector was growing and needed to bond together to build a strong band of HR Professionals.

ALIGNING THE TALENT

INDUCTION PROGRAMME

Every year a large number of Engineering and MBA graduates, as well as certain other fields, selected by the company, are put through one year of comprehensive in-house induction training. The training module right from the first batch, comprising both classroom and on-the-job experience, had been designed to instill the required technical, behavioural, managerial skills and at the same time instigate in them the right cultural and appropriate value systems of the Company.

The training philosophy of the company, that included the induction programme as well, had been based on the belief that 'We do not train to develop resource but develop a good citizen'. In line with the very belief, besides providing inputs on power plant management, industrial safety, etc., adequate inputs for shaping the personality of the employees were added through programmes such as yoga, meditation, theatre workshops conducted by the National School of Drama, business English courses by British Council, corporate social responsibility modules that incorporated association with neighbouring villages and their concerns, etc. These programmes sensitised the new generation with the complete vision and commitments towards the Organisation.

MENTORING

Coming straight from Colleges and Institutions, we knew that the Engineering/Executive Trainees, though brimming with enthusiasm, would need to be essentially oriented to the NTPC ethos, values and cultures. Therefore, we introduced a system to guide and counsel the young talents by providing a personal touch for better socialisation and thus facilitating in an effective integration and assimilation in the organisation.

As such, Mentoring as a formal system was introduced in NTPC in the year 2000 for Executive Trainees for aiding in a smooth transaction in the socialisation process and for aligning them with the culture/values of the Company as well as to build their competence in dealing with work related issues.

Generally, a senior executive at the level of senior manager/Deputy General Manager was assigned with the role of the Mentor. The Mentor would be well versed with the working environment of the organisation, had a good performance background, and possessed a positive outlook. Empathy towards others and the ability to guide was another important aspect to become a Mentor. An extensive training was provided to the identified Mentors in the Organisation to give an understanding of the programme and sensitise them of the crucial role in building talent in the Organisation. When the Trainees were inducted in the Unit for on-the-job training,

Human Resources Function catalysed the process of identification of Mentor as per the guidelines laid down and undertook the role of an anchor by facilitating interaction, reviewing meetings and social get-togethers. Further, the Mentor-Mentee relationship sustained, continued and developed through a well defined structure in accordance with the System. Besides offering a number of opportunities for interaction and building a healthy relationship for socialisation and guidance, the relationship was also publicly recognised through practices like *Mentors' Day* celebration, *Mentors' Samman* on 5th September (Teacher's Day), etc. Organising such occasions and many other exclusive events also brought together all Mentors and Mentees on one platform for experience sharing and recognition. The mentoring relationship further deepened by encouraging out-bound meets and programmes for them. To exchange progress, concerns, views, difficulties and learn from others, and networking, there was a provision for the formation of a Mentors Club. Although the formal Mentor-Mentee relationship was meant for the one year training period, the informal relationship and dialogue usually continued beyond the training period, which eventually contributed substantially towards the building of a strong family culture.

With a focused approach, Team HR created and developed a pool of more than 400 Mentors in the organisation. A number of workshops for training new mentors as well as programmes for refreshing the skills of existing mentors were carried out periodically. This received a tremendous response from our employees and the concept was extended to all the entrants in executive cadre. In order to consolidate the programme, whichever unit I visited, I made sure to have at least a one hour slot kept aside to meet all Mentors to make them share some of their experiences and make them feel that they were doing a very important work in the organisation. Even though some visits to a plant would be short, but I would still meet them, may be over breakfast or a quick lunch and ask interesting and personal question like, when their children's birthdays were, and whether their mentees join the party and so on. This conduct was primarily to generate greater understanding and commitment. I myself would also keep learning in the process and use the experiences and stories of one unit with the Mentors of another. Later, we also added this in our Performance Management System (PMS) by assigning such additional responsibilities and roles played by some executives in evaluation. Even during interviews for Promotions year on year, I would deliberately ask many executives from various Regions and Units about their Mentees, their experiences, their contributions. This inquisitiveness from my side would spread like wildfire and everyone would take lot of interest in the entire process. I would make it a point to mention these and some of the experiences of Mentor-Mentee communications and stories in my interaction in all planned interventions like in Capsule Course, Enhancing Managerial Competence (EMC) and Advance Management Programme (AMP) for different levels of Executives. When combined, these anecdotes helped substantially in institutionalising and culturing mutuality in the Organisation, as people learnt and grew up.

ALIGNING WITH COMPANY VISION AND VALUES

In NTPC we believed that alignment with the Company vision and the Company's Core Values was critical for enhancing employee commitment with the company's objectives. I would often recall the story of the stone cutter and the cathedral in which the stone cutter relates his work to the larger vision of the organisation, and also recall several other stories which held tremendous significance in a corporate context too.

We strongly believed that the core values were the cornerstone of a strong corporate culture. In order to align people to the culture, it was essential that various measures were taken to spread the core values in the company. To enable the employees to appreciate the meaning of core values identified by the Company and practice them in day to day business activities, we brought out Handbooks on Core Values which provided a detailed understanding of each value, its do's and don'ts, primarily to educate and align. We distributed these to all employees and also in all the schools in our Townships.

We strongly believed that story telling was a powerful way of communicating and reinforcing values. An initiative of linking company's core values with moral stories picked up from Jatakas, Vedas, Bible, Hitopdeshas and other scriptures was undertaken. Several volumes of such compilation containing value based short stories were published with the name *Timeless Treasures* in both Hindi and English languages and circulated to all employees in the company. Volunteers kept coming up with a stream of such enlightening and educating stories, motivating and reminding us to refresh our publication. Employees and more interestingly, the families would wait curiously for the next volume to come. In fact, we also started forwarding the *Timeless Treasures* to a large number of schools' principals for their libraries in all cities like Delhi, Lucknow, Kolkata, Mumbai, Hyderabad, etc., which brought excellent feedback from people beyond the realm of NTPC, thus increasing the horizons of our values.

We involved the CMD and Directors through several workshops conducted by Dr. M B Athreya to appreciate, review and own the entire activity and process. The values, which numbered 18–20, were initially restricted to diaries and some documents. Generally not referred to or comfortably understood, these were revisited and focused during the workshops conducted for different levels of employees in PMI, and units. We formulated a set of five focused core values: *Customer focus, Organisational pride, Mutual respect, Innovation and speed, Total quality* . . . **COMIT** (R.K. Nair instantly developed this simple but very powerful acronym) and publicised it continuously. We held value workshops, had the professional circles and workers' all Quality Circles to deliberate and come out with solutions and process of embedding and actualising these. I silently took advantage of the annual promotion interview *melas* for all levels of executives to query and discuss about the Vision and Core Values of the company. This helped in generating keen interest in them; inculcating a desire to learn, be aware of, and to consciously help adhering to the values. During my questioning opportunities these discussions included Executive Directors and the Director on the panel as witnesses and were a great support. We made a request to all EDs and General Managers to discuss HR, the Vision and Values in all Training Programmes in the plant and all coordination and periodic cross functional meetings. I admire the Teams of Directors, EDs, GMs and leaders at all levels that had a sense of ownership within them and supported these experiments in unleashing a very positive People Power in the Organisation. Everyone down the line started talking of the Core Values and imbibing these in their behaviour. We actually extended these values to the families and schools as well, which helped to build up a very powerful support system. I recall, when we introduced the quality circles in schools (Rajeev Jain of Singrauli particularly was extremely committed to innovate and drive these!). The children would take up the values as their projects and bring out very interesting solutions and practices. We found that everyone in NTPC started feeling that they were different and also that they were capable of making the difference.

There were a number of stories and incidents which I used to hear from people about their adhering to core values in practice. I was greatly amused to hear an incident from Avinash (Chaturvedi) during a discussion about some of these activities.

It was a case of a Regional Management Committee meeting, then chaired by G.P. Singh, where two senior officers, one Unit Head and a Regional Functional Head, spoke in very loud tones. While they were hurling accusations and slur on each other, G.P. suddenly got up from his chair, causing the commotion to come to an abrupt silence. He announced that such behaviours against colleagues was a breach of core values and were not acceptable to him and that he would hate, rather detest to be part of such a meeting. With this, G.P. walked out of the conference room and went to his chamber. Avinash narrated that everyone in the room was stunned and later went to G.P., persuading him to resume the meeting and return to the conference room. They gave an assurance of not demonstrating such behaviour and aplogised to each other. Avinash said that the people remembered this incident all over the Region and elsewhere too, perhaps as an example that demonstrated adherence to the Core Values of the Organisation that we were so diligently trying to imbibe in everyone. When such things happen, they certainly penetrate the minds, especially if they are being portrayed by leaders who act as custodians and pace setters of building a strong culture within the organisation.

I am certain, and I know, that there would have been many such examples set by leaders all over the organisation in NTPC that went into the roots, sprouting congeniality, mutual respect and synergy all over, building a strong culture within the work environment.

We came out with a strategy and matrix for effective internal communication, in which we listed all the scheduled meetings and interactions which the top management, including plant GMs, had with the employees, in different official forums as well as unofficial interactions like the Employees Welfare Association, Clubs, Sports Tournaments, etc. For all the official interactions we suggested structuring the content in such a manner that the meeting would start with a recap of the Organisational Vision and Values by the Chairman. For unofficial interactions, we suggested the Project Head asking the people questions related to what the Company/vision meant to the employee, how would they contribute towards realising the Vision, how could they help in internalising the Core Values in the very culture of the Company, etc. We also instructed the Professional Circles and Quality Circles to deliberate on the Vision and Values, and to come up with individual action plans to help actualise, in their own small ways, even at the level of the shop floor. In this way, we encouraged change right from the bottom, apart from leading change and driving it from the top, which was also done through organisation wide HR initiatives. In fact, people power is unleashed when the rank and file gets excited about an initiative such as alignment with the Vision and Values. This excitement can be generated through sustained communication and by leading through example.

With the business strategy of the organisation undergoing major changes, it was imperative that the dream of NTPC to attain its vision be revisited. Accordingly, in 2004–2005, a revisit workshop was organised at PMI that focused on the EDs and GMs as the intended target group. The workshop came up with a new draft of the Vision and Values. This draft was then discussed at various forums across NTPC, covering hundreds of employees, whose opinion was sought. This generated a feeling of involvement and responsibility among the employees. The draft was then discussed by the Management Committee along with the suggestions of employees. The final version, which emanated from the MCM was also shared with the Board of Directors. The revamped Vision and values that emerged from the robust process were:

Vision

"A world class integrated power major, powering India's growth, with increasing global presence."

Values

B-COMIT

- Business Ethics
- Customer Focus
- Organisational and professional Pride
- Mutual respect and trust
- Innovation and speed
- Total quality for excellence

Apart from the above, the Mission statement of the organisation, which was quite lengthy, was also revisited and a revised Mission statement was also announced as under:

Mission

"Develop and provide reliable power, related products and services at competitive prices, integrating multiple energy sources with innovative and eco-friendly technologies and contribute to society."

The initiatives launched during these years started to yield positive results for the organisation. At this juncture, it was important to take feedbacks on the impact of the Values across the Organisation. Accordingly, a Value Survey was conducted through Shri Ram Centre for HR and IR. The objectives of the survey were:

(i) To seek employee's estimation of the efficacy of B-COMIT and their alignment to them.
(ii) To examine the present organisational environment and its role in instituting the development of the values.
(iii) To analyse the effectiveness of existing practices and to inculcate organisational values amongst the employees.

The survey was conducted at all locations (more than 50), including all levels of employees. The data collection was done through a structured questionnaire designed jointly, interviews and secondary data available within the organisation. The questionnaire was divided into 3 sections. The first part captured the demographic data of the respondents, the second part captured feedback on 8 macro dimensions (17 sub dimensions) of the core value actualisation. Qualitative feedback and suggestions were sought in the last section.

Questionnaires were collected from 9165 employees, which is 38 per cent of the total strength of NTPC. Out of this, 4852 were executives (45 per cent) and 4313 (32 per cent) were non-executives. Respondents comprised of a randomly selected sample and represented all regions, departments and levels.

Interviews were conducted with 10 per cent of the total data collected. Additional group discussions were also held with both executives and non-executives in each location. Respondents were randomly chosen.

It was found that the highest ranked scores for both executives and non-executives were the sense of ownership, loyalty and trust and quality consciousness. Some of the common low ranking dimensions were business ethics, entrepreneurship and decision-making.

The strengths of NTPC that emerged were:

  (i) Employees considered themselves as the owner/stakeholder of the company
 (ii) Employees were very loyal to the Organisation.
(iii) There was better trust and mutual understanding among employees. They went out of the way to help and provide support to each other.
 (iv) The organisation set high standards of quality.
  (v) Executives felt that the scope for learning in NTPC was high.
 (vi) Executives worked hard in order to achieve excellence.

The low and medium ranked dimensions were also brought out.

The data analysis based on demographics indicated an interesting trend. Level wise, the senior employees demonstrated that they perceived the values of the company and its actualisation more positively. Similarly, age wise, the younger employees viewed value actualisation at lower levels than the older employees. Employees who had worked in NTPC for more than 20 years had a higher positive perception than employees who had been in the organisation for only 3–5 years. The higher the qualification, the perception appeared to be lower. Thus, based on demographic data, it could be summarised that higher the level, experience and age and lesser the qualification, the perception of core values and their actualisation in the Organisation was more appreciated and, lower the age, higher the qualification and lesser the experience, the expectation from the organisation was much higher and therefore, the satisfaction levels were lower.

The value survey had thrown up a plethora of data, which indicated both the strengths of the organisation, as well as the weak spots. NTPC, moving forward, needed to build on its strengths and also address issues which had come out as weaknesses. A concerted effort was needed and attempted by each employee to foster these values in the Organisation. This enabled the organisation to strengthen its culture and march towards becoming a value based Organisation.

PERFORMANCE MANAGEMENT SYSTEM

Performance Management System was another important tool not just for appraising performance but in clarifying expectations and aligning employees from top to bottom to the Company's goals. We used this tool in helping people to be conscious of actualising various small and big initiatives that helped in building the desired culture. In NTPC, a memorandum of understanding (MOU) was signed by the company with the Government of India every year, setting targets to be achieved in various areas. The target set in the MOU of the company was then percolated down to units, which constituted the Key Performance Areas (KPA) of the Business Unit Heads. The KPAs of the unit Heads were further percolated down to Department Heads and the individuals, thus linking all employees with the overall company goals.

We revisited the entire PMS process with the help of AT Kearny, our consultants for the Organisation Transformation Study, *Disha*, reviewed the entire structure, included a part of the KPAs and KPI drivers specifically designed and measurable to a large extent, and came up with a new yet simple system. The system was extended to all through a large number of workshops, year on year, to become a system that contributed to the Performance Culture in the Organisation.

PACE (Performance and Competence for Excellence), the new KPA based performance management system, had been launched for all executives and is currently under implementation. The system was designed for enhancing the performance oriented culture of NTPC through objectivity, openness and transparency. The key features were as follows:

- The focus of revised PMS was to strike a balance between performance and competence in order to excel at individual level.
- The individual level performances were obtained by cascading of business goals and objectives for the year and thereby integrating individual roles and responsibilities to organisational goals and objectives.
- PACE was also aimed at developing technical/functional competencies along with leadership and managerial competencies.
- It was also used for potential assessment and capturing 'Core Values' being practiced by employees.
- The process was designed to make the system transparent, open and for giving feedback for developmental areas.

We also introduced an evaluation of behaviour, especially adherence to Core Values, which was a unique move and experiment, and also roles in development of many other internal institutions which needed people ownership, like QC, PC, TQM, etc. The system also required people to be transparent and sharing, coaching and counselling role and relationship, which helped in creating a new culture of trust and performance in the organisation. This brought lot of performance orientation, self discipline, much better transparency and communication, as well as stronger value adherence in NTPC.

Apart from assessing performance deliveries against identified Key Result Areas in PMS, we had also taken into account, as generally practiced, assessment of competencies. NTPC also carried on the activity of Competency Mapping and therefore, consequently planning HR activities based on identified competencies, which primarily comprised of knowledge, skill and generally observable abilities defined in terms of attitudes and behaviour, causing excellence in performance. We went developing competency based HR systems for Talent Management and Development. This covered, apart from performance management and assessment, other critical HR Systems like Leadership Development, Succession Planning, Career Development, Training and Development, Recruitment, Rewards and Incentives, etc.

In fact, the PMS became a tool for development of the People and their commitment, and not just a routine assessment. It included areas of

FIGURE 3: Competancy based HR Systems

functional and managerial competencies, potential for assuming higher responsibilities, and training required to develop/refine competencies. Even in the KPA area, we built in a system of mutual discussion at the goal setting stage, mid-year review stage, and the final performance review stage. This was done with a view to improve top-down and bottom-up communication, and to build a culture of openness and transparency. The performance ratings were communicated to the concerned employees, and later linked to financial payouts as well.

NURTURING TALENT

OPPORTUNITIES FOR CAREER GROWTH

NTPC designed a career development system to take care of growth aspirations of the employees. The company had laid down a well defined policy for the career growth of every category of employees, right from lowest level at workmen, i.e. W0 (Attendant) to the highest level of E9 (Executive Director). The career progression had been merit based, taking into account performance and demonstration of core values and potential of employees.

More than the renewed architecture and design of the system, the most important and impactful intervention we made was to dispel the age old belief that performance is not recognised, and that promotions were often results of internal influence on supervisors and extent of the use of external pressures. We worked relentlessly to assure in the process that it was only performance, including attitude and behaviour, that mattered and not the external pressures generated which affected the decisions. We would explain outsiders the relationships or even take the liberty of ignoring them, and made it a point to issue the Promotion orders immediately after completion of the interview process the very same day so that negative apprehensions were not spread which could weaken the trust on system and on the internal Leaders in Organisation. I recall some feedback from an employee that as soon as the interviews would be over, people would flock around the Control Rooms in the Stations even in the middle of the night, on the same day, fully aware that the communication or orders would come instantly. And we would do that! No delay or timelag meant no afterthoughts allowed under pressures of any kind...there were numerous recommendations for promotions, but we would go as per the merit and performance and explain to the external authorities why their recommendations were not promotable. We would, at times, stand up firm against any breach of integrity of our system. The idea was to win and also regain, and also generate confidence amongst Executives that merit and performance were the only virtues that had a say. In one Minister's tenure I almost had to risk my job and even put down my papers, in view of the cumulative impact of pressures exerted for breaching peoples' trust in the system, in the Organisation and of course in me. People would, in fact, facilitate our members not to exert pressures which would be unethical behaviour not only against the organisation but primarily against our own colleagues. This had an impact on the peoples' behaviour and also affected the level of trust in the Organisation and working of its systems.

The review in PMS and Career Development System were not so much in technology and design merely, but primarily on ensuring fairness and trust, a culture that needed to be built, ensured and sustained. This was what the Organisation needed and this was what the People wished for.

OPPORTUNITIES FOR LEARNING AND GROWTH

The need for training in any organisation hardly needs any emphasis today. In NTPC, right from the beginning, training was not viewed as a cost but as an investment. Based on this concept, we developed a systematic and comprehensive Training Policy, which envisaged a minimum of seven man days training per employee, annually.

The company had already created the requisite infrastructure to implement its plan which included an apex training centre, Power Management Institute (PMI) at Noida, 15 Project Training Centres (called Employee Development Centres) and 2 Simulator Training Centres as a great support towards actualisation of this objective.

Training interventions in the Organisation were divided into two components, namely, Planned interventions and Need based interventions that were linked to changing requirements. For career linked Planned interventions, the Organisation had made a strategy that each employee gets at least one week of training input every year. It had also proposed a set of standard modules of different durations for training for both, the executives and non-executives.

Training need assessment had been based on individuals' needs and the organisational requirements, as far as customised interventions were concerned. Each employee had to complete a form devised by the organisation. It was only on being assessed by the Reporting officer and the HODs that the gist of that form came out. Organisational requirements were discussed in the meetings. Needs derived at, from both the stakeholders, were merged and the final training needs of each employee were determined. At the functional or organisational training need assessment, brainstorming exercises were also conducted among functional HODs, training coordinators and training representatives and on the basis of organisational needs, a draft training plan was presented to the Site Management committee. Only after considering the inputs from individual training need assessments, the final plan for project training centre and PMI was determined. We also gave a consultancy assignment to Dr. Ishwar Dayal, a very senior consultant, and professor, who was also Director of IIM (Ahmedabad), to examine and give advice on capability building in PMI to meet the growing needs of NTPC Training and Development.

Training programmes included technical training, imparting new skills, for orientation in general management, for enhancing personal productivity and quality improvement, through service and customer orientation.

Given the changing times, greater emphasis was laid on identifying the need of reinforcing global exposure to create a global mindset, and efforts made to deploy middle and senior level executives to such International programmes were encouraged. Even some workers' teams were exposed to global training and conventions in Quality Circle, etc., conveying a very strong positive message to general employees and also giving them a feel of international practices.

CHANAKYA (AIMA LINES)

As part of company's initiative to provide platforms for developing executives by providing them learning opportunities and also giving them exposure of business decision making, executives from other companies were invited to the Organistion. Initially, a 2 day in-house competition was organised for teams of executives at PMI, Noida. This initiative resulted in 3 teams reaching the finals of the competition out of 150 teams that participated at the all India level competition.

Keeping in view the response and enthusiasm of the employees, a policy was framed to conduct the competition across the company under a special intervention named **Business Minds**. The objectives and salient feature of the intervention were:

- Management Games test the understanding of concepts of business in participants, develop their ability to take quick decisions and give instant feedback to the participants on their overall managerial abilities.
- For executives, the game was more effective than other forms of learning such as conventional class teaching, a case study, role play, OJT or assignment because of its wide coverage, unique delivery and swift learning capability.
- The competition evoked in the management games urged participants to learn willingly and the inbuilt interactivity enhanced the pace of learning.
- The Management Games developed team spirit amongst the participants and helped the participants learn operative and strategic decision making, while being creative and innovative, under constraints of time.
- All executives upto the level of E7 were eligible to participate in the competition.

The top 8 teams of the competition, received rewards and recognitions and would participate in the regional round of Management Games – *Chankaya* conducted by AIMA. These successes brought laurels, learnings and of course immense pride to the winners.

TEAM BUILDING

As part of the sustained and ongoing development efforts of the Talent in the company, and making them capable enough to contribute their best for the Teams' success, a special initiative for developing and maintaining effective work teams comprising of top management (GMs and HODs) in projects had been initiated. This initiative emerged during a discussion with Dr. Suneeta in PMI and was strongly recommended. This initiative included an on-going process of diagnosis, interventions for building work teams, action planning and revive this intervention in all Stations and Projects where our Talent was to perform their best to make a winning NTPC. The programme was carried out in three phases:

Phase-I: Pre Programme Study

The programme was preceded by a study on the dimensions of the working of the team at a particular project/station. Apart from using the findings of the study for designing the workshops, the findings were also presented during the workshop in Phase-II and utilised for action planning.

Phase-II: Team Building Workshops
(Role of teams in the organisation)

Through experiential exercises, the participants gained awareness of the qualitative increase in output when groups functioned as synergistic teams. The sessions discussed the various dimensions of group working which would create synergy.

With the help of psychological instruments and other tools, the group reviewed the effectiveness of its own team and identified the blocks that affected team functioning. The groups also learnt to institute practices for process review on an on-going basis.

Phase-III: Review and Follow Up

There was a review workshop as a sequel to Phase-II. This enabled the team members at the project to review the implementation of action plans formulated at the commencement of the workshop. Building on this experience, the group evolved strategies for enhancing the process of team work at the project. The programme was conducted in association with NIS Sparta, Centre for Cross Culture Communication and I recall it gave excellent results in Dadri and some other units.

DEVELOPMENT CENTRE

- Development Centres were essentially meant to assess the competency levels (knowledge, skills, attitudes, styles, values, etc.) of people. NTPC had been actively carrying on the Development Centre (DC) with a view to promoting a competence based culture and enhance overall organisational development through individual development.

- Development Centres were futuristic in nature as the exercises focussed on competencies and the future potential that is needed at the target level. The assessments in a Development Centre were accurate and objective as compared to traditional methods of evaluation, mainly due to application of multiple techniques of assessment like Leaderless Group Discussion, Interpersonal Skills Exercise, Psychometric/personality test, In-Basket Exercise, Behavioural Event Interview, simulation of real life situations in which actual competencies are reflected, and use of multiple observers for assessment which helps negate individual biases.
- Managers having completed 3 years of service in the grade were eligible for participation in Development Centres. It helped them:

  (i) Gain insight into the competencies required for Senior Level;
  (ii) Understand the nature and level of competencies they possessed;
  (iii) Recognise competency gaps, if any; and
  (iv) Provide beneficial insights in assessing their potential and formulating action plans for self-development.

Long term Educational Opportunities

Apart from short-term training and developmental opportunities, we also created a host of opportunities for acquiring higher qualification during the job. This not only enhanced the competence of the employees but also motivated them for growth and self-development. We tied up with reputed Institutes of the field such as IIT Delhi for an 18 months' M. Tech programme in Power Engineering; Management Development Institute (MDI), Gurgaon for 15 months' Executive MBA; BITS Pilani for B.S. in Power Engineering for employees with Diploma qualification at supervisor/junior executive levels; Government Industrial Training Institutes/Diploma Institutes at local levels for employees with Matriculation/other qualification to acquire Diploma; and also ITI. This enabled employees at the lower levels to enter into the skilled category of employees and take up higher responsibilities in the company. This endeavour created lot of optimism and excitement amongst all levels of employees, who found vast growth and development opportunities with occasions of valuable recognition within the organisation. Thus, what emerged was a learning fever that encompassed everyone in the Organisation. Everybody was busy learning, apart from caring for performance and delivery and it was amazing to see people devote time, efforts and energy in learning and feel very happy and satisfied about it. I recall the convocation of the first batch of Supervisors at Dadri, where hundreds of diploma supervisors were being given a very prestigious degree of Bachelor of Science in Power Engineering by a great Engineering Institution, the BITS, Pilani. Excitement was flowing all over, fuelled by a great sense of achievement, and emotions were abound in the gathering where people flocked, embraced and even tried to touch my feet in acknowledgement and respect! I wished I could have been able to come without those pair of dirty feet! The whole experience made me realise the simplicity of the people who had the potential to create a wonderful family of NTPC, a great Organisation!

RECOGNISING TALENT

NTPC REWARD AND RECOGNITION SYSTEM

NTPC had drawn up a comprehensive reward and recognition system which had a strong thrust on non-monetary incentives. In addition to promotions, the employees' efforts were recognised through a number of ways at individual level as well as team/unit level.

At the company level, a number of awards had been instituted by the name of **NTPC Golden Globe** awards in the areas such as Productivity, Safety, Employee Relations, Environment protection, Rajbhasha, Health services, etc. These awards enthused excitement particularly within the station getting recognition and being rewarded at the national level. In fact, this was instituted early in the mid 1980s at R.V. Shahi's instance but was not being given its due share of recognition and became somewhat less exciting with the passage of time. We revived these awards with greater enthusiasm this time, rechristening it, and created a running trophy and conducted the investiture ceremony with pomp and show. This clicked and was regarded and respected by employees and stations with greater respect and honour.

To recognise individual excellence, a benchmarking project was undertaken by a group of brilliant managers, with leading public and private sector organisations to learn best practices, and came out with a rich set of Reward and Recognition policy for NTPC. A number of awards had been instituted in phases, which included an Appreciation letter, STAR of the month, Employee of the year, Vidyut awards, Power Executive Excellence awards, Performance excellence awards for Regional leadership, Awards for Corporate excellence, Mentors *Samman*, Manveeyata *Puraskar*, etc. These were mostly simply recognitions but used to make people so proud!

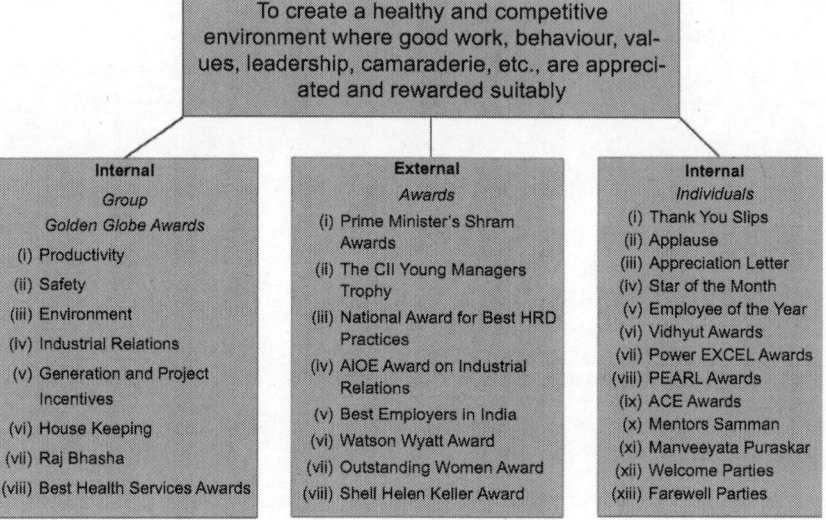

FIGURE 4: NTPC Reward System

RESPECTING INDIVIDUALS AS A PERSON, NOT JUST AN EMPLOYEE

We realised the simple truth that every employee, first of all, is a human being with a mind and heart, having feelings and emotions. She/he wants to be treated with dignity and wants to be valued, respected and does not want to be treated like a cog in the wheel. NTPC very well recognised this aspect of its employees and had formulated many policies which reflected these sentiments. A few such policies included strong welfare facilities in the township, care for the employees' family, schools, hospitals, marriage with support in honey-moon trip(!), gift for newly wedded employees, work life balance provisions and lot many initiatives to recognise and show respect to families and children particularly. These seemed small gestures but had lot of impact on relationship building, based on respect of employees and their families.

Apart from creating various systems and policies for attracting and retaining talent, it is also imperative that a culture supportive of talent is created. In such a culture, talent management does not remain a functional role but becomes an organisational priority. NTPC had been able to create a work environment which was business oriented and at the same time, it was quite informal and open. It followed an open system of interaction in the form of cross functional teams. Even the reward system of the company promoted team work. As mentioned above, we had partnered with NIS Sparta to diagnose the level of Teaming in different stations and take actual Teams to learn to identify the blocks hindering Team effectiveness, and ways and practices to improve Team quality and their effectiveness. This brought out lot of learning as well as ownership amongst the managers and the leaders to drive the positive spirit of togetherness and synergy, resulting into better performance leading to organisational excellence. I would be discussing about various aspects of culture in a separate chapter later.

The Management Committee comprising GM, EDs, Directors and CMD, in one of their meetings, sometime in 1998, had discussed about how to improve the organisational culture. A Committee of General Managers and EDs was set up to look into the matter and submit a report to the MCM. I was appointed as Convener of the Committee. We took feedback from the plants, discussed the issues involved on several occassions and came out with a report called *Changing the Organisational Culture*, which was presented by one of the Committee members in the next MCM. The report contained 19 recommendations under four heads: Becoming Performance Oriented, Becoming People Oriented, Building Mutual Respect and Trust, and Building Pride and a Sense of Belonging, and a time frame for implementation. The MCM accepted the recommendations in toto, and gave directions for their implementation Company wide. Due to various reasons, the implementation of the Culture Committee report could not be pursued in an integrated manner, but most of the recommendations were implemented at various points in time over the next year or so. Thus, for example, a review of Delegation of Powers was undertaken; Joint Goal Setting and Joint Performance Reviews were built into the Performance Management System; a Management Journal *Horizon* was started; systematic training in Behavioural Sciences and Attitudinal Change was introduced on a large scale; and so on.

During this time, we were able to give an HR orientation to a largely technical organisation like NTPC, and also spread the realisation that HR is everyone's business. The hugely successful training course *HR for Line Managers* was introduced, and our technical managers also got sensitised to people issues. We gave a thrust to the free flow of communication across the organisation through our Communication Strategy, which I have mentioned elsewhere. We made yoga and meditation exercises compulsory in our planned intervention training programmes, and we were probably the first organisation to attempt internalisation of values through storytelling. Mentoring was introduced in a systematic way, and HR initiatives like Development Centres and 360 degree feedback fostered acculturation, competency building and openness and transparency. Those were indeed exciting gains and thrilling times!

THE OUTCOME

All these efforts enabled the company to attract talented workforce to join and contribute to the growth, with utmost commitment. The image of the company amongst potential recruits could be gauged from the fact that every year the company had been receiving more than 80,000 applications from professionally qualified Engineers and MBAs/Chartered Accountants, etc., for about 300–400 posts in the executive category. Secondly, the company had very low executive turnover of 0.17, exemplifying a high level of loyalty and commitment to the company.

6

Building Employee Relations Through Partnership

SCENE 1: *Year 1969; A young Personnel Officer, fresh from college and into the corporate world, is in his third week of on-the-job training in a factory set up in West Bengal. One fine morning he comes to office, gets on with his usual training with a lot of enthusiasm and a gleam in the eyes, envisioning a secure future as a personnel officer in a large PSU. Suddenly after lunch, he gets a news that Chief Personnel Manager of a neighbouring plant was being dragged out of the office by a group of workmen shouting slogans and even wielding sticks and rods. They strip and tie the manager in the office lawn on a table and in front of everybody prick his body with hundreds of office pins.*

SCENE 2: *Year 1972: As an Assistant Personnel Officer in one of the washeries in the coalfields, I am returning from a labour court representing the management in one of the labour dispute cases alongwith the general secretary of a leftist trade union. The narrow single track road beyond the dam is looking clean in the heavy rains and the head lights of the Ambassador car. Suddenly, the driver stops the vehicle after sighting a big trunk of the tree on the deserted road. As the vehicle comes to a sudden halt, instantly a bomb hit the windscreen. We immediately jumped out and ran in the slushy field in complete darkness, till we reached a village. Never in my wildest imagination had I thought I would have to dare bullets and bomb as a personnel executive!*

SCENE 3: *Year 1998: A group of representatives of Executives' Association of a large power PSU is attending a workshop in the serene environment of Jaipur. The workshop is being facilitated by HR executives and external experts. Huddled in groups, they are discussing contemporary business problems being faced by the company and brainstorming various solutions. They are also excited about having developed the vision of their association in tandem with the company vision, which read:*

"To be the distinctive federation of world class professionals promoting growth of its members, the organisation and the society".

SCENE 4: *Year 1999: I am invited as one of the guests during the valedictory session of a national level annual convention of a quality forum. Before this I am invited to attend one of the technical sessions in which one team of workmen from my organisation is also competing. A group of seven people, all decked up in their formals, turn up and present a model which they have implemented at their workplace to save more than Rs. 10 lakh in a year. Looking at the quality of their communication skills, level of knowledge and confidence, making an intelligent presentation with the help of a Laptop, it was simply difficult for me to believe that they are from our workmen category. One could not miss the glow of obvious pride on these faces!*

THESE ARE ONLY a few of the innumerable 'scenes' encountered. However, we had come a long way from the days when Scenes 1 and 2 were regular features of industrial relations environment, to the present days where Scenes 3 and 4 have become commonplace in all forms of organisations. It is a matter of big relief for HR professionals and a matter of pride for people like us, who have been witnesses to this transition.

It is a fact that employee development and growth can be achieved in an environment of peace, harmony and trust. In fact, creating systems as well as a congenial environment for ensuring such harmony through building mutual trust and seeking partnership with the employees has been an important role of HR professionals since long.

We had survived the late 1960s and early 1970s industrial relations (IR) scenario and also subsequent times, and managed to keep our ship afloat in the turbulent 1980s, when relationships were very strained and full of strife, with the entire period witnessing unrest of an extent that destroyed industries in various sectors, particularly the Public Sector Enterprises, driving many to be declared sick. Let alone talking of exciting talent in the organisation and creating an environment of learning and development, leading to all round excellence, even thinking about it was next to impossible.

While working in Eastern India and particularly having been associated with Coal and Construction and Infrastructure industries, I had learnt that the Industrial relations appeared to be more of 'Violent relations'. Through senior IR gurus in our times, a tested IR Model developed over experience. Over time, I learnt, developed and practiced an IR Framework which gave sustained results with success throughout the Organisation.

The participative approach of management was adopted by NTPC in all its facets, including industrial relations. The need to manage industrial relations in a professional way was realised early, partly because industrial conflicts have been widespread in the power sector. Moreover, it was evident to all, that unless this complex and delicate area was handled properly, it had the potential to derail all schedules and targets.

The old economy business model was primarily dominated by the typical brick and mortar, manufacturing organisations. Trade Unionism had grown in the country alongwith the independence movement, and hence had been closely wedded to political parties and outsiders. The late 1960s saw the unabated entry of violence in Industrial Relations setting. It peaked up in the 1970s, when the industries entered the professional world. The law and order authorities and particularly the state governments chose to become onlookers, leaving the industry and the political trade unions to deal with the situation builtup like an inferno between them, mostly due to pressures and violent means. On top of it, this scenario was dominated by ills like multiplicity of trade unions resulting in intense inter-union, as well as intra-union rivalries. Most of the setbacks caused to Business, in the arena of industrial relations, were manifestations of such format of prevailing relationships. However, there were no clear-cut recognition systems. Some of the States attempted to legalise a recognition process, but in practice, implementation remained a casualty. These factors kept on affecting relationship and the industrial environment adversely, which could ultimately not become amenable.

The industrial setting also had substantial influence of misplaced philosophies, where trade unions went against any kind of major or even minor changes. Any kind of contemporary technological changes that were proposed, though intended for improvements in productivity, work efficiency and better quality of work life, were, ironically not acceptable to them. For harmony, conciliation and adjudication were the order of the day, which kept the relationship far from satisfactory, as it was always perpetuating the win-lose mind set, devoid of mutual trust, so very essential for harmonious relationship.

Trade Unionism had also spread to Executive Unionism in the industry, particularly in the major Public Sector Undertakings. Though conceived out of a welfare state responsibility, Executive Unions remained far from it. These mega PSUs, as is well known, were supposed to be people oriented and much more democratic in process, but unfortunately started slipping substantially on the grounds of efficiency and performance. The employees' participation, though preached actively, was hardly practiced meaningfully and did not result in the development of a favourable environment of trust that was much desired.

The stature of Worker Directors were also conceived with lot of pomp and show, but remained elusive, with barely a couple of exceptions. Bi-partism did not bring in transparency, alignment and trust in business relationships.

All the features described above in relation to the prevalent industrial scenario, though well intended, did not generate favourable alchemy for the industrial harmony and peace.

Dealing with the industrial relations scenario effectively then was, as perceived, for somewhat rugged IR professionals, who could brave it out or endure these situations. And there were often occasions of physical duress and at times even worse encounters that the HR personnel had to face.

As an organisation or as an individual, such apparently complicated industrial relations, according to our simple understanding, were still understood to be an act or art of directing and controlling Human Resource in employment. It has been referred to as labour relations, employee relations, legal relations, etc., but essentially the professionals still believed it to be basically human relations and that it is merely an adjustment amongst people in the organisation. It is an adjustment in two inseparable limbs, apparently having a conflicting interest but one that is completely complimentary.

Good industrial relations has been understood as an effective cooperation of management and unions, whereas, a poor relationship is nothing but conflicts, indiscipline, stoppage of work, violence, low morale, etc. However, with a little bit sharing of business perspective, alignment to the vision and mission, sitting together in an environment that is transparent and based on a win-win mindset, the environment so created by a wonderful relationship could certainly be ecstatic for the business. This requires mutual understanding that is governed by a fair and honest balance of organisational requirements and human considerations.

This ideal cordial industrial relation is a state of perfect harmony, which had always eluded us. A perfect understanding, harmony and peace for all times, is a myth. It is humanly not possible to eliminate conflicts and differences, that too forever and completely. People have so many disparities and differences in their persona, which vary in diverse situations, with complex emotions displayed in success, failure and opportunities. Thus, people will have grievances, people will have dislikes, and they will have therefore, conflicts and differences. The human being, who is the pivot of the relationship in an organisational setting, exists independently and is capable of intelligent thinking and responsible actions, having an innate sense of dignity as a broad drive to his/her expectations and behaviour.

Hence, he/she is conscious of his/her rights and self esteem and also proficient in demonstrating complex emotions in different situations. This individual also seeks esteem of others, passionately craving for recognition, trust and respect towards his/her dignity. And to top it all, this person is very conscious of his/her material needs and instincts of social existence, seeking an assurance of sanctuary against an impending sense of insecurity of the future. Further, he/she generally wants to join others to secure common interest, and act in groups or teams. The Human being indeed, is a kaleidoscope of emotions!

When all these are satisfied, he/she is very happy, co-operative and productive, otherwise, morose, aggrieved, bitter and even violent on some occasions.

On the other hand, the employer considers, quite unfortunately, all of these innate desires as typical and avoidable evils, and wishes and hopes for wonderland peace and harmony achieved by any and all shortcuts available that could seemingly deliver these in the quickest possible way and time period...and the mirage persists!

Does this leave any IR man, put in position, to remain in and sustain Krishna's described 'calmposure', in all complex and precarious situations?

Is the poor IR fellow left with a dazzling magicwand to mesmerise the workforce into a so called satisfied lot of individuals or groups (trade union), or have a great tune to pipe them to peace, like a Pied Piper?

We often get into tricky and confusing situations, and at times, when the going is good, are very successful in dealing with trade unions through handling few individuals, or vice versa. Success, to some extent, may be possible, perhaps if we deal with the trade unions within the pattern of institutional relationship. This may require an organisation to be equipped with adequate institutionalised fora for sharing and involvement. There is also a need for a platform for determining general values and ground rules for relationships, conscious assessment of strength and weakness of each other and thereafter, their conscious countering and balancing, that would ultimately lead to a determined clear cut point of equilibrium. It is necessary to inculcate an understanding that a relationship that everyone appreciates, does not remain sustainable only on the basis of values and ground rules determined, and that the so called Harmony does not start becoming hazy and elusive, yet once again.

Hence, the Pied Piper has to develop clearer understandings of the values and ground rules that are mutually determined, on the levels of, both,

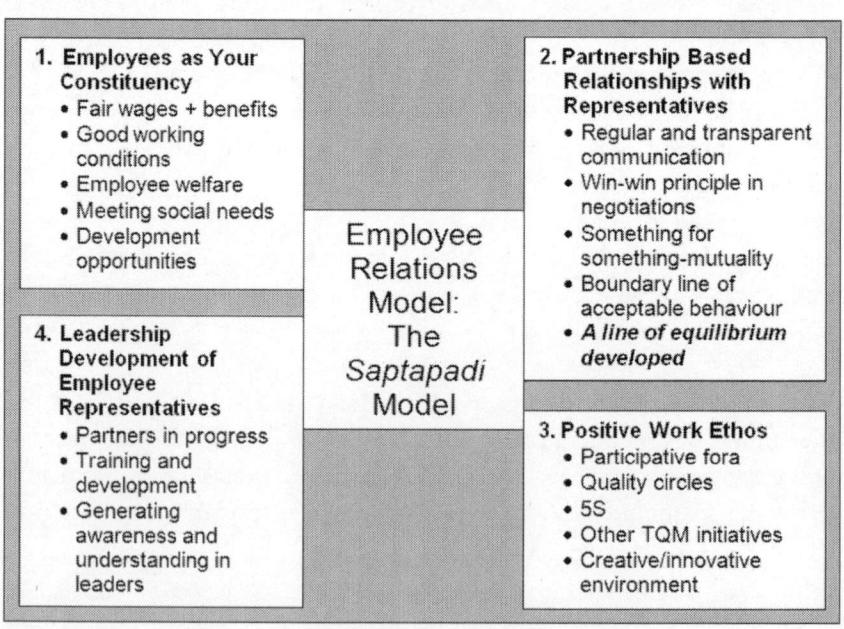

FIGURE 1: Employee Relations Model

individual relationships, as well as institutional relationships. But of course, there has to be a firm belief that whatever is dealt with is the responsibility of the IR Personnel and the field of operations therefore, is their constituency!

EMPLOYEE RELATIONS (ER) MODEL

In course of my assignment with various units in an era witnessing a lot of labour unrest, we gradually developed a broad industrial relations framework which has been tested time and again and found to be delivering results successfully. I had come across this framework while interacting with some very senior IR Professionals of our times from the Asansol coal mines area in the 1970s, the fairly disturbed period. This made sense and we further developed it to create an implementable version. Based on the experiences and inputs of a number of practitioners, we developed the following broad features that were incorporated in this framework:

TREATING EMPLOYEES AS YOUR CONSTITUENCY

There should be an emphasis on a proactive approach to employee relations including compensation and employee welfare.

Fair Wages

The wages and salary structure of employees must have internal, as well as external parity to whatever extent possible. A very proactive approach with required transparency on this subject would help generate the required understanding and trust that form the base of a congenial relationship. NTPC, through its thrust for bringing the best of structure, became even better than ONGC that was a leader amongst PSUs, and was generally considered as a benchmark by the employees at one point of time. We had to make a lot of efforts to bring it to this level of acceptance by the employees.

Good Working Conditions

Though it sounds like the usual small, routine and is often taken as a hygiene factor, the working conditions and environment go a long way in creating a cordial atmosphere. NTPC took special care in creating a work environment which was safe, motivating and exciting. It had evolved a comprehensive norm with respect to environment, detailing all the aspects of office administration, furniture, and standardised working conditions with deference to facilities and services to be created so that a minimal standard of work environment is practiced across all units. With intent to provide the best of hygienic conditions at each power plant and with support of modern equipments, adequate provisions of wholesome drinking water, canteen, rest/relaxation locations, medical facilities, illumination and air were ensured to inculcate a feeling of respect as well.

Responsiveness to Individual Problems

It is essential that problems and grievances of an individual employee are addressed properly by the Supervisor or HR representative. In NTPC, we had created systems for Grievance Redressal to take care of individual grievances. The best practice that brought trust and understanding was that of transparency and the exercise of forming a group to work on solutions. One major concern area where huge expectations and grievances was generated was the desire of the employees to get a transfer to a preferred unit or even region. This was a huge multi-unit, multi-region organisation having 35–40 locations in the country. Employees considered transfers as a big favour, sometimes even greater than promotions! And this also brought in lot of external pressures which in itself was a typical challenge for the public sector environment. A quick response and resolution with transparency through an empowered committee on transfer, with representatives of Association and Management, brought in substantial trust of the people in the Organisation and its management. There was a wonderful balance created between the personal needs and the needs of the organisation. Employees stopped exerting external pressures for seeking benefits which was rampant earlier, embarrassing the organisation, and in the process generating feelings of mistrust amongst employees at large.

Concern for Employees and Family Members
– The Smalls Made Big

In NTPC, a large number of measures were introduced right from the inception to ensure the welfare and growth of not only employees but also their family members. Such efforts included energising Ladies Welfare Organisations, sports competitions for children of employees, coaching facilities for competitive exams for children besides making available good educational facilities at projects. We innovated substantially, with involvement of employees, their families and the HR executives in the field and based on the feedback and appraisals took a lot of initiatives to update the services that were being provided.

As most of the Units were established in remote coal pit head areas, the townships had to be endowed with the best of facilities to ease the concerns of the families. They were handled with a lot of concern and in various innovative ways, coming mostly from them, to win their emotional support and also give respect. Childrens' all round development was handled with new ideas coming from parents themselves: Plant, Regional and National level Quizzes by the best of Quiz Masters like Derek O'Brian, who was retained for several years to establish the practice and generate pride. In the finals, every year, we would invite the parents of the Stations' school children in the Delhi Auditorium, to watch their young ones perform at the national level, that too performing with the no. 1, Derek, as the Quiz Master. It may sound very simple but it did have a great impact on the children, the employees and their families. Sponsoring children to other National level events, News Creation and Daily News reading on our Township cable TV by employees' Children, coaching facilities/support in desired location like Kota, theatre workshops during the summer holidays by NSD, Raising Day participation with art and fanfare, Quality Circles in Schools, Inter School coordination meetings of Principals and HR, and Teachers' Training for continuous development, Rewards and Recognition Schemes for the children including excellent scholarships for higher education...the list could go on!

I recall, year on year, the Raising Day celebrations had a cultural programme delivered by the children and families of all Units and Regions. 200 to 300 children would participate, combine on a common theme or story and perform things like dance-drama in Siri Fort Auditorium, under the able guidance of a choreographer of international repute, who would hop from unit to unit, select, brief, train and integrate them. Children and parents would pray and vie for a seat in the select list. The art, glamour and aesthetics were of such high standards that guests from the city of Delhi would exclaim in awe! So much pride would be generated...attained through achievements and intimacy in relationships. People would work for months. This became a coveted opportunity. I always made it a point to associate myself closely and be visible all over the place. I still recall the evenings after the show or the next day, bidding farewell to 300 participants. The children and parents would become so emotional, having bonded over the period, having connected with each other through a common medium. One could see them hugging each other wishing them farewell, exchanging mail ids and many with tears in their eyes for having formed new bonds.

We found so much of talent in the children that we decided to motivate them by recognising their talent by creating a compilation of the achievements of the children who could also act as examples and role models for others. We invited all those cases of our children who had participated in Quizes, Festivals, Debates, Art, Fine Art, Sports, Games or Academics at State level or National levels. There was an overwhelming response and our mail boxes were full! When *Akash*, a high quality compendium like a Coffee Table Book created by Hindwan and his team, came out as a compilation in the hands of all children and parents, their success stories written in golden words, the townships became abuzz with a sense of achievement and pride! We wrote to each child who was included in the edition, sending them a personalised copy of this Coffee Table Book, and also wrote to all the Principals of each school in townships all over, sending them a copy for their libraries!

Catering to social needs of employees was a prime HR responsibility. The forums were created for helping employees meet their social needs such as Employees Welfare Associations, excellent quality Clubs, and Libraries, etc.

There was another little experiment we did to involve the families on all occasions. Wherever NTPC commemorated or celebrated special occasions like Silver Jubilee, etc., we would ask the spouses about their preference of a gift that they would like NTPC to give. Many a times when we decided to give gold biscuits, or a preferred kitchen equipment, it was of the spouses' own choice. There used to be a wave of appreciation coming from families for even small things like these . . . a sense of belongingness was created without much effort from the side of the management.

PARTNERSHIP BASED INSTITUTIONAL RELATIONSHIP WITH EMPLOYEE REPRESENTATIVES

Regular Communication

Meetings were held every quarter with Unions and Associations of employees at various Units with Business Unit Heads, as well of a particular Region, to discuss and deal with various issues concerning employees.

Decisions and status of actions were displayed conspicuously, as settled periodically. These converted their behaviour to very supportive styles, reinforcing the environment of trust.

Win-Win Principle in Negotiations and Collective Bargaining

At Corporate level there were following separate participative forums for executives and non-executives.

NBC – National Bipartite Committee

The apex negotiating forum was composed of management representatives and workmen representatives drawn from coal-based thermal power stations which have workmen strength of over 500 and have at least one unit commissioned. Besides workmen representatives from project Unions, central leaders (one each) from four National Trade Unions – INTUC, BMS, AITUC and CITU – were part of the committee. We were a PSU of a mega size responsible for industrial democracy. The forum used to meet at least 3–4 times a year or even more frequently, if required. Issues discussed were related to wages and employee welfare.

One challenge we had was for four Central Trade Union organisations and more than 22 Units, we had as many as 50 Unions coming to this forum. Some Units used to send 4 to 5 Unions also, as there was no process or formula agreed to decide the representative character. INTUC wanted check off and CITU wanted secret ballot. This tie went on for a couple of years, though everyone wanted to have one Unit-one – Union to be a healthy format. I recall due to continued personal understanding, Passey (a wonderful support for NTPC) finally agreed to secret ballot, even going against the typical INTUC mandate. The only special exception was made for Korba, MP, which had a state law to determine the representative character. The NBC finally came to terms to a new format of deciding representative character through secret ballot! This was a major milestone achieved in the IR history of NTPC that brought discipline, healthy representation and excellent relationship in the organisation. In most large and multi-unit PSU organisations, this type of understanding in practice was unheard of. Today, it's no longer unwieldy. It practiced one union–one station and gradually related roles were developed and responsibilities were being defined. The Unions became very positive support to the Organisation.

NEFI–NTPC Executives' Federation of India

This is not a joint committee but a Federation of all the Executive Associations from various projects of the Company, with which the management interacted to share information, ideas and concerns of the executive community for the Organisation's benefit. The forum used to meet at least twice or thrice a year. Though the start was fairly rough and challenging, over a period of time, an excellent relationship and understating was nurtured and NEFI was the only association of employees that could voluntarily come out with a Vision in support of the Vision of the NTPC. We had transparent and mutually supportive relationship, even on occasions when executives associations in other organisations or their national federation would call for agitation. The members were very supportive of the Organisation and were ready to put everything on stake for the community and their NTPC.

Line of Equilibrium

With several initiatives to bring in mutual trust, confidence and appreciation, we ensured that a boundary line for acceptable behaviour / conduct of employees was drawn, beyond which discipline was to be actively enforced in the organisational interest. While relationship was founded strongly on principles and acts of mutuality and respect, indiscipline was not acceptable and wrong acts were proceeded against expeditiously, and firmly, including dismissals, if found essential in the organisation's interest. Expediting Departmental enquiries were incentivised; Panel of external enquiry officers was created and announced to expedite disposals of pending cases. It was amazing that Unions and Association themselves were generally not in support of indiscipline and breaking the codes of conduct. We found that a relationship developed where indiscipline of all kinds was condemned and never supported by the Unions and Associations. Even in negotiations a culture of give and take was established and in dealing with so called 'charter of demands', soon a culture of negotiation on principle of 'something for something' emerged and stayed.

All these transformations started moving ahead with a lot of determination and a strong culture of mutual respect that was in the air, was well in view. The organisational climate survey outputs were regularly shared with Unions and Associations to generate a general concern and also bring out an intense feeling of ownership in all of them, to bring the desired transformation and develop a mutually agreed agenda for implementation.

Participative Fora

NTPC had created structured systems for employees' participation in management, which also served as effective two way systems for internal communication. These were all done during Shahi's tenure. The fora had been created as a three tier system – Unit/Plant, Regional and Corporate Centre level. These fora spread across multiple locations in the country including Power Plants and Offices, which began functioning very effectively and with a clear cut agenda and schedule. Some of such forums included:

Each project station had an apex-level Plant Level Council (PLC) and a number of (usually 4–5) Shop/Department Level Councils (SLC). Besides PLC/SLCs, various joint committees were formed to deal with aspects such as safety, township, sports, recreation, etc.

Apex Level Plant Level Council (PLC)

The Council was constituted to discuss plant level issues – information sharing on generation and production targets, productivity, elimination of wasteful practices, inventory reduction, general health, welfare and safety, and any issue referred by shop councils. The members included – Head of Project/Station as the Chairman, three members representing the management and three members representing employees. The effort was to re-energise these councils and committees, enabling effective decision making, implementation, and sharing of information/communication.

Shop Level Council (SLC)

It was constituted to discuss department level issues – Improvement of production, productivity and efficiency, elimination of wastage, improvement in working conditions, safety, etc. The members included – Head of Department as the Chairman, 8–12 members equally representing the management and employees.

Other Bipartite Forums at Plant Level

Various joint committees, represented equally by the management and employees, were constituted at the project level to take care of issues related to employees' welfare. The important joint committees that were constituted were:

(i) Canteen Management Committee
(ii) House Allotment Committee
(iii) Township Advisory Committee
(iv) Plant Safety Committee
(v) Sports Council

While the issues discussed remained the same on plant and shop floors, by and large, an environment of mutual concern, trust and respect was created effectively. A cell in the Employee Relations wing was created to coordinate the meetings, circulate decisions and minutes, follow up actions, notify the actions to be taken, put the status of implementation on the display boards in conspicuous places. Employees at large knew of the decisions taken in these meetings and also of the actions taken for implementation. This brought in a lot of interest in these forums. All these developments generated a very positive work environment and employee engagement at all levels. While the mention of these committees sounds mundane and may appear unimportant activities, the strategy and deft-will was to take up the challenge to make them active, involving and result oriented by the support of implementation of decisions taken and the subsequent follow up. This resulted in the creating of an environment where a small brick like participant took so much pride in every thing and helped build a strong Organisation, where every small brick had its contribution. Hence, we could not leave them unattended as a routine, but made them significant and contributing.

POSITIVE WORK ETHOS

Apex Level Bipartite Fora Related to Productivity

The two apex fora mentioned above basically dealt with issues related to employee wages and welfare, while the following two fora, which met twice a year, dealt with matters relating to productivity, cost-reduction, improvements in working conditions, safety, etc. and were also attended by CMD, Directors and EDs.

- NJPC-NTPC Joint Performance Committee – composed of NBC members, and
- NEFI on Productivity

We ensured that the meetings of their bodies were held regularly and that there was a lot of status and information sharing taking place, plenty of productivity and performance related issues were deliberated and also decided. These discussions used to act as a precursor to many of the Organisation's expectation and demands for process and system improvements. These fora used to create friendliness and lot of mutual understanding.

Partnership in TQM Initiatives

The objective of this partnership with employees was a totally integrated effort to continuously improve quality of all processes, systems, products and services through total employee involvement, to empower them to satisfy their intense desire for creativity, and to improve the employees' level of satisfaction, along-with cultural and attitudinal change. I recall Pran Nath started talking of Quality Circles and Total Quality Management (TQM) in NTPC. Wherever he would visit a station, he would invite one or two QC Team members and see their presentations, encourage them and also guide them. I merely consolidated this movement further, as I considered the initiative to be a very powerful one and realised that this people involvement initiative could do wonders. I converted it into a more intense form and made incentives and recognitions at the Organisational, National and International level rampant. These used to give tremendous opportunities to workers and other employees to innovate, contribute, and to derive a great sense of ownership and commitment.

A dedicated institutional set up was created at all 3 tiers, i.e. Corporate Centre, Regional Headquarters and Plant Level. A senior executive at the level of Executive Director (TQM) was deputed at the Corporate Centre for overall coordination purpose. A large number of executives were involved in the process as facilitators, trainers and coordinators. An apex level Steering Council was constituted involving Directors and Executive Directors. An effective institutional set up was raised at the Corporate, Region and Plant level for these activities. Total Quality Management (TQM) was used as the main tool for bringing in the required transformation.

In order to create an all round interest, concern and commitment, the Company involved various unions of the workers in the process. The professional institutions like Quality Circle Forum of India (QCFI), Confederation of Indian Industries (CII), National Productivity Council (NPC), Institute of Quality Ltd. (IQL), etc., were identified and involved in the process of evolving various initiatives, creating awareness among employees through presentations and workshops and by extending training programmes. The most important factor in the whole process was creating partnership with workers and towards this, various fora of workers' participation in management were fully utilised.

Later, specific targets were fixed and TQM modules were specially included in the programmes organised for employees with committed action plans developed in these workshops by Trade Unions, and later through a series of workshops for involving Plant/Shop level workers. In the initial phase, it took some time to roll in the new culture by creating awareness, education and then building involvement and commitment. But once the Quality Circles started performing, TQM movement got a fresh impetus and everyone including executives and non-executives got fully involved in the 5S and other programmes.

The Company launched the following initiatives very seriously with focus on building quality habits and quality culture across the organisation.

(a) Quality Circles
(b) Five 'S' Programme
(c) Productivity Improvement Initiatives
(d) Suggestion Scheme

Quality Circles

The Quality Circles in the Company started making a difference, not only in terms of productivity gains but also in improving the work culture. Continuous encouragement provided at all levels of management to involve every grass root level employee in this creative endeavour resulted in the formation of more than 900 circles with around 8000 members. Supported by a non-monetary motivational scheme and dedicated efforts of a large number of facilitators and coordinators, a very healthy competitive spirit was generated among the workforce. A number of contests were organised at the project level, regional level and company level to create sustained level of excitement in the Quality Circle movement. An annual QC Convention was organised at one of the stations, which over the years has been recognised as the 'Quality Event' of the year. All case study presentations of the National Convention were posted on the Intranet for wider dissemination. These conventions have been given due recognition and desired importance through full involvement of top management. The Chairman and Managing Director of the company personally ensured attending and addressing these conventions on a regular basis.

The Company has been encouraging the Quality Circles to participate in various Regional and National level competitions organised by reputed institutions like QCFI, CII, etc. High level of motivation, confidence and commitment of the workers in partnership resulted in the employees of NTPC receiving laurels and bagging a number of awards. The Quality Circle Motivational Scheme provided enough recognition and rewards including opportunities for participation in Quality Circle events conducted abroad and visits to reputed industrial organisations within the country. Quality Circles have also provided a platform for the self-expression to shop floor employees. It developed higher levels of alignment with the organisation, generating very positive work relations. Quality Circle activities were started among school children and families as well in order to further build a strong Quality Culture. It became a movement and everyone was excited. One could see thousands of workmen and children standing on all levels of stage and forum making presentations without any hesitation, sharing their learnings and findings with passion and intensity not seen before.

Five 'S' Programme

The Company also launched another employee involvement oriented programme popularly called **5S**. While Quality Circles developed problem solving and team work approach, **5S** activities were for developing Quality habits. The **5S** habits revolved around organising the workplace in an orderly and systematic manner and keeping the workplace clean by following standardised practices and maintaining self-discipline. The Company also initiated a companywide **5S** programme at all 22 projects/stations. The **5S** implementation programme was being regularly monitored and the response had been most encouraging. The employees gave very positive feedback about the gains and success of this initiative and became very enthusiastic about the whole programme.

Productivity Improvement Initiatives

Productivity improvement is the bottom-line of the partnership with workers. It focused on an effective utilisation of available resources and cuts across all systems/processes of the organisation. A lot had been done to push productivity based on different parameters by rationalising manpower and keeping it under check, and at the same time enabling employees to perform more efficiently even with stretched jobs and goals. NTPC HR had undertaken a study through National Productivity Council (NPC), a premier national level professional institute, to design and implement an integrated Productivity Model, linking physical and financial parameters especially with respect to manpower productivity. They were also required to deploy a software package, if necessary, for monitoring and control of the productivity indicators. In the first phase, it had planned to conduct productivity studies and implement a customised model only at few selected projects.

National Productivity Council had also been involved in suggesting multi-skilling measures and conducting necessary studies and training programmes at various projects/stations. The recommendations of the study on multi-skilling were under implementation. The multi-skilling was one of the key initiatives for redeployment required for the purpose of optimising and improving the productivity and efficiency.

NTPC Suggestion Scheme

In all units of NTPC, the Suggestion scheme, guided through a scheme formulated in the year 1984, had been operational to encourage creativity and provide opportunity to employees to come forth with their ideas/views to the management for work place improvement. As per the scheme, all employees could give their suggestions in various areas in a specific format to the suggestion coordinator. A number of projects had also started e-suggestion boxes to make use of the intranet, enabling the employees to contribute and communicate. The feedbacks about the suggestions accepted were also reciprocated to the concerned employees.

Suitable cash awards and certificates were given to meritorious suggestors, who were shortlisted by the Suggestion committee constituted at each unit. Creating a Suggestion Scheme in Factories and PSUs had by then become quite customary but were very essential to generate a higher level of interest and excitement among people at large. A revised model of suggestion scheme with a focus on quicker evaluation, instant awards and other motivational measures was worked out.

The employees of NTPC had been regularly receiving coveted Prime Minister's *Shram Awards, Viswakarma Rashtriya Puraskar* of the Ministry of Labour, which were given for outstanding suggestions given by employees in workmen category, which were accepted by the Management and adopted during the previous calendar year. We used to scale up the level of achievement and recognitions. I recall it was NTPC who started sending winners to Vigyan Bhawan, all dressed up in smart Prince Suits, bringing along their families, parents, etc. Preferring the families over the members allowed and by taking special care, added up to the glamour and pride for the awardees. We would have two-three felicitations of the Shram Awardees in the Organisation. I really appreciate the Directors and CMDs who would be present to felicitate and give respect to them and their families. We would give them a beautiful album and a video Cassette (then) of all the functions including the Prime Minister's congratulatory note. We would interview the spouses or old parents accompanying them to be screened on the company wide cable TV Network. There were systems of giving additional increments, accelerated promotions and above all, special recognitions to the awardees in future functions and celebrations. I also recall NTPC receiving the highest award *Shram Ratna* twice and remember arranging to send these winners with special fan fare to visit most other stations and make presentation of their work, interact with workmen and share their pride. We used to elevate the pedestal of all such recognitions manifold and make them memorable, setting up examples for others in the process and the fact that others too could achieve this by inculcating a feeling of ownership for the Organisation.

The Company was also closely associated in seeking assistance and sponsoring activities of Indian National Suggestion Scheme Association (INSSAN) which organised Regional and National level conventions to encourage suggestors. It has been a matter of pride that NTPC suggestors have won many awards in INSSAN Conventions every year.

All these activities substantially ignited the passion of the workers at large who were provided with several opportunities to bring out their creativity and subsequently get recognised.

LEADERSHIP DEVELOPMENT OF EMPLOYEE REPRESENTATIVES

'Partners in Progress' Workshops/Seminars

In order to align the Unions and Executive Association members about the changing business environment and their roles in helping the company successfully meet the challenges, a series of workshops namely 'Partners in Progress' was initiated for employees' representatives.

In these workshops/seminars, union/association representatives as well as management representatives participated. In these workshops, future plans and current information about business, issues facing the company, etc., were shared by internal as well as external faculty. Joint action plans were developed for the progress and growth of the company and to deal with the important and relevant issues. Apart from workshops at Regional levels, every year an apex level workshop/seminar for unions and executive associations was organised and the action plans drawn in these workshops were followed up/reviewed by workshops at various regions.

The programme included sharing of challenges and opportunities of the company and action planning with the objective of enhancing productivity and quality improvement. The programme had helped the emergence of responsible trade unionism in the company to the extent that strikes, disruption of work, loss of man-hours on account of Industrial relations problems, etc., had become a thing of the past.

In fact, such an initiative had become necessary in the context of the altered business scenario. With the power sector thrown open, we could now expect increased competition from private players and even MNCs who set up shop in India. This, in turn, implied that we had to constantly step up our productivity and profitability, which could only be done by getting all our players on board. Addressing one such workshop, I spoke about the *Saptapadi*, or the seven circumambulations around the sacred fire, and how it forges a deep and lasting union between husband and wife. Precisely the same sort of lasting union, with similar 7 principles and commitments, was called for, between the unions or associations on the one hand, and management on the other, if the institution called NTPC was to prosper and grow (Annexure B).

CONCLUSION

Industrial Relations in the Company continued to be cordial and harmonious. A series of workshops were held, at the apex as well as regional level, for leaders of Trade Unions to sensitise them towards the changing business scenario and the challenges faced by the Company. The overall industrial relation scenario was peaceful and marked by harmony and mutual trust. There had been no major strikes or even cases of serious industrial unrest in NTPC during the period between 1999 and 2005, thanks to its commitment to bi-partism and employee involvement founded on a well designed model of relationship, aiming at creating a total synergy in the Organisation. Collective bargaining through an institutionalised forum had assumed the dimension of productivity bargaining, and the well accepted philosophy of 'something for something' became the guiding principle for negotiations.

This gave rise to a belief in a wonderful employee relations model that we attempted to initiate in NTPC. When tailored, experimented and silently acted upon proactively, with proper assessment and an honest will and transparency, harmony started emerging, and we stood triumphant.

Human Resources players will have to be proactive, sensitive but firm, and act with a well built credibility to generate the synergy desired, for best of relationships. There needs to be a conscious realisation that it is their constituency where they must be successful, rather than anyone else, in begetting the desired peace, happiness and relationship, that emerges as a sustainable one.

7

Building A Leadership Pipeline

IN ONE OF the seminars on leadership, before sharing my views on leadership, I asked the audience comprising middle and senior level corporate executives, to list out the three most critical attributes of an ideal leader as per their opinion and experience. Some of the attributes listed were as follows:

- Visionary
- Highly energetic
- Emotionally intelligent
- Humble
- Highly passionate about goal
- Global mindset
- Inspiring
- Ethical
- People oriented
- Ambitious
- Achievement oriented
- Excellent communicator

After listening to them, I recalled the story of the *Six blind men and an Elephant*, one of the most common fables and shared it with them. Six blind men decided to feel an elephant. The first of them touched the side (belly) of the elephant and said it felt like a wall. One of them held the tail of the elephant and said it seemed like a rope. The third man held the trunk and said it was like a python. The fourth man touched one of the elephant's huge legs and said that it definitely felt like a tree. The fifth man touched the tusk and said the elephant seemed to be like a pointed spear of some wild animal. Finally, the sixth man touched the ears and declared it to be like a fan.

Like the blind men who were forming their own conception of the elephant as a rope or tree, etc., as per their feeling and experience of touching whatever they could. All of them might have been right as per their perspectives and experience but they were detailing only one aspect of a large and complex animal. I explained that the subject of leadership was quite similar to the story. It is like beauty… One can keep describing it endlessly but will know it only when once it is seen. Nobody seems to have all the answers on this vast and complex subject. Leadership is essentially a subjective phenomenon and there cannot be a single perspective on this. However, we do have enough evidence in the corporate, political and social arena to have a fair assumption about what makes a good leader.

Leadership, as one of the most critical factors for business success, needs no explanation. Only people can make your organisation a success and to unleash the people-power, we need leaders who can identify the adequate people, inspire commitment, motivate them to give their best and take the organisation to heights of excellence.

On searching the internet, one may come across almost 3000 books, articles, research papers that are written world over every year pertaining to Leadership. We have enough knowledge available on this subject. Few years back, the importance of leadership had also been established by many empirical studies on business excellence. Jim Collins in his research based book, *Good to Great*,[5] covering about 1400 companies listed in Fortune 500 between 1965 and 1995, says that the first factor for transition from Good to Great companies was *Level 5 leadership* in which he describes the hierarchy of leadership characteristics and states that the most ideal and the highest level is Level 5 leadership which is characterised by a "Paradoxical blend of personal humility and intense professional will". Such leaders are self effacing, quiet, reserved, have a very high ambition for the company, etc. I developed a liking for this model called the *Level 5 leadership* and wanted to develop this model amongst the leaders of NTPC, whether being developed right from the beginning, level after level, or through organised succession plans at higher levels.

One could quote from countless researchers and leaders, everyone sounded right, impressive and best. There have been a number of studies on leadership including the one undertaken in the state of Ohio, University of Michigan studies, and a number of theories have been developed on the subject of leadership including the Trait theory, Behaviour theories, Contingency theories, etc. Besides, a number of concepts on leadership like transformational leadership, servant leadership, etc., have been studied from time to time. In fact, leadership is one of the most talked about, most written about and still the most intriguing subject. Every time we hear about a new theory, there are new paradigms challenging the old ones.

COMMON ATTRIBUTES OF LEADERS

Before I talk about certain characteristics, I would like to talk about certain common myths about Leadership. There are plenty of myths, but there are three which I find are the most critical ones that we need to keep in mind while motivating people to make the best of their Leadership potential:

- Leaders are born and not made
- Leaders are high profile people with big personalities
- Leaders have a brilliant academic background

In my life, I have been particularly inspired by a few leaders from both, political and corporate world, which include Mahatma Gandhi, Konushuke Matsushita, founder of the Japanese company, Matsushita Electronics, later National Panasonic, or Darwin Smith of Kimberley Clark. Indian corporates also had such exceptional parallels like J.R.D. Tata, G.D. Birla, R.P. Goenka, Dhiru Bhai Ambani, V. Krishnamoorthy, E Sreedharan and the likes. In NTPC, we were able to identify good leaders in all roles, functions and characteristics. Some of them were: D.V. Kapur, P.S. Bami, Rajendra Singh, R.V. Shahi, Pran Nath, M.L. Mallik, M.A. Hai, Ojha, Bala, and a few more. They built NTPC as a great Organisation with a wonderful vision. When I started working on refreshing and re-energising NTPC People strengths, we took Organisational Leadership and Organisational Development as our major agenda. For Leadership Development, we planned to develop leadership as a most critical enabling factor, while always focusing on building of a learning Organisation. We wanted to emphasise the following key roles in our leaders who were to take these responsibilities:

- Leader as *Designer* – Design the governing ideas of the organisation: the Vision, purpose, mission, strategy, etc.
- Leader as a *Talent Manager* – Identifying right people, putting them in right roles, motivating and developing them.
- Leader as *Commitment builder* – Gaining commitment towards achievement of organisational goals by sharing and inspiring Vision, recognising performance, celebrating success, communicating openly and freely, etc.
- Leader as *Change Masters* – Preparing people for changes: building capability for continuous learning, innovation, etc., to be able to face change effectively.
- Leader as *Teacher* – Builds/develops Leadership skills in the organisation at all levels, acts as role Model and catalyses development in the pipeline. Similarly, while developing leadership, we were following few planned interventions, to emphasise developing the following few characteristics of a Leader, much more in NTPC, which most of them already had or had potential to develop:

  - *Humility* – So as to respect others and their ideas; learn at all times
  - *Passionate* – Having energy to adhere to goals, determined to persevere in the face of difficulties
  - *Emotional Strength* – To take bold decisions, to maintain right balances
  - *Integrity* – conscious adherence to values
  - *Creativity* – Looking for new ideas, better ways of doing things
  - Concern for people

I rarely came across a single person who had all these characteristics, that were needed to transform NTPC, in abundance, but there were many potential leaders and a willingness to learn.

BUILDING LEADERSHIP IN ORGANISATIONS

Though leadership is critical, it is a fact today that leadership abilities are scarce in today's corporate world. Playing the managerial role demands knowledge and skills to manage complexities which may not be the difficult task. But *finding leaders* who possess a vision, versatility, emotional strength, understanding, execution and people orientation was a challenge for business organisations. Research studies and cases had shown that leadership could be developed and more than the classroom, leadership was developed on the job. Many successful business leaders are often heard mentioning a strong mentor or coach who had played a key role in their development.

Three important ways of building leadership in business organisations would include:

- *Selection* – identifying the set of leadership competencies suitable for the organisation and then selecting the people with these competencies at various levels including CEO level.
- *Training and development* – developing leadership competencies among the employees through regular training, management development programmes, interventions like 360 degree feedback, Coaching, Mentoring, Development centre, PMS, Thomas profiling, Hogan development tools, etc.
- *Developing and providing supportive environment* – Supporting the environment and role rotation and challenges, where the leadership capabilities can flourish including creating culture of entrepreneurship, initiative and risk taking, values actualisation, etc.

These were the areas of focus for creating and adopting a leadership Development model to move the Organisation forward along with an effective leadership.

LEADERSHIP DEVELOPMENT AT NTPC

NTPC had taken a systematic approach to leadership development at all levels. We strongly believed in creating a leadership pipeline and have always laid strong emphasis on building leadership.

PLANNED INTERVENTIONS

Apart from regular need based interventions, the Company carried out planned interventions for transition at various levels. It included *Executive Development Programme* for Supervisors to Executive cadre; Foundation course for Dy. Managers level, *Capsule Course* for Manager; *Enhancing Managerial Competence* (EMC) for Senior Manager; *Advanced Management Programme* (AMP) DGM and *AMPs with Global exposure* for AGMs/GMs and so on. The structure and design were developed by PMI with the organisation's focus on exposure for the identified roles, responsibilities and abilities.

ENHANCING MANAGERIAL COMPETENCE

A three week programme for Senior Managers with an aim to sensitise them with the changes being brought within the Organisation, with special reference to business of the power sector, enhance capabilities to understand strategic issues and to develop holistic cross functional competencies.

CAPSULE COURSE ON GENERAL MANAGEMENT

A two week programme for managers with an aim to provide an understanding of current issues of economy, industry and Company and to develop managerial skills and an integrated perspective of management function.

FOUNDATION COURSE IN GENERAL MANAGEMENT

An 11 day programme for Dy. Managers to provide an understanding of the basics of General Management and to create awareness on various Management theories like team working, communication, delegation, etc. These were conducted at all the Plant Employee Development Centres or in Regions.

STRATEGIC MANAGEMENT INITIATIVE IN LEADERSHIP EFFECTIVENESS (SMILE)

A programme was developed and organised by PMI for Executive Directors and senior General Mangers to address the critical organisational concerns and to formulate an action plan to address the issues that ranged from Business development, financial management, creating performance oriented culture though effective leadership, etc.

An outbound programme was also conducted on similar lines as mentioned above for General Managers to formulate action points for effective learning and Organisational Development.

BUSINESS UNIT HEAD PROGRAMME

A 5-day programme for Business Unit Heads (GMs) with an aim to develop their capacity to identify the challenges of change and the skills required for proactively managing the same.

ADVANCE MANAGEMENT PROGRAMME

A 3-week programme for senior executives at the level of DGMs/AGMs conducted by ASCI, Hyderabad and MDI, Gurgaon. The objectives of the programme were to enhance awareness of the key challenges in the rapidly changing business environment, to provide an overview of state of the art in Management thoughts, practices in functional areas, to provide a conceptual exposure in formulating strategic plans for the organisation and to develop Personal action plans using approaches that would work in the organisation.

Further, in all these planned interventions, sessions were set aside to provide inputs on the Vision and Values of the Organisation, its corporate or strategic plan with challenges, and the plan of transformation undertaken with roles of each level. Senior Executives like Directors, Executive Directors, and General Managers, etc., were involved in attending these sessions with a view to share their understanding and passion with others. These interactions became very powerful inputs for not only generating the needed alignment of all levels to the roadmap, but also for a better understanding of the requirements from people at all levels. The programmes were successful in bridging the gaps in communication which were so much needed in order to move them all in one direction, towards the one goal envisioned for the Company.

Besides the programmes and interventions mentioned above, some other specific initiatives for leadership development were taken, which are as follows:

DEVELOPMENT CENTRE

Development Centres were introduced in 1999 for middle level executives to identify developmental needs for higher responsibility levels by assessing the gap between required versus possessed levels of competencies, and by providing an opportunity for development which was subsequently addressed through specific interventions.

Feedback was given about their strengths as well as the developmental needs. The inputs of these DCs were also used for improving the inputs in the planned interventions. Initially we wanted to bring out individual or even group gaps in competencies by introducing Assessment Centres, but our idea was not to create apprehensions and fear in the minds of people as to how these gap assessments would be used. Hence, we initially made them optional and shared the results only with the individuals concerned, suggesting that they may use these diagnostics or assessment outputs for self development, voluntarily discussing with their superiors, HRD or EDC for a future development plan. In order to generate acceptability, we had to make this programme into a non-invasive development initiative. A similar strategy was adopted to introduce other initiatives like 360° feedback surveys, etc. We were aware of the prevalent cultural status and wanted to introduce these initiatives intended to bring about changes in the performance culture smoothly, changes that were founded on grounds of trust.

360° FEEDBACK SYSTEM

A 360° feedback system had been started for senior executives in the level of AGMs and above and was planned to be cascaded to lower levels of executives first on a voluntary basis and later as a compulsory requirement and as part of PMS, to improve objectivity and enhance development of individuals. It involved seeking feedback from peers, direct reports from superiors besides assessing the regular feedback, as per the PMS, from the direct reporting officer. There were apprehensions in the association and even in some individual executives objected to the introduction of the system, but everyone was gradually won over. Senior Executives at the level of General Managers, Executive Directors or Directors/CMD started appreciating the process and the results of the programme. When T.V. Rao presented my report on the 360° Feedback System, I found it quite interesting and useful. Areas of self development were identified and feedback in the form of suggestions was adopted as an agenda for development. At least the programme was successful in raising issues and concerns, and made the management conscious of their needs. I recall sharing the results with my colleagues in line and HR.

Training on Performance Feedback and Counseling Skills (PREFACE)

To supplement the efforts for a transparent and an open culture and to effectively achieve the intent of performance management, a specific training programme was launched for building counselling and feedback skills amongst senior managers / DGMs, the critical mass of the leadership positions responsible for managing and creating high performing work teams.

DIRECTOR LEVEL COMPETENCY FRAMEWORK

Keeping in view the long-term business strategies and plans as articulated in VISION – 2017, the leadership competency framework of board level positions of NTPC was re-considered and a new leadership and competency framework was evolved with the help of M/s Hewitt after an extensive interaction with the top management. A thorough examination was conducted focusing on Job descriptions, the changing Power scenario and regulatory regime / framework, best in class global practices and the future growth plans of NTPC.

USE OF ASSESSMENT CENTRE FOR DIRECTOR LEVEL POSITIONS BY PSEB

With a clear focus on its commitment for high concern for competent leaders to drive the new challenges and plans of the organisation, and to achieve VISION – 2017, NTPC pioneered the use of Assessment Centres through PSEB for the first time in the country. The Centres were established in order to assess the leadership and managerial competencies of the candidates who appeared for the position of Director (Commercial) and Director (Technical) as an input for the selection process. To supplement the process of assessing the leadership style and behaviour, *HOGAN Development Survey*, a state-of-the-art psychometric tool was also used, with the help of renowned HR consultants Hewitt Associates.

HOGAN DEVELOPMENT SURVEY AS PART OF SUCCESSION PLANNING

NTPC takes the credit of having pioneered the use of *Hogan Development Survey* – a state-of-the-art psychometric tool – for assessing the leadership style and behaviour of General Managers as part of Succession Planning by providing input to the top management. Developmental plans for these levels, based on the Leadership Challenge Report, were also initiated and structured. The initiative was widely accepted by both the participants as well as the top management.

GLOBAL EXPOSURE THROUGH FOREIGN TRAINING

In order to develop world class competent power professionals, the initiative of global exposure through foreign training was being pursued vigorously with the allocation of a budget of Rs. 500 Lakh per year. With this initiative, efforts were made to develop functional competencies in the new business areas such as hydel, distribution and technical competencies in Operation and Maintenance, Erection and Commissioning, and global leadership perspective in key leadership levels by sending executives to reputed global organisations such at EPRI USA, EDF France, CDG Germany, Global Business Schools such as Harvard Business School, Kellogs Business School, etc. Executive Directors and Directors were allowed to be partners in their development journeys and were to select a useful foreign training programme in the Institute of their choice, for acquiring the best of required learnings and desired developments.

LEADERSHIP DEVELOPMENT SYSTEM (LEADS)

A system, namely LEADS had been conceived for senior executives that included Assessment and Development Centres and 360° feedback tools. In addition, systems like Succession Planning, *Hogan* Development Inventory and Strategic Management Initiative for Leadership effectiveness were used.

SUCCESSION PLANNING

A conceptual framework for Succession Planning was devised whose cornerstone was the assessment of core competencies to determine gaps, required skills, and to identify what positions needed succession planning. Formal professional development opportunities were provided through job rotation, job enrichment and job enlargement. Generalised career paths were also drawn up so that the focus would not be on isolated positions. The overall strategic plan of the Company determined the positions that would be included in the succession plan. A matrix was created showing performance, potential, development opportunities and exposure. These were used to place people in leadership positions at different levels in the Company.

Objectives

- To grow leaders from within: Home grown talent
- To identify key leadership positions
- Individual growth and advancement
- Prepare right people for key higher positions at right time and managing transition
- To maintain continuity in leadership roles

Principle

- Succession Planning: 2 levels below Board level positions.
- Identify competent persons based on performance and potential
- Those who were willing to assume responsibility
- Those who had a balance service of 2 years.

I remember the CMD, before taking up interviews for selection, would discuss each internal candidate with HR which included outputs of various instruments including *Hogan*, 360°, and the formal succession plan that was formulated and settled prior to the selection process. This was a big help in leadership development. The Government Directors would want feedback. I recall, the then Secretary Power, Ashok Basu calling me to discuss a couple of appointment of Directors in NTPC, to confer our peoples' strengths and also our development plan. T.K.A. Nair, the then PESB Chairman (now Adviser to the Prime Minister) was seemingly an Administrator with a soul of a wonderful HR professional. While he would at times discuss reports and succession plans of senior Executives, he would also discuss the NTPC system of leadership development and would earnestly want to consciously develop similar structured systems for developing leaders in all PSUs as well. There was a virtual movement of system realignment. We supported PESB for sometime on this leadership development system. I recall the meetings in PESB, chaired by T.K.A. Nair, with CMDs of most leading PSUs and some Directors. They would all be earnestly listening to us explain the leadership development systems in practice, need and methods of some standardisation in Performance Management System, etc. We were being led to the required reforms in HR Systems in PESB, in tandem with changing times. And there were tremendous learnings for us, as well from a host of leading PSUs – lots of bright new pebbles for us to pick up from.

CONSCIOUS CREATION OF REAL-TIME LEADERSHIP OPPORTUNITIES

Opportunities of growth and expansion of the organisation normally offer opportunities of people growth. Growth comes from growing in the same business through *green field* or *brown field* expansions. These create fairly good opportunities of growth for people, particularly by creating new leadership positions. However, greater challenging roles appear when companies have diversified, but within the same sector. These were instances where there was a general comfort of business management, and at the same time provided an exposure of top leadership positions, like CEO and Board level for company executives. We had pushed the strategy of growth within the sector by entering into other critical areas in the energy value chain. NTPC went on growing subsidiaries and strategic partnership for more than two dozen companies, creating positions of CEOs, MDs and a whole list of postions for Directors, wherever a Board was constituted.

The opportunities created through dozens of subsidiary companies involved a lot of excitement and an enormous scope of learnings for our people in senior positions – to get rotated to driving seats and to also explore appropriate developmental opportunities. We always kept the Succession Plan updated and connected to such postings. Around 20 companies created then and later, were successful in providing immense opportunities of Leadership Development.

We have seen large companies taking such strategic decisions to grow their talent into leadership positions through such strategic initiatives which

NTPC adopted. However, we were like parents – to guide them by holding their hands to enable growth and success by true empowerment. We had even procured a large land in NCR to build towers, with a dozen floors for housing these companies, giving them proximity, and at the same time a respectable distance with an intention of empowering their performance.

CONCLUSION

We were conscious of the fact that in the present complex corporate world a single leader or even a group of leaders would not have been able to steer our organisation ahead, but that we needed to develop leaders at all levels. The Company needed to develop *Shared Leadership* and build up leaders at all levels. John Maxwell gave a good illustration of Shared Leadership in his book *Developing the Leaders Around You*[6] by talking about Geese. When geese fly in their 'V' formation, the leader's role changes frequently. We needed to gradually push the culture of mutual trust, creating a solid ground for shared leadership, where the vision becomes more important than glorifying personal leadership.

Further, *Leadership style* (Authoritative, democratic, affiliative, coercive, task oriented, etc.) should be *contextual* or situation specific and specific to circumstances. Daniel Goleman,[7] advocated the criticality of using emotional intelligence by leaders to be successful. He, based on the research of more than 3000 executives about the leadership style that yields best results, concluded that the leader who gets the best results do not use a particular leadership style but a combination of different styles, depending on the type of business situation. So there needed to be flexibility in style, and in our training we emphasised on developing this acumen in our leaders under the development programme. Our idea was to always learn from the best research on the subject that used to bring learning from a large number of tested practices in organisations, bringing success, and spreading the learning in order to not only building individual capabilities but as an organisational capability as a whole. Learning, developing and practicing became a way of life, contributing towards a grand performance culture based on focused values of mutual trust, continuous learning, and commitment to bring excellence all over. *LEADS* developed specific and individual plans of development of leaders and generated leadership inputs required by the organisation.

8

Achieving People Integration In Mergers And Acquisitions

Unchahar thermal power station was acquired by the National Thermal Power Corporation (NTPC) from the government of Uttar Pradesh. Performance was improved dramatically by using de-bottlenecking techniques. Prior to the takeover the Unchahar station had a PLF of 18 per cent; in six months thereafter it went up to 35.5 per cent and in twelve months to 73.7 per cent. We don't know who are the heroes and heroines who made these achievements possible through teamwork!

– Dr. A.P.J. Abdul Kalam in India 2020 [8]

IN THE YEAR 1992 NTPC acquired Unchahar Thermal Power Station of Uttar Pradesh Rajya Vidyut Utpadan Nigam (UPRUVNL) having a capacity of 420 MW with Plant Load Factor (a measure of capacity utilisation) of only 18 per cent. Today it is rated amongst one of the top ten power stations in the country. The compliment coming from Dr Kalam was a rich tribute to the team members of NTPC who achieved this turnaround after successfully integrating the culture of a State Electricity board to its own.

Uttar Pradesh State Electricity Board had accumulated a huge amount of losses and outstanding liabilities over the years. In order to settle the outstanding dues, UPSEB decided to sell Unchahar Plant to NTPC, for which the discussions began in 1991.

Around December 1991, a team of NTPC officials reached Unchahar to have an assessment of the overall situation and prepare the ground for the future course of action. They had discussions with employees and their representatives apart from the management. Generally, it was observed that employees had the following threat perceptions on the issue of takeover:

- Job insecurity
- Fear of getting step brotherly treatment
- Transfer to other locations of NTPC
- Fear of unknown culture
- Changed working conditions

With this background NTPC's major thrust was on communication which entailed the establishment of the following features along with the policies of the Organisation:

- Assurance that no layoffs would be done and there will be job security
- Benefits like advances be extended
- Promise of enhancing technical know how of people

There had been an attempt by the UP Board to get into a deal with the Dalmias in the past, which failed following very stiff resistance and protests from employees and Unions. These protests were also marked by violence and assaults. NTPC did not want this opportunity slip away, which would have not only improved the capacity addition, but would have also improved the books of accounts fairly, that was loaded with outstanding receivables. However, we were also aware of the past incidents and did not want any resistance from the employees which would hamper the takeover. I recall how, along with Babbar, the Co-secretary and Gopal, the Chief-Legal, I spent months in Lucknow's Clark Awadh, the only respectable Hotel then, working on this difficult transfer. My job, integrated with that of the other two, was primarily to understand the conditions and generate workable strategies and also generate acceptability amongst the large number of Unions and Associations, particularly amongst the employees. We convinced the Government that we would not absorb the Executives or Engineers of Utpadan Nigam at all in this takeover as we had already a surplus. We, in the perceived low time for NTPC, when growth was apparently not feasible in the opened up economy and the sector, were seeing an opportunity of growth of the organisation and its people. This was agreed to by the Government and we started our work with complete focus on the Unions and workmen in order to win their confidence and trust. I recall how we facilitated a group of union representatives and some opinion makers to visit our Stations in Shaktinagar, Vindhyachal and Rihand, and also interact with the unions. These visits were encouraged to impress upon them that they were joining a cultured family where employees were treated as family and excellence was the culture in work and delivery. I wish I could write on NTPC's takeover learnings in detail separately sometime!

Soon the final stages of the transfer arrived, with all legal clearances and Ordinance in place. Though rigorous efforts had been put in to create appreciation and support of workers, executives and the Trade Unions, because of history of Dalmia case, we took enough security precautions, not aware of the actual mood of the employees. I recall, on the final day, we moved in from Lucknow and Rai Bareilly to the plant and Township in a convoy accompanied by police protection and CISF from Rai Bareilly ITI Unit. But, our transparent series of communication had worked and created a somewhat positive mood that enabled the establishment of cordial relations with workmen and Unions, which facilitated the transfer. There was some resistance from some Executives in handing over, which did not last for long.

After the takeover, the efforts were made not only convert all promises into reality but do more than promised. Welfare measures were taken to improve the township life by developing schools, upgrading hospitals, markets, creating facilities like cooperative societies, power supply, garbage collection systems, dish antennae, etc. This started improving not only the quality of life in townships but also enhanced the process of building trust and relationship. Various participative fora such as Plant level committee, Shop level council, safety committee, etc., were created which gave the employees a feeling of sharing in decision making. A large number of Training programmes were primarily organised not only as a measure of creating learning platforms but also platforms for communicating the changes that were taking place to bring in the NTPC Culture. A number of visits were organised for employees to other projects of NTPC which gave them the opportunity to interact with employees of other projects and broaden their perspectives, as well as to learn the culture and systems of NTPC. The achievements were publicised widely amongst employees and also celebrated in various forums, functions and visits of senior officials of company. I recall some of the HR leaders like Sachhidanand, Nagakumar(now in Tatas), Amar Nath Verma(now in NSCPL), Rajesh Sahay (now in WIPRO) and few others, who were part of the entire operation. They contributed and learnt from Unchahar and would always remember the lessons Unchahar taught us as HR personnel.

The transformation of the plant and people was carried out at an amazing speed, with immense support of people there. There was again immense learning in this takeover which was not sudden and surgical like BTPS and that too without the development of any basic unwillingness.

TURNAROUND OF TALCHER THERMAL POWER STATION

Similarly, in the year 1995, the company took over Talcher Thermal Power station from The Orissa State Electricity Board (OSEB). Based on the experience and learnings gained in the previous takeover at Unchahar, we took a more systematic approach during the takeover of Talcher Thermal plant. For example, the process started with conducting an *HR Due Diligence* programme after the intention of the deal was made public, which helped us to collect a lot of information before the actual takeover took place. Some of the details collected were:

EMPLOYEE AUDIT

- Number and type of employees at the site
- Overall talent of the employee base
- Strength of technical/marketing/functional talent
- Ability to recruit/retain employees
- Ratio of regular Vs contract employees
- Manpower growth plan through fiscal year
- Likelihood of key employees remaining post-acquisition

CULTURE AUDIT

- Assessment of work environment
- Stated or implied values of company
- Morale/pride of employees
- Degree of shared vision among leaders and employees
- Frequency and results of employee surveys
- Communication style favoured

- Effectiveness of teams
- Degree to which the organisation applies learning
- Attractiveness to potential new hires
- How and when the company celebrates successes

MANAGEMENT AUDIT

- Management style at company
- Decision-making process used
- Importance of values to manage the company
- Overall management capability
- Management training conducted

COMPENSATION/BENEFITS AUDIT

- Compensation philosophy
- Compensation components
- Grading system
- Performance evaluation system
- Salary review process/frequency
- Stock option distribution/holdings
- Wage agreements
- Pension and other social Security

INTEGRATION ISSUES

- Compensation plan blending
- Benefit plan blending
- Employee communications plan
- Geographical considerations
- Likelihood of employees to relocate

Subsequently, after the announcement, steps were taken such as Employee Mapping and Placement, fixing Compensation packages of newly acquired employees, attending HR and business integration meetings, understanding potential issues and educating leadership/management accordingly. Based on above inputs, an HR strategy was drawn to deal with the same. Here we were required to retain a few executives also, and we chose the junior most of them to be absorbed, as it was much easier to change their mindset and assimilate them in the NTPC work culture.

Communication strategies were intense and similar to the one used and developed in Unchahar. I remember, after the approval of the government and consent from the Hon'ble Governor, Orissa, as our convoy marched in the Talcher Plant, the executives and workmen welcomed all of us with loads of flower bouquets and garlands!

Prakash Rao, the chosen Station Head and Saptarshi who was chosen as Station HR Head, did a great job in this absorption and transformation. They were so successful and effective that after the Unchahar and Talcher turnarounds, I used to suggest to Saptarshi, Prakash Rao and many others in their teams that NTPC should continue takeovers of the so called sick stations from the Boards and transform them through our experienced and expert group. Infact, not only would have NTPC gained through these acquisitions, but nation too would have immensely benefitted by such changeover mass activities.

TAKEOVER OF TANDA POWER STATION

Besides the takeover of Unchahar, another power plant from UPSEB was undertaken in the year 2000, namely the Tanda Thermal Power Station in which, once again, similar steps were taken and the deal was completed quite effectively. We did not take any of the Executives of the Board, and took only 50 per cent of the workmen. The decision of selecting the workmen was on the basis of seniority, as their retirement could be sooner, and fresh induction in future would provide new workmen if at all needed, to adapt to the NTPC culture. The takeover was not as smooth and peaceful as Talcher. The environment was not friendly as there was resistance and we even had to march in with the support of an Army Contingent comprising of their Core of Engineers. Our Engineers and those from the Army were welcomed by complete darkness and an inoperative plant. They had to work very hard for hours to bring them on line. The experience and learnings here were somewhat different. Saptarshi slogged here to use our rich experience to transform the mood and culture of the former state employees, which obviously took lot of time. The transition was lengthy but we were able to win the confidence of the people and families.

CONCLUSION

Due to an adequate manner of dealing with the people issues and integration of employees with NTPC culture, all these plants are working at very high levels of efficiency. There has been no conflict or industrial unrest as such. The learning gained in each such venture was adding to the repertoire of NTPC in consummating such deals with considerable ease. There was a huge learning for the entire HR Team. A model of taking over ownership and turning around was developed as an added strength of NTPC, though slightly different in model and experiences in Badarpur, which started primarily as a management contract.

Seeing the success of NTPC in turning around underperforming power stations (Unchahar, Talcher Thermal, Tanda), we could think of creating a dedicated Turnaround Cell of an experts team, or even a subsidiary company, which would be on call to go to power stations that the Company acquired or set up Joint Ventures (JV) to run in alliance with others. Ultimately, it is people power that creates these experts, for strategy, planning, technology, finance, HR, etc. Skills and competencies can be developed in an enabling environment, where freedom exists to grow and learn, and whereby conscious design and opportunities are created. These abilities reside in the people alone, and it is them who make the difference. Similarly, we were able to offer training programmes on turning around ailing power stations to other organisations in the power sector. The well known quote "Give a man a fish and you feed him for a day; teach him to fish and you feed him for a lifetime" comes to mind. It would be a great service that NTPC would be able to provide to the power sector, to impart its turnaround ability to other players, anytime.

9

Leveraging Organisation Culture For Enduring Business Success

Culture is the soul of the organisation. I think of the structure as the skeleton, and the employees as the flesh and blood. And culture is the soul that holds the things together and gives it life force.

– Henry Mintzberg

ORGANISATIONAL CULTURE HOLDS tremendous significance for sustainable success and for achieving any enduring change in the work environment. This fact has also been established by many studies, and creating a sustaining culture which supports the business and HR strategy comprises an important aspect of the role that HR functionaries' have to perform in the current scenario.

CULTURAL TRANSFORMATION AT NTPC

NTPC had been witnessing a boom time till the end of 1980s – a phase that witnessed rapid expansion and virtually unchecked career progression, providing growth opportunities galore, not only for the Organisation but its employees as well. However, the New Economic Policy of Government of India in the 1990s actively encouraged and solicited private investment in the power sector. As mentioned earlier, some of the upcoming projects of NTPC were redirected to the new stakeholders. Suddenly it seemed that brakes had been applied to organisational growth, and consequently on career growth as well. The new fast track companies looked glamorous and offered similar glamourous looking, yet challenging career opportunities, luring the skilled professionals. I recall headhunters operating to target NTPC. There were advertisements that openly targeted experienced people from NTPC, preferring them over others. Some people left in quick succession and the attrition rate of NTPC went up by 2.5 per cent. Apparently this would not have had any major impact but as narrated earlier in this book, a few prominent people in the organisation at the visible positions also left, giving rise to rumours and cynicism about the future of the Company. Overall, the Organisation witnessed a phase of low morale with an increased employee turnover. The Company needed to bring back the passion and excitement amongst its workforce and rejuvenate the overall culture. The management rightly became concerned with the pressing issues.

In the beginning of 1997, as I have mentioned earlier also, the Management Committee set up a Committee of Senior Executives to deliberate on improving the morale and the organisational culture. This was an initiative coming from an apex forum involving the CMD, all the functional Directors, the Executive Directors and General Managers of functions and Station or Projects. This was an opportunity provided to us for identifying a wish list for bringing improvements in the organisation by drawing support of all seniors. This group identified four areas for improvement, presenting a list of recommendations of number of initiatives in these areas. The four areas identified were as follows:

- Performance orientation,
- People orientation,
- Building mutual respect and trust, and
- Building pride and a sense of belonging.

PERFORMANCE ORIENTATION

To revitalise the performance-orientation in the culture, the memorandum-of-understanding (MOU) concept under which NTPC had been signing agreements with the government every year guaranteeing its performance, was extended to the Regions, Stations and the functions at the Corporate Office. Every Regional ED signed an annual internal MOU with the Corporate Centre, guaranteeing the performance of his Region in terms of generation, project implementation, and other parameters. Similarly, the corporate functions like Finance, Human Resources, Contracts and

Materials would sign an MOU giving their targets which, naturally, were stretched ones. The Internal MOU concept brought about a sense of ownership at the regional leadership level and, through its emphasis on collective endeavour, helped the organisation in building both cohesiveness and performance-related excitement, bringing about significant improvement in the working of the organisation. In order to bring clarity to and ownership of the targets, the system of joint goal-setting was introduced, wherein the superior and the sub-ordinate mutually identified goals and targets in the key performance areas.

The company went in for driving Total Quality Movement (TQM) in a big way to spread quality culture in the organisation. It created an institutional set up and a framework within which TQM tools and techniques could be used effectively. ISO, **5S**, SA-8000, Six Sigma, Think Tanks, etc., were some of the programmes that were implemented to bring about the desired changes in the Organisation. It undertook TQM through both *Process Improvement Programmes* such as Benchmarking, Business Process Reengineering and new framework for Business Planning, and *Employee Involvement programmes* such as Quality Circles, Suggestion Scheme, Think Tanks, etc.

PEOPLE ORIENTATION

Though performance was always accorded a high priority, it was also ensured that adequate thrust was laid on the people aspect. Such a 'People first' approach was firmly established over the years in the cultural fabric of the Company. We forged the four pillars of HR strategy, i.e. Competence building, Commitment building, Culture building and Systems building and around these four pillars, an integrated model of HR, being portrayed as a Business Partner, was developed and implemented by Team HR.

With the introduction of this model, a host of HR initiatives aimed at making the organisation more people sensitive were inducted into the system. A number of steps were also taken to make the HR Department more responsive. Keeping this objective in mind, programmes like Customer Focus training to HR staff, HR Policy Manual on intranet, simplification of HR rules and systems/processes, computerised HRMS, HR Benchmarking, etc were launched.

A lot of thrust was put on communicating the achievements and future plans of the company so that the employees could take pride in being part of the family of the leader of the Indian Power sector, thus kindling a sense of belongingness in the people. Appreciation and praise by dignitaries such as World Bank Officials, the President and Prime Minister of India, etc., were highlighted at a number of forums. A corporate film, Tamso Ma Jyotir Gamaya (From Darkness to Light) was produced in the silver jubilee year 2001, which was directed by noted film maker Shyam Benegal. This film has been a great motivator for employees and helped in reinforcing the culture of the company. I recall how R.K. Nair, the Chief Corporate Communication came up with the idea of roping in Shyam Benegal, who had created a beautiful documentary on SAIL in the 1970s. When we met him in his Sahyadri Films office for making a similar impressive film on NTPC, Shyam Benegal laughed it out saying he was no longer in documentaries and said he could suggest few others who would agree to take up the project. But we were determined to have him and urged upon him through a series of meetings in his Bombay office. Our persistence finally paid off and one day he ultimately agreed saying he would do one like Manthan if he was allowed freedom to create his own story for NTPC and would not tolerate any interference of any sort during the making of the documentary lest his creativity was marred. We were overjoyed. It was a pleasure to see his enthusiasm as he went through tons of reading materials on our company that he desired to study. Shyam Benegal first of all decided to visit 6 stations himself, and accompanied by his story writer Mishra, would sit in market place, Dhabas, offices, clubs and meet employees and even family members, listening to their stories and experiences. We were surprised to see him getting personally involved in the assignment. Though it had been an uphill task of convincing him, but once he did, his passion was very evident as he remarked that NTPC's story was very attractive.

There were waves of excitement in all stations and the people of NTPC, who would eagerly wait for Shyam Benegal's visit to listen to their stories. What he finally created was amazing, a master piece and poetry on celluloid! It was a story carved out by Shyam Benegal and his story writer Mishra, out of real experiences and feelings of people and hence it was easy for the masses to relate to the story and through it to the Vision of the Company for '**Powering India's Growth**'. I also recall when we invited Shyam Benegal to the premier show in Scope Auditorium, he gladly agreed. As the only speaker on stage, next to the screen, Shyam Benegal introduced some of his character artists and went on to share some of his experiences in the making of this great film for NTPC. He said that he was amazed and was full of tremendous respect for the thousands of its people who had raised such a great organisation with so much of care and ownership, something that is not generally seen in corporates, and especially in the Government sector. This was the year 2001, and we continued screening the film year after year on Zee, Star, Door Darshan, etc., and would invite the families to see. We were ourselves so excited about it.

We also strengthened the feeling of 'care' amongst employees by extending a large number of welfare measures for the employees and their family members. It provided quality primary and secondary schooling facilities to the children of its employees and also the neighbouring community in its townships spread across the country. Towards this the company tied up with leading educational societies of the country including DPS, DAV, KVS, Chinmaya, Society of Jesuits, etc. The company provides infrastructural support to the schools set up in the townships. Altogether, more than 50–60 schools had been established across the country through such arrangement. I recall, the young and brilliant engineers of NTPC would have high expectations and once in the mid 1980s, in a small gathering in our Korba unit, some of the youngsters urged me to work towards establishing standard schools in Township for providing quality education for the children, like the Delhi Public School, etc. Delhi used to be far away to send the children to study. I arranged a meeting with Lugani,the virtual head who could take a decision on this on behalf of the DPS Society and requested him to open a branch of DPS in Korba. He was very excited at the prospect and immediately sent Mrs Chona and another teacher colleague to Korba with me. I recall my journey with them to Champa and then to the project, where the infrastructure was hardly developed. During the entire journey I kept rationalising the short comings and challenges of the terrain. They wanted a new modern school building which we didn't have till then. I thought that Chona and her team would give a negative report. But on the contrary, they recommended the proposal to the management and this became the first DPS for the children of NTPC! The employees in Korba were overjoyed. A few more branches soon followed suit in quick succession in the other stations.

The company also provided opportunities for people to learn together as a team, with a view to institutionalising learning in the cultural fabric of NTPC which included Professional Circles, NOCET, *Chanakya*, *Horizon*, the management journal, etc. I recall that the Quality Circle movement created a genuine interest and excitement amongst workmen and even executives. Once, a young executive of an Association casually expressed why a similar opportunity could not be initiated for executives to develop and demonstrate. Praveen Kumar passed away early but the idea worked when I rolled out Professional Circles (PC) without worrying much about its format or structure. We gave a slogan to the programme, 'let's meet and share knowledge!' And PC provided a strong platform that grew tremendously.

I remember, AIMA made me a judge for their Best Manager contest, in either the 1998 or 1999 contest (I am unable to remember exactly when). The write up came for the assessment and I dumped on Indranil Mitra, my Staff Officer, to make my recommendation, and then I also sat through the presentations with a committee of judges. It was a good learning opportunity for me as well. And while sitting in the hall for the prize distribution, I asked Indranil why couldn't we have something similar in NTPC to energise the youngsters and get their contribution on challenging organisational issues raised by us and also recognise them? And thus emerged NOCET! Indranil came out with a draft and we rolled it out immediately. The Chairman would choose topics and along with the Directors, agreed to sit for the whole day during the finals as member of the board of jury, accompanied by some external experts. This programme became a matter of prestige and we could see young girls and boys coming up in plants, Regions and Corporate level competitions, presenting their research work. There used to be excitement amongst the young executives to see their teams perform at the National Level. Every year we would publish a compilation of their work as a book with pictures.

In corporate HR, I started inviting the young and junior ETs in my office room once in a fortnight or a month and just gossip over a cup of tea. This used to be an excellent opportunity for sharing ideas and an excellent learning experience.

Even for formal Training and Development, the whole system at NTPC was revamped and a structured training plan with level-wise interventions and need-based programmes was put in place, giving a target of a minimum of 7 days of training per employee per year. All planned training interventions were further enriched by including modules on value actualisation, corporate social responsibility, and yoga and meditation at all levels.

Spreading people orientation across the entire company was vigorously pursued through HR for Line Managers Programme, System of HR Ambassadors and Nodal Officers, Communication Strategy/Matrix, Tips on Effective Counseling, and guidelines on Development of Subordinates, etc.

BUILDING MUTUAL RESPECT AND TRUST

HR also took steps to preserve the culture of bipartism and promoted leadership development of employee representatives, rejuvenated the Workers' Participation Scheme, and settled the issue of equitable representation of employees. As a result, the participative process had become part of the culture of the organisation.

The Organisation provided a lot of opportunities for experimentation and risk taking. Such opportunities were created at all levels of employees. The creativity was duly appreciated, rewarded and the good ideas were implemented at the workplace.

A lot of emphasis was put on internal communication. We developed various modes of communication and utilised every occasion as an opportunity to communicate and to keep in touch with the employees and stakeholders, and also to identify the pulse of the people through various surveys. The communication involved both sharing of information and obtaining feedback from employees. The following mechanisms were used for the same:

Top Management Communication and Interactions

- Address employees during visits by CMD, Directors and EDs;
- Open house meetings in Units;
- Strategic communications meetings with executives;
- Interactions in Training Programmes like Advanced Management Programmes, EMC and General Management Programmes for senior leaders of the Company.

We always put our motto of 'People First' to practice everywhere. We wrote to all Regional EDs and the station General Manager, and persuaded them to start all meetings by reviewing HR matters, aligning those present on organisational development and also talking about positive achievements and appreciating the station GMs and Regional EDs who supported the initiatives with utmost sincerity and enthusiasm.

I would even write to the station General Managers to visit their Training centres at least once or twice a week, and address the gathering during the inaugural or valediction assembly, or even take an interesting session for the sake of interaction and communication. They were always enthusiastic to support such practices and later started enjoying and improving or adding to the programmes themselves. I was known to be a supporter of station GMs as I would often take their side at corporate level. I once recall, two General Managers sitting outside the Directors' office. I inquired if they were waiting for me and they replied that they were waiting to meet their Director (Operations). I went down for some work and on my return saw them still waiting outside. I brought them to my room asking the PS to call them if the Director (Operations) was ready to call them. We had tea and discussed many things. As one of them had an afternoon return flight to catch, he apparently was getting restless. He wasn't able to leave for the Airport, as he was conscious of leaving without meeting the Director (Operations) after the morning meeting in EOC was over. I suddenly rose, took the two of them with me and went to the Director's (Operations) room, lightly saying that they had just come to convey their regards before leaving for their stations. Ojha was very good natured, took me very sportingly and closed his meeting with soft apologies. Ojha was always very supportive of my indulgences and always took things in his stride, very innocently and with respect. I'd always get ready solutions and understanding from him. This also built up a natural support from his operation people all over. What a favour!

We ensured an Advanced Management Programme for all senior and middle levels by regularly inviting the Directors' support by arranging for their visits to PMI, ASCI, IIMs, etc., for interaction with senior and middle level executives in MDPs.

Magazines/Newsletters

- NTPC News
- *News Flash*
- *Horizon* – a management magazine.
- Power Scan giving sectoral developments
- Project house journals and newsletters/ leaflets on HR News, etc.

Nair was an innovator and also a perfect executioner accompanied by a great sense of sincerity. During discussions, we found that NTPC News used to take time to be compiled, so he brought out the great *News Flash* which was an instant success! When we wanted to create an NTPC News for Cable TV, *Power Vision* was born…and people used to eagerly wait for it! I recall Nair and I visited the Rourkela Steel Plant to benchmark Cable TV practices as early as 1986! This became a reality and a dream come true with Nair's support. Charan initiated and helped institutionalise this idea on robust footing in Rihand. This was a great achievement and was a runway success amongst employees and families in the Township, more particularly amongst the school children who became News readers in *Pratibimb* and also started creating small clips and serials. I used to collect loads of VCR copies of *Pratibimb* and send them to all Station GMs and HR to screen and also emulate. This practice spread in a far better manner than I had imagined.

Messages

- CMD's message – on New Year, Raising Day and other special occasions.
- Director's message on special accomplishments, festivals.
- Power Station General Manager's message on New Year, Raising Day, Festivals, Accomplishments, Quarterly house journal, etc.

Video

- 1980s was the time when TV channels and networks were still in the developing phase. Anything we did by utilising this media was very much appreciated. We used this extensively and proactively for the development of our programmes and practices.
- *Power Vision* – a bi-monthly video newsletter professionally developed and taken out in Hindi/English by Corporate Communication, show casing companywide activities.
- *Project Video Journals* – Power stations encouraged bringing out their in-house video journals also.
- CCTV was a facility made available at all power stations and Townships, wherein information related to power generation, new circulars, cultural programmes and events were shown, apart from entertainment. The news was read by children of the employees, which was an encouraging and motivating factor.

- *'Silver Jubilee Film'* – Tamso Ma Jyotirgamaya was produced by Shyam Benegal, highlighting challenges/hardships faced by employees during the making of the Organisation.
- *Power Station Videos:* Some of our Power stations had produced videos on the history of development of that project to a station and the challenges and learnings from it.

Company's Intranet

- NTPC launched its Web Page giving all the relevant information regarding the company, its growth plan, latest achievements, circulars, vacancies, forms and formats, etc.
- A web page for Power Management Institute was also created which gave details of the forthcoming training programmes, training calendar.
- *Project/Unit's Intranet:* All the projects/units had a local web page giving information about various activities of the project like all HR documents, plant performances and data related to the operating efficiencies, etc.

These were new technology based initiatives and they infused instant liking and pride amongst employees.

BUILDING PRIDE AND A SENSE OF BELONGING

Corporate Communication undertook the creating of a standardised identity Manual to bring greater oneness and identity all over. It was fortunate that Corporate Communication was part of HR and we could work together very closely, utilise their professional support in communication and branding, which was a boon in our transformational initiatives. To create distinct cultural identity, this became a major support to HR.

We further developed and refreshed the *NTPC Song* in the Silver Jubilee year when Shyam Benegal and Vanraj Bhatia recomposed it for *Tamso Ma Jyotir Gamaya*. While reviewing it, the Board members who constituted the subcommittee on celebrations, agreed to change only the song size to limit the rendering time to one minute but in the same tune. We prepared, created a master and gave guidelines for singing on important occasions like VIP visits, meetings, Raising Day, etc.

I recall conceiving the song during Shahi's time in 1985 when we wanted to celebrate the tenth Anniversary with a cultural meet in Delhi. It was a competitive meet to start with at Siri Fort. And we wanted to start the show with a song on NTPC. Rameshwar Prakash, a junior HR guy in our Team, I recall, came with the lyrics one day to PMI (Kailash) where we used to have rehearsals in a room with the Music Director, Chote Lal. The first tune of an NTPC song was born. It had 4 stanzas and was almost 4 minutes long. This song was performed for 3–4 years, when we would sing it once in a year during the Annual Cultural meet at Siri Fort. And then one day Urmila Mukherjee, a very sensitive HR colleague with excellent sense of aesthetics and art, came with an idea to revamp the tune and size of the song. She located a Music Director in Chittaranjan Park and we adapted a tune which had more speed and regimentations of the rhythm, cutting down the size to perhaps 2.5 minutes approximately. This version of the song was sung for a few years more but we started singing it on other functions, apart from Annual Cultural Meets.

We sent a guideline to use this as a company song with a protocol format for the song's delivery. We made a booklet with not only the lyrics and tune but also the details of the size of lead group, their instruments in support, the presentations and the occasions when it could be sung. Within the next 5 to 6 years the song started becoming like a stale, routine ritual, which was however, given due respect when it was sung. In our long service award function of Hyderabad when the compere announced for this song before commencing the programme, I saw some people stand up with the others following them and by the end of the first stanza the entire audience of guests, employees and families stood up and sang! And with passion!! This gave an idea to give a formal structure of presentation to the company song, when everyone must stand in respect while the song is rendered, and also sing with the coir. The mass or audience response in large functions was amazing. We started printing the lyrics with the programme of the occasion and distributed it in the audience and on stage. I recall Atal Behari Vajpayee, the then PM, being the Chief Guest on Foundation Day of Kayamkulam. After the NTPC song was sung, with the large crowd standing at the call of the compere, Vajpayee picked up the leaflet during his address, and read a stanza, appreciating that when the employees had a strong resolve like this, there was no chance that the organisation could ever be defeated!! How can we ever forget the strength we got through such appreciations, for NTPC? It makes us energetic and proud even today!

Besides, an *NTPC Flag* was designed for creating a sense of identity. One could see employees passionately owning the flag and the company song. Even caller tunes of the company song on mobiles were passionately retained by employees retiring from the Company.

A unique initiative was started by the name *Sparsh,* wherein a dedicated group reached out to the families of the employees during difficult times like when employees were hospitalised for any illness, this group would work towards establishing rapport with the family of the employee, arranging medical aid including blood and ensuring best medical care. Apart from this, they also sent flowers, greeting cards to employees at their homes on special occasions such as Birthday, Marriage day, etc. If someone was transferred to Delhi, *Sparsh* would immediately contact the employee asking if he or she would need transport pick-up, home on rent or a Quarter, admission in school or any other support, being new to the city.

To provide recognition/appreciation and motivation for performing better, the company set up a separate Group called Cell for Awards and Rewards (CARE) for internal and external awards. This generated a healthy competition, as well as gave occasions to celebrate. The culture of fun and celebration was consciously built to enhance a sense of belongingness amongst the employees. Every achievement, whether by an individual or the company, was celebrated. Employees winning internal or external awards were felicitated and given recognition through gifts, publication of photographs in house journals and other in-company publications, etc.

We glamorised all external awards received by employees. A lot of data and information sharing about host of awards at state level, national level and in various fields of Management was created. We asked CARE to help the employees to put their best presentation or entry forward and win prestigious awards. I remember when Dilip Krishna of Singrauli won the prestigious Prime Minister's *Shram Ratna* award for the first time, we celebrated throughout the organisation. We even got TV channels to interview his wife about her wonderful contributions in enabling the attaining of the first *Shram Ratna* for NTPC family and screened it all over our Cable TVs. Dilip went from station to station proudly making presentation of his work and achievements in order to motivate everyone. It was in the present year, i.e. 2013, when I was directing a training programme at the great BIMTECH campus for batches of employees, that I suddenly saw seated at a dining table, Dilip and his wife after more than a decade and half! He hugged me with tears rolling down his eyes . . . uttering that I was his Krishna helping him to achieve! He meant this compliment to all those leaders of NTPC, irrespective of levels, who held the hands of all the Dilip Krishnas to rise and win!

QUALITY OF WORK LIFE

Quality of Work Life is becoming an increasingly popular concept in recent times. It basically talks about the methods in which an organisation can ensure the holistic well-being of an employee instead of just focusing on work-related aspects.

It is a fact that an individual's life can't be compartmentalised and any disturbance on the personal front will affect his/her professional life and vice-versa. Therefore, organisations have started to focus on the overall development and happiness of the employee and reducing his/her stress levels without jeopardising the economic health of the company.

Each organisation has its own way of achieving this, but NTPC focused on this, which became a winning strategy right from the beginning.

In NTPC, being an organisation that developed coal pit head power stations, it was not only a part of people strategy that needed the company to put a premium on excellent Talent to accept and enjoy life in such remote locations, rather it became a culture and habit to always provide for best Quality of work life to people in order to create a vibrant and comfortable work environment, balancing with a respectful and caring family life. Right from the beginning the cultural life, including quality clubs, entertainment programmes, particularly cultural programmes involving employees and the entire family at local and national or company level were always organised. Parents would not feel happy only with the quality of schools and education which was always provided by the best of institutions, they always associated themselves in all extra-curricular learning opportunities for the children in remote townships. Some of the very useful and attractive activities for School children in our towships were also coming through the following:

(i) Executive Clubs
(ii) Welfare Centres

(iii) Year-long sports, welfare and cultural programmes

(iv) Raising Day Function of 200+ children in direction of National level choreographers in Siri Fort of such Reputed Auditoriums

(v) Annual Theatre Workshops for children

(vi) TV News Reading Training to present News on Cable TVs

(vii) Creating Bal Bhawans equipped with the best of activities, while mostly engaging House wives

(viii) Bringing the best Children Films by tie ups with Film Divisions

(ix) Ladies Clubs creating opportunities of operating Kindergarten Schools

(x) Developing School Teachers out of a large number of educated Housewives by providing them with Training in order to address the issue of not only meeting the shortage of Teachers in remote Townships but also enabling development and employment opportunities for Women

(xi) Quizzing, Training and competition opportunities at Plant, Regional and National Levels by the country's best Quiz Masters, opening up learning opportunities for children

(xii) Training and enabling Quality Circles in Schools

(xiii) Arranging special coaching facilities for final school children

(xiv) Children Scholarships enabling better performance and opportunities

(xv) Rural Children Sports and Games opportunities

(xvi) Sports Promotion Board to guardian excellence

(xvii) Sports and Athletics Scholarships to state and national level identified children or adults from our and neighbouring schools

(xviii) Most innovative and dynamic Health, Environment and Safety Policies and systems, ensuring best of medical facilities

(xix) Best of working conditions

(xx) Best of modernised quality Canteens

(xxi) Music during breaks

(xxii) Regular Yoga at Work Places, as well as in all Training Programmes and Townships including Meditations trainings

(xxiii) Wedding gifts for employees on their Wedding day by a company representative at the venue and extending other facilities like Cars, Guest Houses

(xxiv) Celebration of Birthdays, Welcome/Farewell parties

(xxv) Option to take a holiday on marriage anniversary or birthdays in family

(xxvi) One of the first ones to introduce Paternity Leave for Male employees to support and care for Families

(xxvii) Special long leave to Female employees for caring for the young children at home,

(xxviii) *Akash* and other opportunities to recognise children performance at State and National Level in Art, Fine Arts/Music, Games, etc.

(xxix) Sensitive to spouse employees in postings

There were many more . . . We were always innovative, and were continuously learning from the best practices of other performing organisations in these areas to enable better quality of Work Life and also empowering our Stations to experiment and create or improve these continuously.

CONCLUSION

Due to continuous efforts, NTPC had been able to create an organisational culture where performance was paramount and all employees, besides being proud of it, were committed to meet all the challenges faced by the company. As part of the management, we would take forward one good step on recognition, reward or celebration, but people would take tens of such steps demonstrating great cheer, mood and passion of being NTPCian. The 'can do' attitude was all pervasive in the culture and the employees took a lot of pride in being part of NTPC as reflected in a large number of surveys.

10

Facilitating Corporate Citizenship

Praja sukhe sukham rajyaha prajanamcha hitehitam...

> – Only in the happiness and welfare of the people lies the happiness
> and welfare of a king (Interpretation of Kautilya's approach
> enshrined in Kautilya's *Arthashastra*)

THE CONCEPT OF Corporate Social Responsibility (CSR) in the present context means that the organisation must be aware of its responsibilities towards the communities and societies it operates in and fulfil those responsibilities. It implies that the focus of an organisation should not be limited to increasing shareholders' value but should be widened to take care of the needs of various other stakeholders of the company to create long term value and for sustainable development. These stakeholders include employees, project affected people, community, local government, customers, shareholders, etc.

While there is no denying the fact that business organisations exist primarily for economic profit, it is also true that a business organisation is also an organ of the society and a symbiotic relationship exists between an organisation and the society. Various constituents of the society contribute to an organisation's creation, survival and growth. Therefore, the business organisation must discharge its obligations towards the society and justify its continuance by fulfilling its responsibilities to the society.

CSR activities not only make good business sense but also contribute to the long-term survival and prosperity of companies. In this era of globalisation the concern about long-term health and sustainability of communities is on the rise. Consumers are increasingly aware of the impact that business activities have on individuals and communities. In turn, there is an increasing awareness in the corporate sector that good corporate citizenship is good business. Companies that have earned good reputation among consumers through good social and environmental performance are benefitted in many ways, some of which are: enhanced ability of the company to attract better talent, motivated employees, increased customer loyalty, less volatile stock values, reduced litigation and environmental costs. The involvement of corporates in social and environmental issues can have an immensely positive impact and contribute to the larger goals of sustainable development which is vital for the nation as well as the planet.

At Global level organisations such as United Nations, International Labour Organisation, OECD, etc., have also formulated various guidelines setting voluntary principles and standards of responsible corporate conduct in areas such as the environment, labour standards and human rights.

In India, the concept of CSR is age old: as brought out by the Doctrine of *Rin* (Debt), Gandhiji's Trusteeship concept, etc.

I recall my school days when most of the teachings to us were based on famous couplets on moral values and valuable *shlokas* from scriptures. One of them, which I still recall, is on the principle for *Moksha* based on discharge of debts (*Rin*). It talks of one of the principles in our acquiring *Moksha* that each human being has to discharge his/her total debt or the *Rin* to become eligible for acquiring it. These *Rins* that the teacher recited are *Dev Rin* (the debts to the God or metaphysical power as we may say), the *Pitri Rin* (the debts of our parents), the *Rishi Rin* (the debt of knowledge and learnings borrowed from our teachers) and the *Bhu Rin* (the debt of earth/ motherland of the total environment) which enables our overall growth. Hence for our growth and for our well being, each one of us, especially the *Raja* and the *Shreshtha* has a major responsibility to discharge the *Rin* which we are competent or able to do so. This may seem to be somewhat philosophical but I always had the conviction that this is an undeterred principle which requires us to give back to the society all our debts which has enabled our growth and well being.

I also recall Sanskrit word *Shreshtha* which means the best. It was the title given in the Hindu period to those who were given the responsibility of raising wealth through commerce and industry. They had certain enjoined responsibilities primarily for the society. The title Shreshtha later became *Seth* that was taken to mean people of high order or with wealth in the society or traders in today's meaning. As I recall these teachings, I realise that the basic purpose of furthering the vision or objective of a corporate should primarily be a responsibility to the society, else one is not a businessman or *Shreshtha* or *Seth* in the true sense. For acquiring the true position of *Shreshtha* the person given this role or responsibility had to be inclusive and had to be caring for the society.

Further, Emperor Ashoka, the ambitious and ruthless king, after having concurred Kalinga faces the biggest truth of his life. As he passed the roads and the alleys of Kalinga, seeing piles of dead bodies, weeping widows and orphan children, he is overcome with a social sense that perhaps he was the only one to be victorious, whereas, the millions who died, or were maimed or uprooted from their origins, were not included in his journey to the pseudo victory. He began hating his victories which had been exclusive for him, but not inclusive of the others in the society. The realisation descended on him and he transformed himself completely thereafter.

The company would have to determine a total transformed role and responsibility in the wake of the essential needs of the society and would have to appreciate that they had grown primarily because of society and its resources and hence their contribution and their impact have to be essentially inclusive.

I always believed that these principles have to be embedded in the very existence of companies and their behaviour towards the society, their wealth, health and the environment have to be commensurate.

CORPORATE SOCIAL RESPONSIBILITY – NTPC EXPERIENCE

NTPC has been a socially committed organisation since its inception and had adopted a systematic approach to CSR and had always played its role of a positive and sensitive visionary to address the issue of CSR. NTPC's mission statement included "To be a responsible corporate citizen with thrust on environment protection, rehabilitation and ash utilisation". NTPC had formulated specific policies to fulfil its responsibilities to all its stakeholders, namely, employees, community, environment and society in a very systematic and comprehensive manner. NTPC had also formally expressed its support to Global Compact – a UN initiative for encouraging and promoting good corporate practices and learning experiences in the areas of Human rights, labour and environment.

NTPC had comprehensive human resource policies covering recruitment, welfare, recreation, training and development, career growth, rewards and recognition, medical facilities, safety and social security measures for the employees. It also boasted of a strong institutional set up for employees' participation in Management at various levels. NTPC's Recruitment policy incorporated adequate provisions for preferences to SC/STs, OBCs, physically challenged persons, Ex-servicemen, etc., and the company was always very proud to perform exceedingly well on them.

The Safety policy had also been formulated and communicated to all employees. Guidelines had been formulated for reporting accidents, dangerous occurrences and for constituting committees to conduct inquiries and prevent their occurrences in the future. Personal protective equipments had been standardised and provided to all employees working in hazardous areas. All projects/stations had prepared Disaster Management plans to ensure the safety of people and protection of environment in case of any disaster. Regular Safety audits were conducted at all projects in association with external agencies in fulfillment of statutory obligations and maintain safe working environment. Being an HR person, it gave me tremendous advantage to display corporate people sensitivity in creating all policies pertaining to safety and their enforcement. If Quality Circles' usefulness prompted me to create the professional circle, it also led to use people involvement by creating Safety Circles. Though innovative and seemingly little at the time of inception, Safety Circles were powerful institutions instrumental in the development of other processes like Safety Stewards, Safety Audits, etc.

NTPC also contributed generously towards the various relief funds in times of calamities such as the cyclone in Orissa, earthquake in Gujarat, Kargil war, etc. In addition, NTPC also used to send teams of doctors and engineers to provide medical assistance and for undertaking restoration works on such occasions. NTPC was conferred the prestigious Platts Business Week and Global Energy Award, 2002, for community development programme of the year in recognition of its efforts made during the earthquake in Gujarat.

Subsequently, NTPC became one of the pioneers in creating a clear CSR policy of its own as early as in the year 2004, setting apart 0.5% of its annual profit every year for CSR budget. This was a very pragmatic move and I admired our leaders who supported this proposal in the Board. This drastically started changing the internal mindset in the organisation and also made the employees feel very proud. Later, I learnt that some features of the CSR policy were also supported and adopted by the Government of India.

RESETTLEMENT AND REHABILITATION EXPERIENCE

It is very true that infrastructure development projects displace people and give rise to severe social, economic and environmental changes, which if not addressed adequately, affect the socio-cultural fabric of the local community structure, weakening their social networks, affecting their cultural identity and traditional authority and the potential for mutual help. It has been well recognised and accepted that the old minimalist and charity or welfare oriented approach is no longer acceptable to people displaced by these projects. In fact, the resettlement and rehabilitation (R&R) process is increasingly seen as a development process in which consultation with, and participation of, all stakeholders is required for truly effective implementation. NTPC had to set up power projects in remote and underdeveloped parts of the country, displacing the local population from their land and homesteads, upsetting their settled agricultural life. The Organisation learnt how to do effective R&R the hard way, preserving the interest of the Company while at the same time trying to give a fair deal to the project affected persons (PAPs).

Resettlement and rehabilitation has not been the core competency of an industrial organisation like NTPC. But a corporate has to adopt the principles of addressing the R&R issues. In conformity with its core values, NTPC displayed rare tact and sensitivity in addressing the human and social issues related to R&R. Being a learning organisation, NTPC was successful in building the required capabilities and replicated the strategies of addressing the R&R issues of its projects in a region, in its new projects. There were a lot of opportunities for taking on challenges and undertaking experiments and innovations on the spot. We were empowered and were hell bent to reach a different level of excellence, delivering success in the area, in order to ensure the so much essential harmony all around to provide confidence, strength and support to the Project executives to execute projects. In fact, there was so much of learning and innovation from them, that too with so much of sincerity, involvement and passion, that solutions were incessantly flowing. We had to merely ignite their passion and extend support where ever needed. The team, then supported by Dinesh Agarwal, virtually turned out to be a teacher for me, such was my learning experience. I recall on my return to NTPC from IPCL, Vadodra in 1993, when I was not assigned a portfolio, I was asked by Pillai to look at R& R which had been given to be part of HR perhaps as per the suggestion of World Bank. That is where I met Dinesh Agarwal for the first time. I found him to be a man with profound knowledge, immense clarity and utmost dedication. We assumed lot of powers ourselves, started taking decisions in the wake of making a sincere organisation along the guidelines and principles set by the World Bank. Support from the Bank instantly started to be extended to us and we took this as a big opportunity for further development of the Organisational objectives. The interaction with the World Bank and its representatives like Michael Cernia, Tjarda Storm, David, Sam Thanganaj and others, helped us gain exposure and the experiences that we had were a great learning in building capabilities and a road map to success in the R&R area. We learnt to develop a flawless Rehabilitation Action Plan (RAP) that was easily acceptable to the affected population, NGOs involved and above all, the World Bank. Of course, we learnt things the hard way but the success became an enduring one. These experiences could be summarised into seven key learning points which need to be kept in view while addressing the R&R issues even in the most complex of situations.

BUILDING ADEQUATE DATA BASE

For successfully addressing the first pre-requisite of R&R issues, we undertook to build an unambiguous and complete data base of PAPs everywhere. Often the land records were not updated. There were cases of expired landowner and second generation legal heirs. The issue of encroachment of government land through generations was another issue. In many cases, the matter was taken to courts. There were issues of aliases and also repetition of same name / alias, resulting in duplicate entries. Thus, building an unambiguous list of PAPs in a transparent and consultative manner was essential though very challenging. It had also been observed that creating a family tree was extremely useful in avoiding duplicate names/ aliases, etc., and to bring transparency and clarity.

Minimise Land Requirement

Earlier, the land for setting up the projects was acquired liberally, keeping in view its easy availability and the lack of tools for adequately assessing the need and requirement for future expansion. Under the changed scenario, the land requirement was to be assessed carefully not only to minimise the problems of land acquisition but more so for minimising the environmental and social impact. We had been updating Rajendra Singh, the then CMD, with the working of the project and he readily agreed to support the process and issued guidelines in Principle to Engineering, Regions, Projects, etc. The key areas that were critically looked into, while planning the new projects, were the main plant area, ash disposal area and the township area, as given below:

- Review the layout of the project to make it as compact as possible. The open areas may be minimised to the extent feasible, keeping in view the environmental requirements.
- Reassess the land requirement for ash disposal area. The ash dykes could go vertically up to the extent feasible keeping in view the utilisation of ash in the future, in accordance with the governmental norms and regulations.
- The land requirement for township needed reassessment by considering compact layout and rising vertically by adopting the concept of multi-story buildings even if the initial cost was high. This required a change in attitude and freedom from the regulatory norms for public sector undertakings by considering not only techno-economic aspects but also the environmental, social and aesthetic aspects.

Avoid Acquisition of Homesteads

Shelter – a house – is a basic need of human beings. A house is not only used for living but for all social, cultural and religious needs. Thus, every nook and corner of a house is filled with memories, more so when the house is an ancestral house. The trauma of displacement faced by the homestead ousted could be better understood in the above perspective.

Thus, it was of paramount importance to avoid acquisition of house. But at the same time, adequate care was to be taken so that the habitation was not surrounded by the acquired land, or the approach to common resources like river, forest, etc., or approach road to other neighbouring villages and highways was not blocked.

In situations where acquisitions of houses were unavoidable, it was observed in small thermal projects like ours that cash in lieu of a plot in the resettlement colony along with the free transportation facility was a far more prudent and acceptable option, which enabled affected people to settle at the place of their own choice. This gave them the choice of living with their kith and kin instead of forcing them to learn to live in created resettlement colonies with 40'–60' plots in which they even lost the opportunity of free and flexible living, which they enjoyed in their village hamlets. By having an option to move out for settlement to a place of choice, it was found that they felt happier to get an opportunity of restoring their lost rural, social and cultural fabric.

Safeguard the Acquired Land

Taking the actual physical possession of land immediately after the land acquisition and safeguarding it from encroachment had been of paramount importance. This not only helped the company but also the affected population. If they were allowed to continue living in the acquired area even after acquisition and not shifted immediately, the affected people continued cultivation and got the usufruct, thus remaining dependent on the acquired land, and alternatives to cultivation were not explored by them in right time and compensation money was also exhausted over a period of time. In case of houses, additional construction was done to accommodate growing families. Since the land had already been acquired, no developmental activities were taken up by the governmental agencies, thus depriving these people of the basic amenities. At the time of vacation, on a subsequent date, may be even after lapse of few years when the land was actually required for the project work, these people felt embittered at being displaced without any concomitant R&R benefits at that time. There were also issues of outsiders or the other affected people encroaching into the land vacated by a part of affected people who availed of the R&R benefits. Hence, there were always chances of avoidable strife commencing which could assume serious proportions, with the likelihood of new dimensions getting added. Thus, it was both in the interest of the affected population and the company that the people were rehabilitated and resettled as required and settled immediately and actual physical possession of acquired land taken as soon as the formal acquisition process was complete. This was a good learning and we reoriented our practices accordingly, instead of postponing the problem.

DO REGULAR CONSULTATION AND MAINTAIN TRANSPARENCY

Consultation and transparency are the backbone of any democratic process and good governance. In the situation of displacement, when the PAPs are going through trauma and uncertainty, even prone to exploitation by certain outsiders at times, consultations and transparency had been the most viable process of winning the trust and confidence of affected people. The lack of consultation and transparency also provide enough space for the most precariously spreading misinformation and mistrust, vitiating the environment.

We further observed that while the informal consultation is effective and preferred to a more structured and formal one, the dynamics of the groups becomes quite different, more so where the outsiders take the role of self-proclaimed-leaders and well wishers. In such situations establishing a formal mechanism of consultation and transparency becomes imperative. There was a need to ensure that the consultations are objective and realistic with no space for false or tall promises, which could only result into the creation of higher expectations, uncertainty and imminent problems and strife in the later stages of rehabilitation.

For consultation, a Village Development Advisory Committee (VDAC), comprising of the representation of State Government and local bodies, head of village Panchayat, representative of the PAPs and the company, was constituted. All R&R issues including the process of planning and implementation of action plans were discussed and the committee was informed of the progress made. The records of each meeting were prepared and circulated to all members. This practice initiated by NTPC was appreciated by the World Bank and the Government of India, and both extended it as a good practice for others to emulate.

For transparency, Public Information Centres (PIC) were established in the area where the PAPs were residing. All relevant data, land records, socio-economic survey reports and rehabilitation action plan were available for the information of public. Registers were kept to record the queries and grievances of the PAPs as well as the action taken by the R&R staff of the company to resolve the issues. This resulted in the creation of improved and cordial relationships and created a conducive environment. The PAPs were able to realise the limitations of the organisation and, on the other hand, the project authorities were able to appreciate the genuine concerns of PAPs. These measures resulted in mutual trust and amicable resolutions.

INVOLVE PROFESSIONALS

It was accepted that the R&R issues needed the competency in understanding the socio-cultural aspects and the individual and group dynamics of affected people including the psychological and behavioural aspects. Therefore, we considered the deployment of professionally qualified sociologists. This experiment created a good impact on the PAPs. They were seen as independent players for understanding the needs and requirements of the affected people and bridging the critical communication and relationship gaps between NTPC and affected people. They sensitised the NTPC Management and also provided vital inputs during the process of planning and implementation of the R&R activities. Living in the villages mostly, the appointed sociologists also earned the faith and trust of the local people. Based on these experiences, the sociologists were deployed in new projects right from the initiation.

The professional organisations/NGOs were also deployed for providing technical and administrative support to the affected population in their endeavour of establishing self employment schemes. This reduced the dependency syndrome to a great extent. It was observed that the involvement of devoted and experienced professionals provided greater impetus in creating understanding with the affected people and in implementation of the agreed R&R activities.

'LAND FOR LAND'– MOST FEASIBLE REHABILITATION OPTION

Traditionally, the profession of cultivating one's own land is considered to be of prime importance, placed above the professions of being rulers and administrators or working for others. Land is not only an economic capital but also a social capital as it establishes the social status of a rural person. Initially we went through tough experiences of making various Income

Generating Schemes (IGS) either brought in by our sponsored NGOs or established Institutions or taken out from those prevalent amongst the villagers. Extensive training in skills of work, entrepreneurship, marketing, etc., were provided and initially a lot of support and hand holding continued. But with an exception of a few, the majority of the affected could only sustain this for a substantial period of time. On the other hand, only few jobs were available in the Company, that too not in unskilled category, as part of rehabilitation. Hence, it was felt that giving the affected jobs as an alternate occupation should not be kept as an option for rehabilitation at all, as it would only create insatiable expectation among the PAPs, who would begin refusing to accept any alternate means of rehabilitation.

Thus, land was found to be the most preferred and viable option. Initially, there were several impediments in implementing this option. We wanted to make it participative and wanted, therefore, to make a Land Purchase Committee (LPC). Getting the nomination for members from among the affected people for the land purchase committee was difficult. People did not have trust in the committee members. The big land owners, whose land was proposed to be acquired, demanded to be treated like other PAPs and expected R&R benefits. The government land which would have been free of all encumbrances was not available. The affected population was also demanding large quantum of land uniformly, irrespective of the quantum of land acquired. They also demanded it as land in lieu of job in the company and were not ready to return the compensation already received. Hence, providing land for land on 'willing buyer–willing seller' basis was considered by us as the only workable option and as a responsibility of the company. The affected population and the mediating NGOs unfortunately remained aloof blaming the failure of implementing 'land for land' on the company.

For resolving the issue, an alternative approach was conceived, wherein the option of 'land for land' was to be operationalised directly between the willing buyer (PAP) and willing seller. Negotiations were held with the affected population through a third party for fixing the market rate at which good quality land would be made available. This amount was further enhanced by grant of exgratia. However, the compensation paid earlier was adjusted as decided earlier. The balance amount was deposited in a joint bank account in the name of the PAP and NTPC and the money was subsequently released only for purchase of land, so that it was not squandered away. People were free to identify land in the neighbouring villages/district/state and bring a letter of intent of sale. The actual land transaction fee payable to the government was also paid by the company as per the entitlement. Additionally, land development charges were paid, which acted as inducement. Most of the people bought the land successfully with the help of kith and kin. Thus, 'land for land' (on willing-buyer and willing-seller basis) became the most successful and viable rehabilitation option happily accepted by PAPs, the Government and NGOs. This strategy was replicated in other Greenfield projects and was found to be highly successful.

CSR or R&R however, cannot always be dealt with on the same model or pattern of relief in all cases. The personnel involved in HR, CSR or R&R have to adapt themselves to situations. However, the basic philosophy and the mind set by which the issues are dealt with are much more important. HR's success, with people first motto, shall always learn substantially from the success stories of dealing with CSR and R&R related challenges, thus generating the much desired harmony which in turn becomes the solid foundation for developing peace and property of internal people recourses.

All our learnings led us to instantly keep changing and adapting our policies and rules. Later, our several Rehabilitation Action Plans were much different than the initial ones. NTPC came out with a detailed R&R policy in 1993, which was revised in due course of time. The policy also became a fair guiding factor to the development of the National R&R policy in NPRR 2003, which was published in 2004, and the same was again revised further.

11

Creating HR Leaders Amongst All Functions

Companies may do all right things for keeping employees happy through ESOPs, welfare facilities for family members, paid vacation and other incentives but if the relationship of the employee with the immediate superior is not good, the employee will not be satisfied or stay with the company.

– Marcus Buckingham and Curt Coffman
in *First, Break All the Rules*[9]

AS EVIDENT FROM the above findings by the Gallup consultants, it is not only HR that can attract and retain best employees, it has to be engrained into the culture of the organisation. Hence, HR needs to develop HR competency in not only its own team but among all Line Managers, leaders and the CEOs.

In NTPC we were able to realise the power of this wisdom long time back and started with a number of initiatives to sensitise line managers to people issues and equip them with skills to look into various aspects of HR like training, reward, motivation, counselling, communication with people, etc.

Thus, with a view to involve line managers in HR initiatives and for quicker resolution of issues, certain systems such as *HR Circle* were created at projects/stations which comprised HR Ambassadors, Mentors, etc., enumerated as under:

HR AMBASSADORS

In each Project an executive from line in each department was nominated as HR Ambassador to act as interface between HR department and the employees of the concerned department. The executive would act as a useful link of communication between employees and the organisation. These HR Ambassadors acted as a focal point for HR initiatives such as NOCET, Professional Circle, TQM activities, *Horizon* and primarily communication and feedback, etc. At one time, I recall, there were more than 350 HR Ambassadors in various units of NTPC. They were excited to innovate their roles as well and continuously built up this as an institution of support and relationship.

MENTORS

A Mentoring system had been formalised in NTPC in which each new Executive Trainee was attached with a Mentor who helped in the socialisation process by sharing company information, helping to assimilate into the company culture, clarifying doubts and also sharing company's expectations. The Mentors were trained through experts before being attached with the Mentee. At one time there were more than 500 Mentors who were involved in the system and enjoyed their role and benefited through this scheme. It was proposed to train/prepare more and more Mentors and attach them with employees being placed in E1 grade as Mentees also, with innovative roles enabling this transition.

EMPLOYEE INVOLVEMENT FACILITATORS

Various facilitators for initiatives such as 5S, Quality Circle and Suggestion schemes, had been identified from various departments for coordinating these activities in their departments. They were trained, inducted, periodically reviewed and also evaluated in some initiatives. This added to the HR brigade and further inculcated the sense of ownership in people development.

TRAINING COORDINATORS

Training Coordinators had been identified for each department for communicating and coordinating training activities in respective departments including training need analysis, training plans and ensuring/follow up training inputs to people of their department. The coordinators from line were sensitised through training and alignments for delivering this new role in people development, and they immensely enjoyed contributing towards it.

HR NODAL OFFICERS

In all the units executives of HR department had been identified as nodal officers for various departments of the Unit and they acted as a medium for disseminating HR information as well as addressing HR related issues of individuals of that particular department. These HR Nodal Officers used to make regular visits to the department assigned to them to find out the HR issues of people of that department and tried to solve them promptly. The idea was also to step up a good rappport and communication with the regulatory. It was amazing to see them communicating and dealing with the issues/challenges with so much of ownership and passion.

PROJECT NODAL OFFICERS

As per this system, the executives of Corporate HR were nominated as Nodal officers for each project who looked after the HR matters of that particular project and facilitated speedy communication and resolution of issues. They were expected to visit the assigned stations periodically to interact and get firsthand information and feedback regarding various people related issues, connect with corporate HR and resolve them. They became a significant link and an identified officiating person between the Unit HR and the corporate HR to sensitise and bring faster resolution and responses.

INTERVENTIONS FOR HRISING THE ORGANISATION

With simple experiences I was confirmed that success of an Organisation needed an intensely sensitive HR, and with them a number of equally sensitive Line Managers.

I tried introducing a number of programmes and attempted sensitising and involving line guys in HR roles at different levels.

HR for Line Managers' Programme

A special programme was designed with an objective to align line managers with HR functions and empowering them to take care of people issues of employees working with them. The template of the programme was designed after seeking inputs from department heads and other line managers. The programme provided a good overview of the HR initiatives of the company and created a good HR bent in the minds of the line at different levels. A large number of line managers were covered through the Regional HR getting resource support from institutions of repute like MDI, IIML, IIM Kozhikode, IIMK, etc. This made a lot of positive impact, creating substantial alignment of line with HR and developing a genuine symbiotic relationship.

Team Building Programmes

A series of structured interventions were introduced across the company with the help of external agencies to foster team spirit not only amongst the members of department/group but also between various departments and units. The process involved a validation study and analysis of impediments to build high performing teams, formulation of action plan to overcome barriers and facilitations with review and feedback, primarily of Site Management Committees, etc. This significantly helped in bringing synergy amongst individuals and the departments, having a positive impact on not only productivity but the overall HR climate of the company.

Value Actualisation Training

A series of workshops were conducted across various units to promote the awareness as well as implementation of core values of the company. The list of the company's core values included elements like mutual respect and trust, organisational pride and customer focus which significantly helped in improving the people orientation in the company. A series of a 3 day programme, **'Adventures in Attitude'**, created a lot of positive excitement in building a sensitive ground to revive the values, behaviours and a strong culture based on trust and respect. We covered perhaps more than 5000 employees, who also shared and made an impact on the environment by adapting improved behaviours.

COMMUNICATING HR PLANS AND PERSPECTIVES

We had given a structure to all Units' weekly meetings or the Quarterly Regional Management Meetings to give and devote the initial one hour for an update on HR plans and delivery status invariably, so that people at their critical levels start appreciating and associating in HR deliverables on a continuous basis. We initially suggested a standardised structure of presentation and discussions. Similar practices were started in the Management committee meetings at the Corporate. I recall scheduling time slots in the meetings of the Board of Directors around every six months to apprise the Board on HR plans, new initiatives and action status to encourage their involvement, positive support and valuable inputs. During my tenure the Board had stalwarts like Deepak Parikh, Dr. Pradeep Khandwala, Dr. Pachauri and some very empowering Government Directors as well.

SUBORDINATE DEVELOPMENT

We knew that a powerful learning change was required in the Organisation that would come by creating commitment and ownership in the minds of everyone, making them responsible for developing teams or subordinates.

We brought in focus change in the Performance Management System with assigning specific weightage for the KRA by the name of Subordinate Development at different levels. We started communicating and educating our people as to what was meant by subordinate development and what initiative options they have to choose from, in order to develop everyone in the team. We even went to the Plants to substantially renew and review the seriousness of the subordinate development and raise its effectiveness.

CONCLUSION

With a large number of such systems and interventions, a right ambience had been created in the company where all executives felt that managing people in their team/department was primarily their responsibility and not that just of HR. The company was also increasingly taking measures to empower line people with managing people processes. All these initiatives bridged the communication gap and brought in silently, substantial involvement in HR from all levels, generating a deep sense of ownership and drawing their explicit and tacit support whenever needed.

12

Managing Change:
The Only Constant

CHANGE HAS ALWAYS been the hard fact of corporate life but the existing business environment has made it more frequent and discontinuous. Almost all the companies tend to be affected by changes due to various factors, internal or external to their environment, including forces like mergers and acquisitions, introduction of new technology, company's decision to enter into new business or new markets, corporate restructuring, etc. This has created a very critical challenge, as well as an opportunity for HR professionals to become change agents and manage change successfully every time.

In 1995 I met a young professor, Dr. Sumantra Ghoshal on a PSU invite and heard him speak to a large number of public sector leaders. He was a wonderful story teller and narrated astonishing stories of corporates, mostly Indians, who had delivered wonders to change and transform themselves to achieve even the impossible. This story teller used to come out with tales of breath taking ambition and extraordinary speed. He talked of a 'corporate disease of satisfactory underperformance' and elaborated in his book, *Managing Radical Change*,[10] written alongwith Gita Piramal and Christopher Bartlett. This book thereafter became like a Bible for me on managing change in corporates. He talked of 'the idea of Radical Performance', establishing that companies can come out of the state of satisfactory underperformance and deliver radical performance, despite all challenges, in order to make managers believe – really believe – that radical performance improvement is possible. It is not only possible for small and medium-sized firms, but it is also possible for large, established companies.

And, it is certainly possible to achieve such non-incremental improvements within a reasonably short period of time, though not within a quarter or a year but it definitely would not take ten years either to achieve the target performance.

He mentions that there exists a religion in management which is called 'incrementalism' and which implies that things happen at a slow pace in companies, particularly big ones with large number of employees. Like the analogy of 'Supertankers' which move slowly in the long turns, the big companies have to have patience to see change and the employees cannot be pushed too much to be quick.

He adds that most of the Indian managers believe in this religion and practice it as they have found it true most of the times in an environment of 'bureaucratic dominance', 'crippling regulations' and poor infrastructures. They do not believe in 'radical change' as they find these words 'too unIndian' and 'too childish' and find it difficult to change their faith from 'incrementalism' to 'radical change'. Yet, he says, there were some leaders like Dhirubhai Ambani who never believed in this religion.

According to him, in this deregulated market economy, a company that fails to keep pace with the market will die soon, which is already happening to some of India's great old companies, and at the same time, in this kind of market economy, it is also possible for a management, which is focused and determined, to transform the company quickly and more effectively than what was possible in the past.

Dr. Sumantra Ghoshal goes on to say that radical performance is possible under all circumstances even in unattractive industries, even when the industry is shrinking, even when the competitor is much bigger and stronger, or even when a company is already very successful. He even emphasises that charismatic leadership is not a prerequisite for radical performance improvement, and discussed by what all it may take to achieve radical performance improvement. He also mentioned that there was no universal formula that could be applicable to all companies universally, and gave examples of how some companies had achieved exceptional corporate performance. One of his major messages was that to sustain superior corporate performance one needs to develop the ability to manage the strain between two symbiotic forces, i.e. the need for ongoing improvement in operational performance and productivity by bringing about constant rationalisation in the prevailing activities, and the requirement for growth and expansion by constantly revitalising the strategies, organisation and the people. I realised that this had to be a very successful and certain strategy for transforming larger multi-unit and multi-business companies, particularly in the Indian Public Sector.

There is nothing new about either of these two needs. The problem is that most managers see the processes of rationalisation and revitalisation as mutually exclusive. Rationalisation is often unpleasant – 'sour'. Few managers enjoy closing plants, selling businesses and sacking people. Revitalisation, on the other hand, is 'sweet'. Most managers love growth; they love dreaming up a vision and driving their organisations to match their dreams. And, most go for either one or the other, hoping to either cut or grow into the high-performance league.

But, he adds that, those companies, find that these two processes are symbiotic, which achieve radical performance improvement. The resources like people and money required for growth are provided by the 'rationalisation process' and the hope and vigour required for enduring the challenges of improving productivity are provided by the revitalisation process. He asserts that growth and productivity improvement go hand in hand. Growth without productivity improvement would be like building collapsible castles on sand and productivity improvement without growth would be draining the organisation of its energy and creativity. So, according to him, a 'sustained superior performance' can be achieved by taking both the things together. We strategised our transformation agenda in NTPC on this valuable learning.

Dr. Ghoshal goes on further to quote M.R.R. Nair (also of SAIL and Ispat Group repute and one of my effective Mentors), that successful transformation required a fundamental change in the behaviour of people, that no organisation can achieve a radical improvement in its performance without revitalising its people with a process that changes the mindset of the people. But if achieving this is difficult, Dr. Sumantra Ghoshal goes on to say that revitalising people is not so much about changing their fundamental attitudes. The challenge of changing behaviour at work is much more about changing the context that managers create around their people. In the NTPC we addressed both these issues as major scaffolding provided by HR to support organisational transformation. The responsibility for creating the behavioural context was entrusted to the senior managers, and of course, the Team HR. Dr. Sumantra Ghoshal suggests that this behavioural context is 'The smell of the place' that managers create, and goes on to describe the important characteristics like constraint, control, compliance and contract in the old and traditional companies to stretch, support, trust and establish self-discipline in renewed and transformational companies.

I wanted to create this context change, this new smell of the place in NTPC, a huge organisation which had always performed but which, I honestly feared, was slipping in to the syndrome of satisfactory underperformance, if not a confirmed disease. When we met people from all levels, when we saw strife springing day and night, when we saw the output of Bodh I, we saw the NTPC emerging into a typical traditional company, showing characteristics like constraint, control, contract and compliance which needed to change the 'smell of the place' developing characteristics like stretch, support, trust and discipline so that they eventually create a smell of the learning, collaboration, commitment, initiative, persistence, confidence, ownership and so on in this mega Organisation, spread all over the place and pushing in to the total value chain of power business. And this was the time when NTPC sensed the term competition, if not so much in volume, but much more in setting and achieving performance benchmarks. The government invited the so called 'Fast Track' companies, all big and daunting names... Enron, Cogentrics, AES, National Power; and to top it all, the energy sector, which was so conveniently safe, particularly for PSU's like NTPC, was thrown open for a host of Independent Power Producers (IPPs) ... and there was a clamour for attaining it when the gates were opened. All types of companies jumped into the race for exploring business opportunities. We at NTPC did not accept the changing scenario easily, but we were getting aware of the change that was slowly seeping into the industry and the market and we needed to do something fast and immediate to regain, recapture and revitalise our market share.

MANAGING CHANGE AT NTPC

The later part of the 1990s and the early part of the new century saw many states undertaking reforms including unbundling, corporatisation, introduction of Electricity Bill 2001 and the entry of private players in the power sector. All these developments led the Company to choose, to change, to enhance its competitiveness and leverage the opportunity in the market. We decided to engage the renowned management consultant, M/s AT Kearney in January, 2002, to advise the management in the Organisation Transformation Exercise. The Study was named Project Disha, which would give the company a direction to excel in the new environment.

The study was undertaken to provide recommendations in the area of Business Strategy, Information Technology, HR systems, etc. The study involved extensive participation of all stakeholders and a regular communication.

The recommendations of the Consultants were also incorporated in formulation of *VISION 2017*, the 15 year Corporate Plan of the Company till year 2017. As part of Project *Disha I* implementations, a number of initiatives were under the process of implementation including the revised Performance management system and the integrated Enterprise Resource Package (ERP). Communication resource persons from various units were identified and trained to communicate to the people the intended changes and prepare the mindset of people. The implementations of *Disha I* were affected by dedicated groups for each initiative led by senior executive of the Company.

We went on moving on the path of fast growth and diversification of business. The Company had already entered into hydel generation, coal mining, electricity trading and electricity distribution, and planned to enter the field of nuclear generation and transmission, spanning the entire power value chain. NTPC aimed to become a fully integrated power utility, powering India's growth to lead the economy of the nation.

In this corporate plan, we took the responsibility of becoming the *Best in Class, becoming a Sector Architect, a Catalyst of India's Growth and also an Overseas Ambassador!* And thus we move forward.

DEVELOPING CHANGE CAPABILITY AT NTPC BY MAKING IT A LEARNING ORGANISATION

One of the most important roles for HR today is building a learning organisation, so that the organisation is ready for change always. A learning Organisation is one which is able to continually upgrade its capabilities and adjust readily to the changes in the business environment. It also had a built-in mechanism to continually adjust its own structure and processes according to the changing environment and of course the increasing and dynamic employees' requirements. In a learning organisation, there is nothing constant except possibly its core values. Indeed, the essence of a learning organisation is the realisation, capability and readiness to adapt to change at any time.

The NTPC attempted to be a learning organisation with a strong heritage of institutionalised learning mechanism, which extends to fit the mission, values and culture of the organisation. The Power Management Institute played a pivotal role in achieving its mission by acting as a catalyst to champion the individual and organisational learning activities. PMI had been responsible for the training and development interventions of the entire executive cadre of the corporation and the non-executive fraternity of the Corporate Centre, apart from providing constant support and assistance to all the employee development centres at the projects. Apart from this ambitious mandate, PMI has been able to attract impressive participation from other organisations in the power and allied sectors. It partnered HR particularly to research, benchmark and fathom the depth of the changing environment that was incessantly impacting the Organisation and the smell of the places.

HR had undertaken several research and development initiatives in line with the organisational and sectoral needs and many training programmes conducted at PMI were driven by the research findings of the projects. The high quality programmes of the institute helped develop ethical, knowledgeable and technologically competent business professionals. With an impressive infrastructure, the Institute was capable of conducting large number of programmes concurrently. Based on research and the findings, we were able to forecast the future needs and wanted to renew and create a larger campus that would be better equipped to manage the personnel. We were fortunate to have an abundant and learned faculty. The recommendations of Dr. Ishwar Dayal had also been well received and we started working on them (The recommendation of Ishwar Dayal on PMI is in Annexure E). The recommendations were primarily adopted to guide and hold our hand, with the intention of taking PMI, the primary and perhaps the most important learning and development Centre, to greater heights and to acquire a new strength and capability of its own. This would enable PMI to continuously envision the future and keep creating newer strength and capability in NTPC, which in turn was destined to play a much greater role not only as a catalyst of growth in the power sector but also as an enabler of building a new winning economy in India and becoming an ambassador of the country for making it a global giant.

SOME SPECIAL INITIATIVES

KNOWLEDGE MANAGEMENT

We knew that NTPC was creating tremendous amount of very rich and valuable knowledge day in and day out. This was in functional areas where NTPC kept learning ardently especially in the engineering, project management and operation, maintenance and substantial applied research areas. We needed a robust system, preferably IT based, for storing and retrieving knowledge, when needed.

We sent teams of Engineers and Executives to some of the leading companies to see their Knowledge Management (KM) systems and centres, and inspire and enable a KM Centre in NTPC as well. Our executives visited GE's Bangalore Centre frequently and brought the learnings and their rich model to be established in NTPC.

In the NTPC a number of initiatives for creating and disseminating knowledge had been initiated and a systematic approach to KM was also in the process of being instituted. Schemes such as Professional circles, NOCET, Quality Circles, M. Tech in Power Engineering, B.S. in Power Engineering, Think Tank, Benchmarking, etc., had been formulated to support learning and knowledge creation and transfer. A comprehensive training policy had been formulated to impart training of a minimum of 7 days per employee annually to enhance their knowledge on a continuous basis. In order to foster a culture of learning extensive recognition and incentives, schemes for learning, including acquiring higher qualifications had also been formulated.

The Best Practices Manuals had been prepared at the Corporate level as well as various Projects/Stations, documenting the best practices in various areas. At different Projects/stations, a Best Practices Centre had also been set up. PMI also came up with compilations of case studies which were based upon the experiences of employees of the company in various areas of their functioning. Job rotations were undertaken systematically to provide

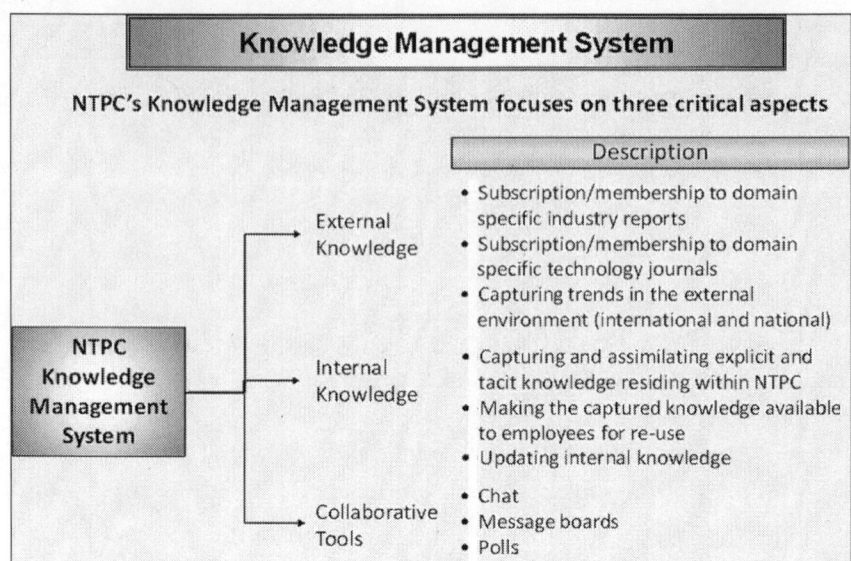

FIGURE 1: Knowledge Management System

opportunities to acquire experience and knowledge in various functional areas. Meets of various functional group heads such as O&M, Finance, HR, Contracts/Materials, FQA, Legal, IT, etc., were frequently organised to share practices and experiences. The Annual O&M Conference had risen to international levels where representatives from different international organisations participated to exchange their experiences.

The Organisation Transformation Study (*Disha*) team had also forwarded a number of recommendations in this direction to implement integrated Knowledge Management system in our organisation. The recommendations were made with a view to effectively manage our knowledge asset and actualise the HR Vision of making NTPC a Learning Organisation. The programme was implemented in the organisation and a few areas were taken up as knowledge domains. The structure for an e-based integrated Knowledge Management system was being put in place.

NTPC OPEN COMPETITION FOR EXECUTIVE TALENT (NOCET)

NOCET, started in the year 2000, was yet another small catalyst to charge the Organisation. It was introduced to provide opportunities to our

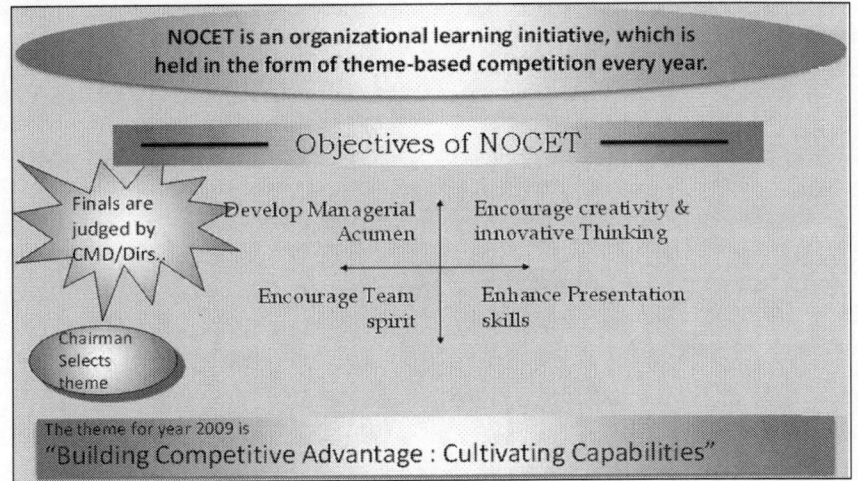

NOCET is an organizational learning initiative, which is held in the form of theme-based competition every year.

Objectives of NOCET

Finals are judged by CMD/Dirs.

Develop Managerial Acumen

Encourage creativity & innovative Thinking

Encourage Team spirit

Enhance Presentation skills

Chairman Selects theme

The theme for year 2009 is
"Building Competitive Advantage : Cultivating Capabilities"

FIGURE 2: NTPC Open Competition for Executive Talent (NOCET)

executives (up to E6 level) to team up and deliberate on contemporary topics of organisational interest, carry out primary research and present the recommendations to the top management. One could see the knowledge, research and, above all, the concern and excitement created among the employees. Nearly 100 teams of young girls and boys, worked together on contemporary and futuristic challenges set before the organisation and shared their knowledge with NTPC as a single entity, including the top brass of its leaders. This not only upgraded the presentation skill / analytical thinking / team spirit of the executives but also acted as an effective tool for upward communication, providing input to the top management on critical issues of the Company. It was conducted every year in which deliberations were made by the executives working as teams on a particular theme of organisational interest.

CHANAKYA BASED "BUSINESS MINDS"

As part of company's initiative to provide platforms for developing executives by providing them learning opportunities and also giving them exposure of business decision making, was done by executives from other companies. Initially a 2 day in-house competition was organised for teams of executives at PMI, Noida. This initiative resulted in teams reaching the finals of the competition out of 150 teams that participated in the all India level competition.

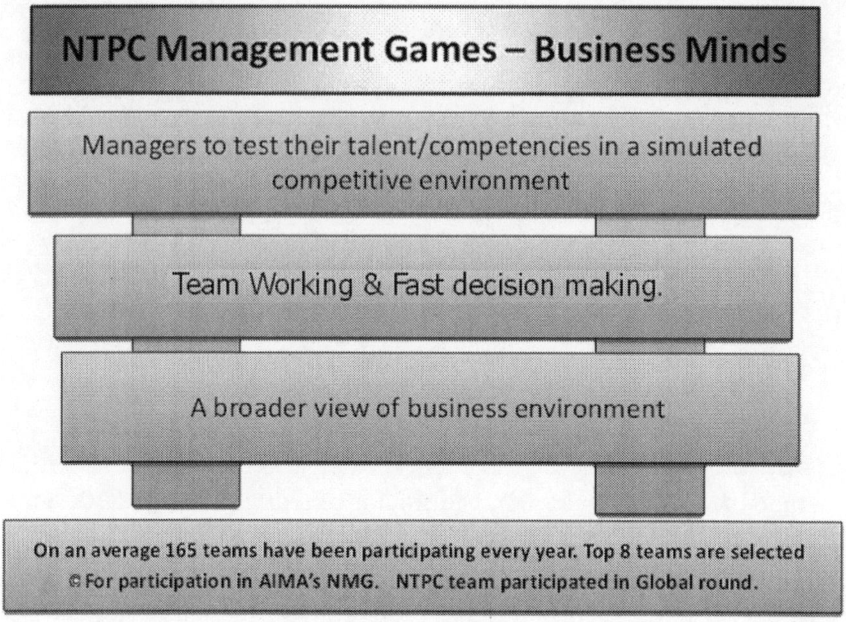

NTPC Management Games – Business Minds

Managers to test their talent/competencies in a simulated competitive environment

Team Working & Fast decision making.

A broader view of business environment

On an average 165 teams have been participating every year. Top 8 teams are selected © For participation in AIMA's NMG. NTPC team participated in Global round.

FIGURE 3: Business Minds

Keeping in view the response and enthusiasm of the employees, a policy was framed to conduct the competition across the company under a special intervention named 'Business Minds' that was introduced in 2013.

PROFESSIONAL CIRCLES

Professional Circle (PC), the initiative introduced all over the NTPC during 1997–1998, provided a forum for executives of a particular discipline to network and share their learnings and experiences on the latest developments in the profession, issues of importance to the company, etc. This also provided an excellent opportunity for the employees to communicate their views/ideas on important issues. At one time, about 300 Professional Circles were active in various units of the NTPC encompassing all departments.

Every year competitions were organised at project level in which two PC teams were selected to represent their respective projects at Regional level convention. Finally, an Annual convention of Professional Circles was organised in which presentations are made by participating PC teams in front of senior executives including CMD, Directors and eminent academicians/consultants. The presentations, as well as write up of all the participating teams are distributed in form of CD as well as a compendium and also put on the intranet.

SYSTEM'S REVIEW GROUP

A dedicated group, namely System's Review Group, was created to continually look at systems and processes in various functional areas including contracts, engineering, finance, HR, etc.

While all these were initiated at different levels, they also catalysed a momentum all over the organisation. Everyone was beginning to change, without putting in much effort even at the individual level. Change was taking place silently – from the lowest level to the highest. Making it happen was every individual's responsibility, who in his own way, was changing the smell of the place, changing and lowering the level of ownership, changing the concept of knowledge and learning, and helping to transform NTPC, that had been known for its 'can do' attitude to convert any kind of impossible task into a reality.

STRATEGIC VOLUNTARY RETIREMENT SCHEME (VRS)

While we were laying emphasis on creating a culture of performance a number of executives were also identified to be consistent non-performers among the relative ranking in the Organisation's performance matrix. They were repeatedly rated below 3 on a 5 point assessment scale. We addressed their issues individually, as well as in groups and found they had challenges in growing, and were repeatedly falling short in the career development system. This resulted in lot of cynicism amongst them, eventually having a very negative impact on the environment. We started focusing to develop a plan and special training programmes for them with an intensity and at the same time also addressed to turn around their attitude which was seemingly turning negative. We created 'Kshitiz' as a learning intervention to drive this mission. While these measures were being taken, many of such identified people suggested that they be given a Voluntary Retirement Scheme (VRS), the so called 'Golden Handshake', so that they may look upon alternative pastures of opportunities and growth. On examining this suggestion, we found that announcing a generic VRS would further give a very negative message among the non-performing executives and also put a premium on the exit of better performing executives, to the keenly watching competitors, who were ready to jump on NTPC talent. When we examined the VRS, the Law stated that if we announce it, this would have to be executed for everyone as the scheme was allowed only in case of surplus management which was not applicable in our case. In fact, we required more talent as we were also growing at the same time, we did not want to risk putting premium on exit and at the same time wanted to support and relieve the so called non-performers, who wanted the 'Golden Handshake'. The Government and Tax Authorities had indicated that there would be no tax relief on payment of such a large sum of money under the 'Golden Handshake' or VRS Scheme, if announced by NTPC, not fulfilling conditions of surplus management and for a very limited and a few hundreds of people only. We approached the CBDT and related Government officials, presented the case and position of NTPC as a performing PSU. Ultimately and amazingly, a special decision for NTPC was taken by extending tax relief to the employees even if VRS was allowed only to the identified employees who were not getting growth opportunities in the organisation, in view of their performance. This was a major breakthrough and when the scheme was announced, a large number of executives, who were low on the PP Matrix and were not getting career development opportunities, left NTPC for better opportunities with a Golden Handshake. This was an excellent move for dealing with such cases with the so called 'iron hand with a soft glove'! The VRS became an amazing success and big facilitator to our efforts of transformation in managing competence and commitment of employees referred to by Dave Ulrich, whose philosophies and practices gave us ideas for developing the strong and successful HR model that we had envisioned.

Strategic Partnership through HR Score Card

With a view to align and integrate HR strategy with the business strategy (*VISION–2017*) and position HR as a strong strategic business partner, the HR Score Card based on the principles of Balance Scorecard was designed and developed during 2003–2004 and is being implemented in NTPC HR function as a strategic tool. The process was helped by leading HR consultant M/s HEWITT. During the implementation of this process, the top management views, expectations of key customers and line managers were mapped and taking into account all the diverse perspectives, the HR strategy was realigned and fine-tuned, keeping the long-term business imperatives and their impact on the Human Resource of the company. After extensive deliberations with the involvement of HR leaders from the Corporate function, Regional and Unit functions, the Corporate HR Scorecard, Regional HR Scorecard and the Unit HR Scorecard were designed, developed and finalised in January 2004. The HR Score Card that had been designed cascaded to the regions and units since April 2004. Further, the key measures were also implemented in the Key Performance Areas under **PACE** for all the HR functionaries.

PART IV

PEOPLE FUNCTION:
THE ROAD AHEAD

13

People Function: The Road Ahead

HR FUNCTION HAS a strong reputation for getting a seat at the table given the importance of people factor and intangibles in the success of a business. But it also mandates that HR truly demonstrates business leader behaviour and moves beyond the functional domain. The road ahead for HR function would simply imply the utilities to move from a Functions approach to that of an Organisation approach. HR needs to have a helicopter vision, a bird's eye-view-of the business and the environment within which it operates in order to get a larger perspective while planning and casting HR initiatives. Business requirements have to be broken into people imperatives which form the nucleus of all businesses.

To achieve its objectives, HR has to occasionaly deviate from its traditional transactional roles and adopt integrated transformational roles, such as that of a system designer, talent manager, internal consultant to line managers, change agents, etc. HR has to constantly discharge tactical responsibilities, and at the same time passionately engage in strategic roles in the area for developing great people, a wonderful environment and exciting culture of performance and celebrations with the aim of creating a sustainable winning organisation.

Our Team HR learnt and adopted these roles, introducing and implementing the People's model in NTPC in order to make it 'People First' organisation. The Team HR strived hard towards justifying their roles to achieve the desired change.

SYSTEM DESIGNER

HR as system designer would imply designing HR systems and HR strategies for achieving the organisation's business goals and realising its business strategy. HR professionals have to assess and articulate the needs – explicit or implicit of the employees as well as the organisation and develop appropriate systems to fulfil those needs that broadly include the following systems:

- Identify and retain right people.
- Achieve organisational goals through effective PMS.
- Address employee aspirations through proper career development system.
- Facilitate organisation renewal and enhance organisational capabilities through learning mechanisms and Knowledge Management initiatives, creativity booster, etc.
- Building strong culture of commitment through creating Values and Vision in line with the business needs.

Team HR also designed HR Systems/processes that align with the needs of the business and integrate diverse HR initiatives in a common business focus. This role involves diagnosing critical organisational capabilities and developing those capabilities in people.

The alignment of HR with the business however, had to be organisation specific, tailor made to suit the company's core values, culture and strategic purpose.

INTERNAL CONSULTANT

As internal consultants, Team HR attempted to 'HRise' the line and spread HR competencies throughout the organisation and also empowered and counselled line managers on various HR issues. Line leaders at all levels started appreciating people aspirations and speaking HR language.

CHAMPIONING CAUSE OF EMPLOYEES

In the age of outsourcing, usage of technology and assigning various roles to line people, HR managers/professionals need to effectively coordinate the people issues throughout the organisation, often acting like a master conductor of a grand symphony orchestra. Due to the efforts of Team HR, all groups, formal or informal, Unions or Associations, started voluntarily enjoying orchestrating the same tune, same rhythm of building NTPC as a great organisation.

CHAMPIONING THE COMMUNITY DEVELOPMENT

HR championed, defended and propagated issues such as values and ethics, code of conduct, human rights, labour standards, building of society, etc., issues that affected the employees all across the organisation. HR played a driving role in helping the organisation fulfill its social obligations and in being more accountable to all the stakeholders – employees, community and society – besides the shareholders. HR played an important role in promoting good Corporate Governance practices.

IMPACT ASSESSOR

Further, HR performed the role of measuring the effectiveness of HR systems/processes, the value system that they worked hard to establish and demonstrate to the line managers how HR adds value and helps the organisation to achieve its goals.

Lack of quantification of results or contribution of HR is often viewed as a hindrance in establishing its worth in the eyes of line managers and shareholders. It is essential to quantify the contributions of HR and measure the achievements. Quantified results bring credibility to HR Function and enable all stakeholders to appreciate the need and importance of HR. At NTPC, Team HR undertook to measure not only the growth in employee satisfaction but also worked towards reducing the man-days lost due to strikes to zero. The productivity of manpower on all kinds of parameters kept on rising by leaps and bounds like million units generated per man, profit per man, etc. (Annexure D).

CHANGE AGENTS

In the present era change had become an inherent part of corporate life. Mergers and acquisitions, alliances, takeovers, downsizing, etc. became the norm of the day. All these procedures entail a tremendous change that affect the organisational structure, its way of functioning, behaviour of employees and so on.

During such dealings in NTPC, we, as Team HR, had an important role to play in employee retention, integration of culture, managing communication and managing the overall change that was inevitable. HR professionals had to act as change agents and work towards building the organisation's capacity to handle the changes successfully.

We made sure that initiatives were defined, developed and delivered in a timely manner. The fundamental values of the organisation were debated upon and appropriately adapted to align with the changing business situations. As change agents Team HR was able to turn the resistance and fear of change to excitement about new opportunities by being consultative, sharing, transparent, generating sufficient trust. All these roles were played very sincerely and in a planned manner. Some of the HR personnel took extra time to take on their roles as compared to the rest, but all had an important input in bringing the transformation very effectively.

HR COMPETENCIES

To perform these roles and other new roles that would be coming their way, HR professionals need to master certain competencies, development of which was addressed by us very sincerely and in an organised way:

(i) **Knowledge of HR processes:** HR professionals must have an excellent knowledge of HR processes such as recruitment, training and development, performance management, etc. Possessing specific skills such as counselling, coaching, good communication skills and ability to work with the team/line managers are an added advantage in the performance of the roles.

(ii) **Business Acumen:** HR professional must have a comprehensive understanding of the business of their organisation. HR professionals must have a clear idea of all aspects of the business because almost every business issue has people implications. This involves knowledge of not only the products, services, values and Vision of the organisation but its customers, competitors, market situations, as well.

(iii) **Strategic thinking:** For a good HR professional, one must demonstrate an ability to make directional choices and balance between present and future. The professional should be able to take the long-term perspective into account. This enables him/her in making sustainable improvements and changes.

(iv) **Execution Excellence:** A complete HR person will have to demonstrate an ability to implement the plans and strategies and consistently deliver on time. He/she has to be continuously prepared to deliver excellence in both tactical and strategic roles.

(v) **Change Management skills:** HR professional should be proactive and anticipate change. The professionals should have an ability to see through the change, diagnose problems, build supportive relationships with others, propose solutions and encourage others to implement change successfully. They should also take a leading role in the cultural transformation process by challenging the existing culture and frame and help in stabilising the new culture suitable for the organisation.

(vi) **Customer focus:** In this age of thrust on customer orientation it is imperative that HR professionals should also have a strong focus on their goals and have commitments to internal customers, i.e. employees as well as external customers including community, consumers, suppliers, etc.

(vii) **Personal credibility and image:** It is one of the most important qualities of the HR professionals.

- They should be seen as role models by their colleagues in practice of the core Values of the organisation.
- They should evoke trust, respect and confidence from others and demonstrate a high level of integrity.
- Create optimism in the Organisation. The HR personnel have to be dealers in hope and trust.

Most important of all is the mindset of HR professionals and his/her conviction and credibility that assist him/her in delivering the roles. According to me this should be guided by the philosophy laid down in *Kato Upanishad*:

अमंत्रम् अक्षरंनास्ति नास्तिमूलम् अनौशधम्।
अयोग्यः पुरूशोनास्ति योजकस्तत्रदुर्लभः।।
                                                — ऋग्वेद

(Every letter can be turned into a 'mantra'; every root can be used as a medicine. Every human being has some value and potential. Rare is the

person who lends an enabling hand for development and actualisation of these potentials.)

This ancient Sanskrit shloka exemplifies the attitude that HR professional must bring to their task. We must make the rare breed plentiful through spreading people orientation throughout the organisation.

(viii) *Avid and continuous learner:* The HR person shall have to be a born learner taking in everything from anywhere and anyone, and build upon it, innovate and utilise for actualising the great smell of the place as desired to make a great organisation.

CONCLUSION

I recall I was always paranoid about my lack of knowledge and that made me humble enough to learn from all directions, all sources, be it my teachers, mentors, coaches, advisors, consultants, elders, friends, particularly juniors, team, professionals, articles, books and training programmes attended, be it practices seen, benchmarks learnt and developed and so on. I had been like a little adolescent pebble picker who would bend down every where to pickup pebbles – round, supple, rough, any colour and size, and put them to my use or store them for better days. In this journey there were several instances when I virtually could pick up plenty of gems and even real diamonds and use them like mine. But I always felt that I was not dishonest anytime as, while putting them to use, I added value to them and used these gems for my organisation and my people, who were the true beneficiaries. However, I would always avoid using them for mere show or display, which always seemed somewhat vulgar to me. Nor would I ever use them just for the sake of fitting them in the value chain just because they might look colourful and glamorous, like a feature creep adds features innovating in say, the mobiles today, and creates or adds them, not mindful of the fatigue it could cause on the users (One Page Talent Management).[11]

I would always like HR to be creating simple but innovative designs, keeping in mind the extent of impact they may create on the users and the people. Our intent was to primarily recreate the smell of the place in NTPC, working on developing the characteristics like stretch, support, trust and self discipline, and boosting continuous learning. It was seen that developing these characteristics prompted forward looking innovation, deep commitment and a strong sense of ownership in the organisation, primarily rekindling the people power, the core of any organisation's life, health and longevity. NTPC's return of all the developed characteristics was only through these small yet continuously learnt pebbles of initiatives and experiments that brought smiles on every face with rekindled brightness.

ANNEXURES

Bodh 1: Conclusions And Recommendations

CONCLUSIONS

We live in a world where perfection is the ideal goal but difficult to achieve. More so in organisations like the NTPC which has been managed by design to serve a lot of socialistic orientations with the resultant overmanning and lackluster standards of performance and accountability, etc. This baggage comes in the way of continuous efforts of the HR management and others in NTPC for seeking improvements and achieving the ideal goal of seeking positive perceptions of all the executives/non-executives in a larger number of personnel policies/dimensions.

In such an environment, achieving a high level of Job Satisfaction and Organisational Commitment (accepting a mean score of 1.95 and above as a benchmark of satisfactory level) is in itself an achievement. The NTPC management, particularly the HR officials, needs to be complimented for the same. It further leads us to believe that NTPC can build on these fundamental strengths to seek further improvements in the perception of employees on other dimensions. The management may, however, need to be cautious that the executives do not use these very strengths in a negative manner, in the sense of complacency creeping amongst them. It must be on its toes to oversee that the executives keep on deriving Job Satisfaction to build on positive energy for themselves and others, towards the benefits of the organisation. Likewise, a largely positive perception on safety and security and monetary benefits must be utilised by the management to positive outcomes.

A high score on lateral trust is reflected in the fact that executives of this organisation are ready to help each other. NTPC needs to further examine whether this exists amongst the 'in groups' or to a larger entity of management. Further, are these 'in-groups' working towards organisation or personal benefits. Executives, at times, indulge in favouritism to pat each other at the cost of the organisation and respond to this as a manifestation of lateral trust. In case we link up this high perception of lateral trust with the other perceptions, obtained in a limited manner through the qualitative data, we find that along with this, there was lack of cooperation among different departments.

All the high-ranking dimensions need to be continuously strengthened as well as probed further to get in-depth details.

The fact that there are many other dimensions on which the perceptions of the employees are not highly satisfactory is a matter of concern and an in-depth examination is required to prepare specific action plans. As mentioned both by executives and non-executives, during the interviews (with a cross section of employees), that they joined NTPC with a lot of enthusiasm but very soon seemed to lose it. Employees had come to learn that it was not hard work but maintaining relationships that counted and thus their motivation became low. Complacency seemed to have set in. Generally, organisations tend to provide more money and welfare measures, etc., to their employees to boost their morale. But there is a limit to the extent to which any organisation can go on giving more and more of these.

The managerial challenge, therefore, lies in creating a motivational package of intrinsic rewards that can address the higher order needs of employees. These intrinsic rewards are recognition, involvement, freedom, opportunities for personal growth and advancement, opportunity to utilise one's abilities, to experiment with ideas, to trust and be trusted, etc. Some of these dimensions were taken care of in NTPC while most were managed that well.

RECOMMENDATIONS

Over all, NTPC has well designed policies and systems. However, there is room for an improvement in their implementation. Hence, one of the prime recommendations is that NTPC should ensure through 'regular system implementation reviews' that systems are properly implemented down to the grass-root level. Developing and having implicit trust in one's people, providing them freedom to project different viewpoints, involving them in target setting and in preparing action plans to achieve the targets, and their active participation in self-initiated projects will go a long way in implementing policies in their letter and spirit. While the above are over all recommendations applicable to most policies of NTPC, some of the specific recommendations concerned the following areas and dimensions:

VISION, MISSION AND VALUES

While the executives' knowledge of the Vision, Mission and Values was perceived to be high, these were medium to low on the efforts of the organisation to promote the same. The literature of some of the successful companies like Hewlett Packard, Sony, Motorola, 3 M, reveals that such companies have stood steadfast with their core values. These values have helped them to formulate and implement their Vision, Mission, etc. Such values in these companies do not change with market ups and downs, technology, and change of leadership at the top and have survived the test of time. To the corporate management, the values become the core purpose, the *raison dietre* of their existence. The management continuously strives to inculcate these values along with the Vision and Mission amongst their employees. It is a difficult task but is achieved by the management practicing them and being the role models.

Indian companies have also picked up the learning from the Western world about the core values being the fundamental management practice. Some companies have succeeded while many others have given only a lip service to these values. Companies like TISCO have changed course and formulated newer visions. For example, TISCO had steadfastly held on to the value of caring for employees as a tool of achieving excellence. It altered course to become one of the most admired steel companies in the world. In the process, the company had changed its core value from 'we also make steel' to 'we make steel'.

The executives of the NTPC gave an average or a medium response to the organisation's efforts of promoting Organisational values. It is, however, important to highlight that if according to their perception the corporate management is not doing enough to popularise and internalise core values, what are they doing about it? Why are the executives, many amongst them the seniors, are not doing their bit to do the needful? Their own understanding of the core Values and Vision did not go beyond verbalising it. This does not mean that the senior management at the corporate level can not play the role of popularising and internalising the core Values of the organisation. In this context, the example of SAIL is relevant. Somewhere in mid 1980s, the top management felt that one core input for revival of the company was to inculcate core Values and formulate a fresh the Vision and Mission of the organisation. The Vision was evolved through a large number of interactions with the corporate level officials, plant level executives and trade union leaders. The whole exercise of formulation of Values and Vision took about eight months through the involvement of a larger community of employees so that they perceive the Values and Vision as their own.

Core values of NTPC of Customer focus, Organisation pride, Mutual respect and trust, Initiative and speed, and Total quality along with its 'Vision' to be *"one of the world's largest and best power utilities, powering India's growth"* are inspiring enough. It is important to note that NTPC has made changes in its Values, Vision and Mission. The attempt has been to make them sharper and focussed to meet the imperatives of the new economy. The implementation of these values and the role of State Governments (its customers) which still operate with socialistic orientations, send confusing signals for effective implementation. Today, the Central Government has come out of the socialistic orientations but States do not even bother to pay their dues along with encouraging over employment and political interference which leads to an in-built laxity to demand, and thus gets a value orientation amongst a section of the employees. Such an environment becomes an impediment to the implementation of core values and their inculcation. The employees have been bred (not necessarily by the management of NTPC) into a culture, which has been influenced by the policies of the Central and the State Governments. Also, the executives' salary package (cost to the company) is very high. They enjoy security of job and some of the groups derive job satisfaction not necessarily by working positively but thriving in the environment at the cost of the core Values and Vision.

The study team is of the opinion that such extraneous factors have contributed to the executive's medium perception on the dimensions of core values, vision and mission of the organisation. Given these limitations, the management task becomes all the more difficult. Sustained communication by the senior leaders, not only by HR department, along with the top leaders to be seen as role models, will help in building values.

TRAINING AND DEVELOPMENT

NTPC has a deep commitment to developing its employees. It is through training and development that the foundation of the inspiring visions is attempted to be achieved. The basic philosophy of training is to make it as an instrument in transforming NTPC into a learning organisation. There is a continuous attempt to streamline the function and in March 2001, the corporate officials consolidated and codified it to streamline and rationalise. The Power Management Institute at the Apex level is the nodal agency and provides specialised training. The training Centres, simulator training Centres and HR group at the corporate and Regional level complements the efforts of the PMI. An in-house faculty takes the lead in teaching at the Power Management Institute. Outside faculty is invited to provide specialised inputs. The executives (in some cases non- executives also) are also sent to outside programmes for specialised inputs. Additionally, the executives of plants invite faculty/institutions to conduct training programmes for larger groups within the sites.

According to the perception of the employees, this activity is providing the desired results although the mean rating of the executives' perceptions on the dimension of providing adequate training is on the medium side. Non-executives gave low rating to training and development.

As is well known, there are the following three major components of training.

1. *The Training Need Survey.*
2. *Training Programme (design, content, faculty, etc.)*
3. *Evaluation in terms of the integration of learning into the tasks and roles.*

Training Need Analysis (TNA)

There is a system of identification of training needs in NTPC. Executives identify their training needs once in two years. This data is analysed and becomes the basis of training inputs.

The method followed for the TNA needs to be improved and must contain the following elements.

- Organisational Analysis
- Task/Role Analysis
- Person/Executive Analysis

Identification of training need is therefor a holistic exercise, which requires inputs from a cross section. Training needs of the newly promoted executives should be identified. Some training needs may be identified for all levels of employees, accordingly providing training in Interpersonal Competence. One example of this is 'HR for Non-HR' for all the executives.

The problem/issue of availability of identified executives (as per the TNA) needs to be sorted out. Many a times, the seniors are not able to spare the identified executive due to one contingency or the other. One possible alternative is to finalise and intimate the training calendar along with the list of participants to every one concerned much in advance (preferably a year long schedule). The seniors may be instructed to adjust the work schedule accordingly.

Training Programmes

- The programmes, their design, content and faculty should emerge from the TNA.
- The requirement of faculty members, their background, levels, etc. needs to be constantly reviewed to suit the training requirements.
- Presently, there is a dependence on the outside faculty. Involvement of outside faculty per se is welcome and the attempt by NTPC is to get the best faculty. Many a times, however, the search ends on the basis of availability rather than merit. Outside faculty is not involved in the design of the programmes nor do they know the session inputs being provided by others.
- The selection of internal faculty should be based on specific criteria appropriate for a teacher/trainer. Having followed this strictly, they need to be trained continuously. Let us take the case of IIM (A). The faculty has a right blend of academics and practitioners. A sound background of academics is continuously enriched by an interaction with diverse exposure and linkage with a cross section of industry. In the case of NTPC, one needs to ask such

questions on a continuous basis to get the right mix of internal faculty.

How much of all this is being followed is a matter of further examination:

Training Evaluation: Evaluation needs to be carried to know the quality of the inputs and their applicability into practice, i.e. the tasks and roles performed by them at work. In NTPC, evaluation is carried out immediately after the training programme. The integration of learning into the task requires a deeper examination by the management. Some of the essential pre-requisites for achieving this objective are as follows:

- A culture in the organisation which allows employees to integrate learning at work. In NTPC the trainee mostly goes back and there is little scope, encouragement and persuasion to implement new ideas.
- Preparation of a brief action plan by the executives to implement new ideas. This may be backed by the management followed by its periodic review, meetings and discussions to look into the inhibitors and facilitators.
- Continuous evaluation of the person's abilities, attitude, etc., which determine actions of individuals.

DEVELOPING EFFECTIVE COMMUNICATION

The communication system was moderately perceived (close to low ranking dimensions) by the executives where as non-executives gave low ranking to this dimension. Developing good communication is, therefore, essential in order to generate trust, cooperation, commitment and feeling of belonging. It is important that all policies, including the Vision and Mission statements be clearly defined and explained to all employees. Clear statements of responsibilities, authority and accountability, as well as criteria for promotions, transfers, and other matters that affect employees at large must be spelt out.

Information sharing is so crucial for effective performance. Usually people consider information as power and that sharing information diffuses power. Therefore, some leaders resist sharing information. This is a failure on the part of leaders. A **system of regular feedback and interaction gives**

employees a sense of participation in the decision-making process. Another advantage is that it helps in rectifying the problem at a very early stage.

Management may need to be **transparent** and enhance their capacity to communicate freely, promptly and effectively with the employees and also allow them to put forward their views and suggestions. Information Technology (IT) may help in facilitating internal as well as external communication. The act of sharing information relating to financial performance, strategy and operational measures conveys that employees are trusted.

Internal Communication

Internal communication is one of the important corporate functions, which links many functions. Research studies indicat that organisations overlooking linkages between Human Resource development and internal communication failed to achieve efficiency in organisations. HR effectiveness is closely linked with the quality of communication within an organisation.

HR Line Manager Interface

In the present scenario there is a greater need for the involvement of line managers in the HR function. Some line managers could be appointed as HR coordinators. They could also assist in the identification of respective areas and training needs. Let us take an illustration. Usually, line supervisors and human resource executives are responsible for implementation of career development programmes. Line supervisors are responsible for the assessment and development of their subordinates and for assisting them in attaining the desired position with the help of varied measures especially counselling. The human resource executives play a significant role in promoting the development of career paths to satisfy the needs of people. Proper coordination of these two is essential for the development of people.

During these interface meetings, HR and line managers could debate about each other's roles and consultations. They could also debate what each other could do to make the other group effective and efficient. At the end of these interactions, a MOU highlighting an Action Plan could be generated.

Interdepartmental Meetings

Data of the present study revealed inter-departmental differences resulting in dissatisfaction. This interface could take place periodically to share each other's concern and priorities. Such interface meetings would help to appreciate each other's viewpoints and evolve a common agenda for organisational effectiveness. Some of the suggestions for more interactive communication are:

- The department heads may meet monthly to review how each department is contributing to the systems goal.
- The members of a department may assemble to discuss how they will handle specific problems; they may employ brainstorming technique.
- The members of one department may meet with members of another department to give them some new data/information.
- The members of departments may meet to discuss a conflict inherent in the department or between departments.
- Train people in communication skills.
- Ensure top management's support in developing and maintaining the system.

Open Forum

Open Forum would provide opportunities to employees to interact with senior management teams during various professional, organisational and personal meetings. Thus, employees will be encouraged to share their sentiments, dilemmas, concerns and suggestions. Data emerging from these deliberations could be used for action planning, teamwork and positive work culture. Though NTPC has some such systems, but they were 'perceived' by employees as not functioning very effectively.

ROLE OF MIDDLE MANAGERS

In NTPC, E5 level emerged as most dissatisfied. It is indicated in research studies that job satisfaction is relatively high at the start and end of the job duration and low in the middle period of the job.

The survey done by Business Today (1996) has quoted many examples where many organisations shed the entire middle level to adopt flatter hierarchies.

On the other hand, J N Armolia, Executive Director (Personnel), Ashok Leyland, points out "Middle Managers are the backbone of the company. If retrained, they are the biggest assets, otherwise they are liabilities".

Since NTPC will not shed its middle managers, they should be a special focus of development. The more strategic role of middle managers may require in nature. **The organisation needs to conduct a deeper analysis.** However, some of the suggestions are as follows:

- Retraining facilitates for development of multiple skills, which may enable middle managers to work in cross functional teams as well as develop inputs for strategic business decisions that could be of help to the top management.
- Leadership and team building qualities may be developed.
- Some of the middle managers may be asked to take the role of mentor for junior executives.
- Middle managers can also conduct induction training for management trainees.
- Some middle executives may be chosen to take larger responsibilities, which may help in succession planning.
- Some middle managers may act as internal faculty to impart technical training to its employees.

ROLE ANALYSIS

The data of the present study gave clear indication that employees were not clear about their roles and responsibilities. With the help of Role Analysis technique, the role descriptions relating to various operating positions could be articulated. Such role analysis clearly identifies for each position its purpose, prescribed elements and discretionary elements, which together constitute the Role Boundary. These help in result orientation and exercise of discretion within the framework of policies/rules of the organisation. Along with this, their accountability norms must be specifically prepared and followed.

WELFARE MEASURSES

While NTPC has provided a liberal package of welfare facilities like housing, medical, education, etc., these were yet perceived moderately by executives and accorded low ranking by non-executives. While welfare is an integral part of the agenda, the NTPC management may decide how far it can go to appease the employees. A few specific suggestions which came up during interaction are as follows:

- Concrete steps need to be taken to improve the standard of education in schools at projects.
- Reputed educational institutions may be invited to set up school with a CBSE system so that children do not face difficulties in case of their parent's transfer.
- Residential school for NTPC employees' children.
- Some seats at good colleges to be reserved for NTPC employees' ward, especially those who are posted at sites.
- Medical facilities to be improved upon especially at Gas plants and aken-over projects.

STATUS DIFFERENTIATION

In any organisation there are bound to be some status differentiation. However, this has been perceived as more pronounced in NTPC. It was felt that, NTPC is projecting itself as an Executive-based organisation, which is percolating down the line – be it supervisor or workman. The non-executives perceive a drift between executives and non-executives. They are not feeling as a part of the total organisation. *Whether it is a part of the management design or by default, needs to be checked.*

For many years there was no or very negligible recruitment at supervisory level. At workmen level also most of the work had been done by contract labour. The kind of status distinction that is emerging and gradually creating a feeling that they are less valued is not good for any organisation. Certain measures in this direction would be appreciated:

- The act of sharing information, consulting them in decisions affecting them, and involving them in decision making process wherever necessary creates a feeling of belongingness.
- In the present scenario of NTPC, workmen have very less chance of moving to supervisory or executive cadre. A workman would remain a workman throughout his life. This is creating a social

taboo amongst them. *Can NTPC designate them differently such as – Associate?*

AREAS OF IMMEDIATE CONCERN

Scope for Advancement

NTPC is providing high job security and adequate monetary benefits to its employees. In both the categories there was dissatisfaction regarding scope for advancement. They felt that they had very limited avenues to grow in the organisation. Of late there has been growing interest in the use of career planning and management succession as instruments to resolve problems such as stagnation, alienation, disinterest in work and demotivation, and as a tool for insuring the supply of managerial skills from within the organisation as and when required. These programmes or plans shape the progression of individuals within the organisation in accordance with assessments of organisational needs and performance and potential of individual members of the enterprise. Some suggestions are as follows:

- Offering a package of diagnostics to help identify a career path and then provide counselling and training to move towards it. The Organisation may use relevant techniques to test the manager's aptitudes. The organisation may match their individual competencies against the competencies which future jobs will require. Attempts are made to do so through discussion with the manager's boss. Both self-assessment and its validation by the supervisor are taken into account in evolving individual career plans.
- Testing of managers to identify their skills prior to putting them into a career plan.
- Exposure to varied functions to the manager to enable him to find out his best career option.
- Facilitating career choice without dictating which path to choose.
- Making executives/non-executives aware of the competencies required for varied career options.
- Some thinking is required for career growth of the Medical and Chemistry group, considered as 'specialist group'. Creating further avenues in their career growth.
- Some of the non-executives had pursued few courses and acquired diplomas or degrees with the hope to get advantage in their career

path. But later on they came to know that those courses or institutions were not recognised by NTPC, resulting in wastage of money, time and efforts on their part. Therefore, proper communication is required about various career paths and career schemes to channelise their energy in the right direction.

Promotion Policy

Promotion has emerged as one of the foremost areas of concern. Every employee aspires for promotion in the quickest possible time. The opportunities of promotion have to match the organisational structure and its needs.

Underlying the responses on promotion policy and appraisal system, the following four areas of concern came up:

- Feeling that the practice was not consistent with the policy.
- What superiors said to employees was different from the decision taken on promotion. In the past, promotions were somewhat regular. As growth of NTPC stagnated, this is no longer true.
- All this had negative consequences on the organisation, apart from its consequences on work. When a person is not promoted, the children are discriminated by those of their colleagues and this influences family/social relationships, particularly in the projects.
- There is subjectivity in the promotion. Factors in the environment such as favouritism, casteism, personal liking, etc., also influence promotion decision.
- Most of the above mentioned opinions may also be due to the 'perceived' lack of transparency while implementing the promotion policy.
- Denial of promotion is seen as 'rejection' of the person. Hence, it is demotivating. Therefore, there is a need to create confidence in the selection process for the promotion.

There are two ways to frame any action plan based on the responses. One is to have a detailed open house discussion to understand the 'why' of the perception. The open house discussion forum should help in either authenticating or rejecting this perception along with bringing other issues if any, of the 'why' of this negative perception. Such open house discussion should be used to communicate the details of the process along with understanding their specific needs of transparency. The twin actions for the management should be on understanding, through a two-way communication process and framing policy to reduce the perceived subjectively.

The management may also debate whether the Promotion Policy itself needs to be anlaysed a fresh. While doing so, NTPC may, among others, think on these lines:

- For operations, clerical categories, seniority can be used as basis of promotion.
- For middle level – technical, supervisory and administrative personnel, seniority cum merit can be used as criteria for promotion.
- Merit can be used as a guiding force for promotions to higher levels of technical, managerial and administrative positions.

Some more specific suggestions are as follows:

- NTPC has three clusters of jobs at executives level—E1–E4 is a working level/junior executives; E5–E6, managers and senior managers/middle managers; E7–E9, top executives. The percentage of promotion at the lower level should be much higher than the senior level. Since this is working level, promotions within cluster will not make much difference.
- NTPC may have more stringent selection process at cross-over points compared to promotions within the cluster. At the time of moving up from lower cluster to the next cluster, relevant training to prepare them for the higher position needs to be seriously implemented.
- Promotion from supervisor to executives could involve a written test to assess their technical competence. Those who are promoted should be put through rigrous training capsules on technical, managerial/behavioural aspects of their personality.
- Project experience should be made mandatory for middle/senior level managers in NTPC and taken into consideration at the time of promotion to higher positions. As in the Banking Industry, two years of rural posting is a must for higher promotion. In services also, field posting is must.

Performance Appraisal

Performance Appraisal, like promotions, has been a major source of discontent in industrial organisations. In this respect, NTPC is no different from other organisations. Yet, it is important that the system is implemented in a manner which provides the desired result for the organisation and is perceived as fair by the employees.

In NTPC, except for E-6 to E-9, appraisal process assesses largely the performance at the end of the time period. As per the policy, the appraisal is conducted both by the appraiser and the appraisee. The moderation committee sorts out issues in case of differences of opinion. However, the whole process lays emphasis on the past performance of the employee. There are certain distinct suggestions in this regard.

- NTPC should utilise the performance appraisal largely as a tool to improve performance. The Appraisal review should take place at the time of giving the work rather than the completion of work or a time period. Continuous review of identifying strengths and weaknesses of the executives, the environment and support services should become the prime focus of the appraisal process. In other words, the focus of appraisal has to shift from *Past* to *future*.
- The management must prepare a continuous action plan and implement the same to improve the required abilities.
- Strengthen the moderation committee and make it transparent where the appraisee and appraiser see the process as transparent.
- The appraisee has to involve the appraiser and sort out the differences at that stage.
- The roles and tasks must be made very clear to the Executives. This may include specifics of responsibilities (making them clear at the time of assigning work) and expected tasks to be accomplished. Specifying KRA's may further help. This is more applicable for the E-1 to E-5 levels.
- PA is an important tool of developing and motivating employees. The appraiser and the appraisee must, therefore, perceive this activity as one of the important policies and undertake the same accordingly rather than performing it in a mechanical manner.
- Appraisers have a habit of giving an average rating to a larger section of the appraisee. If this is so in NTPC, the appraiser must be trained.
- Supervisors/appraisers can be trained with a view to improving their

ability to evaluate subordinates and discuss evaluations with them effectively.

- Feedback sessions relate the communication with appraisee with the explicit purpose of improving his/her performance. There is a need to train appraisers to improve skills to communicate appraisal and the feedback process should form a part of the career development plans of appraisees.
- Training of an appraiser formed a pre-requisite to the acceptance of the appraisals, objectivity and uniformity and building skills to provide feedback to the appraisee for the development. Such training would help in eliminating appraiser bias and developing interviewing and counselling skills.

The details of many recommendations may be worked out once the Organisation takes a decision to introduce a comprehensive performance management system.

For effective implementation of the recommendations of any survey it would be appropriate to share the results down the line and get the support for these kinds of activities in the future also. This will create an atmosphere of trust and openness, which is sine quo non to ensure the cooperation and commitment to the process.

It is also not so much the policy but its implementation, which needs to be examined and improved. The senior most executives must show more professionalism for their success. Finally, in case the management decides to conduct an in-depth examination in certain areas as well as formulate and implement the package or part of it, there will be a merit in involving an outside consulting organisation.

RECOMMENDATIONS

The following suggestions are based on the overall functioning of the NTPC:

- From the quantitative as well as qualitative data one thing had emerged that NTPC had very strong systems but the implementation was not good. Hence, there is a greater need of rationalisation of implementation of policies and practices across the country.
- Management must try to remove biases, favouritism and nepotism. This can only be possible when senior executives are perceived as fair,

frank, unprejudiced and just. They have to stop nurturing sycophancy. It must draw the attention of seniors to build credibility of their actions while implementing the policies.

- Transparency to be maintained, rules and procedures should be well communicated to all.
- All out effort should be made to inculcate feelings of trust and confidence among supervisors through objectivity and fair approach.
- Performance appraisal system should be more objective and transparent.
- Provide frequent feedback on performance/areas of improvement.
- Job rotation policy to be strictly implemented. It should be used as a tool of HRD and not as a mechanism of punishment. A well thought of rotation policy may be drawn and publisied appropriately.
- Supervisors in shifts should be rotated after every 5–7 years.
- Though welfare facilities were good, still concrete steps need to be taken to improve the standard of education in schools at projects.sa '
- Residential school for NTPC employees' children. Some seats at good colleges to be reserved for NTPC employees' ward specially, those who are posted at sites.

- NTPC has three clusters of jobs at 'Executive level—E1–E4 is a working level/junior Executives; E5–E6, Managers and Senior Managers/middle managers; E7–E9, top Executives. The percentage of promotion at the lower level should be much higher than the senior level. Since this is working level, promotions within cluster will not make much difference.
- NTPC may have more stringent selection process at cross-over points compared to promotions within the cluster. At the time of moving up from lower cluster to next cluster relevant training to prepare them for the higher position need to be seriously implemented.
- Associate outsiders in committees appointed for promotion to maintain the objectivity in the promotion process; emphasis should be given to competencies at higher levels.
- The interviews for the promotions are round the year. It would be better if a specific period is earmarked to carry out the promotion related matters rather than having it through out the year. There should be dead line on the date of promotion upto E6 across the country to reduce the ambiguity in the minds of people.

- The DPC constitution should be broad based to obtain objectivity in the process.
- Promotion from supervisor to supervisors could involve written test to assess their technical competence. Those who are promoted should be put through rigrous training capsules on technical, managerial/behavioural aspects of their personality.
- In the case of Supervisors who are not moving out of corporate office there should be some provision of slowing down their progress. Project experience should be made mandatory for middle/senior level managers.
- Related to promotion is the Performance Appraisal procedure. Though NTPC has a good Performance Appraisal system but the implementation part is very poor. NTPC may go for potential appraisal or 360 degree appraisal. In Performance Appraisal, subjectivity elements would always occur. Executives should be trained to be more objective in their evaluations.
- Stringent actions should be taken against those people who indulge in Confidential Report (CR) manipulations.

- A thought needs to be given to the problem of Medical and Chemistry group, considered as 'specialist group' by creating further avenues in their career growth.
- For effective implementation of the recommendations of any survey it would be appropriate to share the results down the line and get the support for these kinds of activities in the future also. This will create an atmosphere of trust and openness, which is sine quo non to ensure the cooperation and commitment to the process.

Certain recommendations for the medium ranked dimensions are as follows:

- Training Need Analysis in consultation with individual and reporting officer should be done much before the fiscal year, and people informed much in advance to avoid substitutes being sent for training. Evaluate training effectiveness on a regular basis, through scientifically established methods.
- Training should be given to the supervisors who are promoted from supervisory level.
- All levels of employees should be provided training in Interpersonal Competence.

- More thrust should be given to practice the core values. Senior supervisors should act as role models. If required 'Values Labs' may be conducted to enable employee to understand the concept of values and also identifying individual values and organisational values. Further identification of gaps and then bridging the gap between the two set of values.
- Restructuring should be done as per the corporate plans.
- Participative Forums should be properly implemented. NOCET should not become just for HR people. More involvement of the supervisors at all levels is required. More and more open house OD approaches may be followed.
- There should be clear statements of responsibilities, authority and accountability with delegation of powers. The authority and accountability should go together.

To conclude, the data revealed certain strengths and weaknesses of NTPC. Some of the major strengths and weaknesses are highlighted below:

STRENGTHS

- Job security
- Good pay package
- One of the NAVRATNA companies
- One of the best in power sector
- Systems based organisation
- Supervisor based organisation
- Technical competencies of the people
- Man power / MW ratio is an example for other organisations
- Very good at crises management

WEAKNESSES

- NTPC has very good policies but implementation is not proper
- Lack of openness and transparency
- Groupism, nepotism, casteism and favouritism are influencing decisions
- Leaders are not perceived as 'role models'

- Employees at project expressed their dissatisfaction over the role played by Corporate employees
- NTPC structure is widening at middle level
- Less information sharing at inter-project level
- Information technology not used optimumaly

Strengths should be sustained and weaknesses to be minimised.

Saptapadi: A Commitment Of Everlasting Partnership

1. "ॐ ईशा एकपदी भवः"
   "Om Isha Ekpadi Bhawah…"
   (With the promise to nourish each other, we take this first step.)

2. "ॐ उर्जे द्विपदी भवः"
   "Om Urje Dwipadi Bhawah…"
   (With the determination to grow each other in strength, energy, we take this second step.)

3. "ॐ रजसपोशय त्रिपदी भवः"
   "Om Rajasposhay Tripadi Bhawah…"
   (With the promise to preserve our wealth and prosperity, we take this third step.)

4. "ॐ भयोभव्यः चतुश्पदी भवः"
   "Om Bhayobhavway chatuspadi Bhawah…"
   (With the vow to serve you with happiness and harmony, we take this fourth step.)

5. "ॐ प्रजाभयः पंचपदी भवः"
   "Om Prajabhaya Panchapadi Bhawah…"
   (With the promise to care for our healthy and worthy progeny, we take this fifth step.)

6. "ॐ ऋतुभयः शशटपदी भवः"

   "Om Ritubhaya Shashtapadi Bhawah…"

   (With the vow to be together forever in all responsibilities, in all seasons, all stresses, we take this sixth step.)

7. "ॐ सस्वै सप्तपदी भवः"

   "Om Saswey Saptapadi Bhawah…"

   "ॐ ईशा सखा सप्तपदी भवः"

   "Om Isha Sakha Saptapadi Bhawah…"

   (With a promise of everlasting friendship and like ideal companions who think and act alike, we take this seventh step.)

Few Examples In NTPC Employee Discussions On Principle Of 'Something For Something'

1. Reduction in overtime to zero, except in most essential circumstances.

2. Manpower Rationalization: reduction of number of locations in Stations.

3. Reducing closed holidays from 12 to 8 and increasing restricted holidays from 2 to 6 optimising with higher availability of work and employees and at the same time better flexibility to employees.

4. Revision in prices of items in all canteens to enable recovery of cost of raw-materials, cost reduction, and all round improvements in Canteens.

5. Electricity metering in project/station townships to regulate expenditure, which was never there.

6. Sharing and practicing greater concern on safety issues.

7. Agreement in NBC for optimising utilization of manpower by extending responsibilities with multi-skilling traiing.

8. Unions supporting the movement for anctualisation of the Vision, Mission and core-Values of the organization.

9. Facility of LTC and medical restricted to self, spouse (only one), two surviving children (below 25 years) and parents subject to members being dependant on the employee.

10. Introduction of Economic Rehabilitation Scheme as a security measure to ensure that there is no request for jobs from dependants of employees who die while in service but not on duty.

11. Revision of Contributory scheme for post-retirement medical facilities with post-retirement medical facility through appropriate Medi-claim Insurance policy. Also, provision for medical facility through Medi-claim Insurance Policy to spouses of deceased employees.

12. Entitlement for company accommodation linked to grades as opposed to Basic Pay for new joinees. C-type entitlement raised to E-3.

13. House Rent Recovery linked to revised pay for executives, supervisors and workmen from W-8 to W-11, as opposed to pre-revised pay as in the past.

14. Examination of only such representations for resolution of anomaly in the case of workmen and supervisors, as a result of annual increment, where a senior employee drawing higher basic pay than a junior employee as on 31/12/96, draws less pay in the revised pay-scale than a junior employee for a continuous period of 12 months, provided both are in the same grade.

15. Introduction of new grade of W-0 below lowest workman grade of W-1 for induction in unskilled category.

16. Parity between workmen in grades W-8 to W-11 and S-1 to S-4 as regards pay-structure, allowances and recoveries, thus reducing the dissatisfaction caused as a result of inability of workmen to move to Supervisory category because of very few vacancies and ensuring that the organizational requirement of skilled workmen vis-à-vis Supervisors is fulfilled.

17. Promotions to E-1 from S-4 as opposed to S-3.

18. Unions agreed to encourage all workmen to become members of Quality Circles within a year's time and also helped in pursuing other TQM initiatives, like 5S, obtaining ISO certification, promoting suggestion scheme, etc.

Indices Of Performance Improvements In NTPC

OPERATIONAL EXCELLENCE

- No. 1 in capacity utilisation globally
- Six plants operated at PLF of >95%
- Dadri stage-I achieved highest ever PLF of 100.59%
- Gas stations registered highest ever PLF of 78.38%

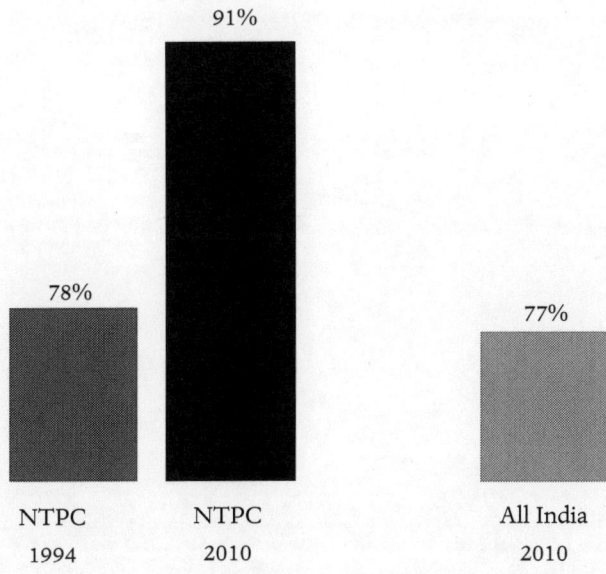

Figure D1: Operational Excellence

Table D1

Taken Over in the Year	Station Taken Over and Transformed	PLF % at the Time of Takeover	PLF % in 2009–10
1992	Feroze Gandhi Unchahar TPS	18	97
1995	Talcher TPS	19	91
2000	Tanda TPS	15	92

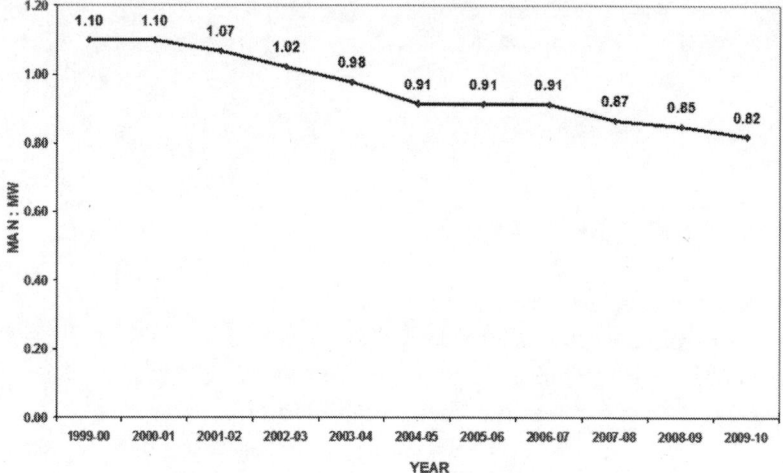

Figure D2: Man/MW Ratio Over the Years

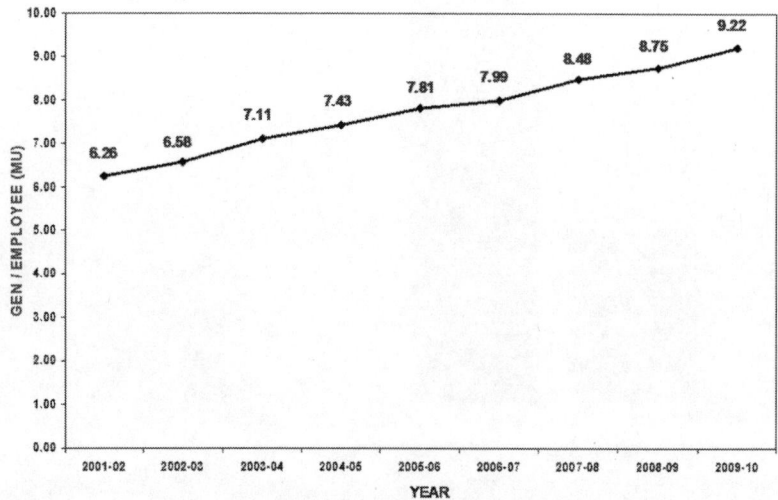

Figure D3: Generation per Employee

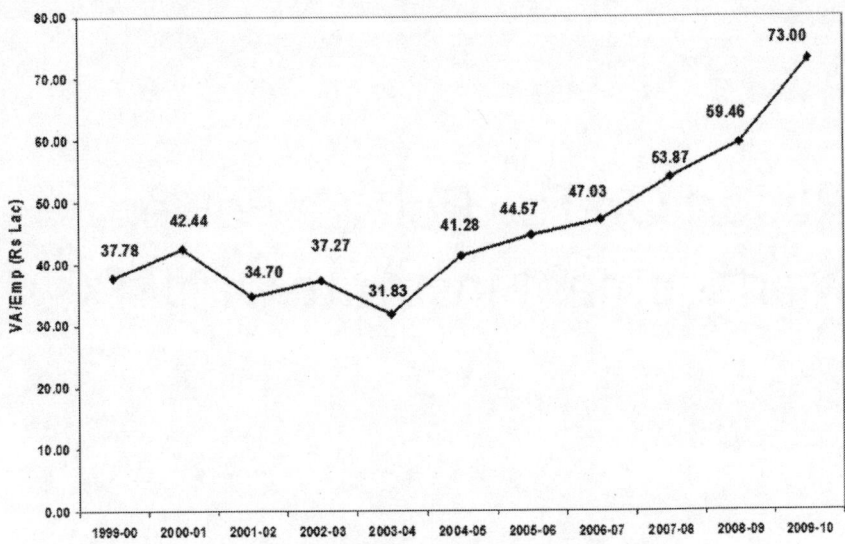

Figure D4: Value Added Per Employee

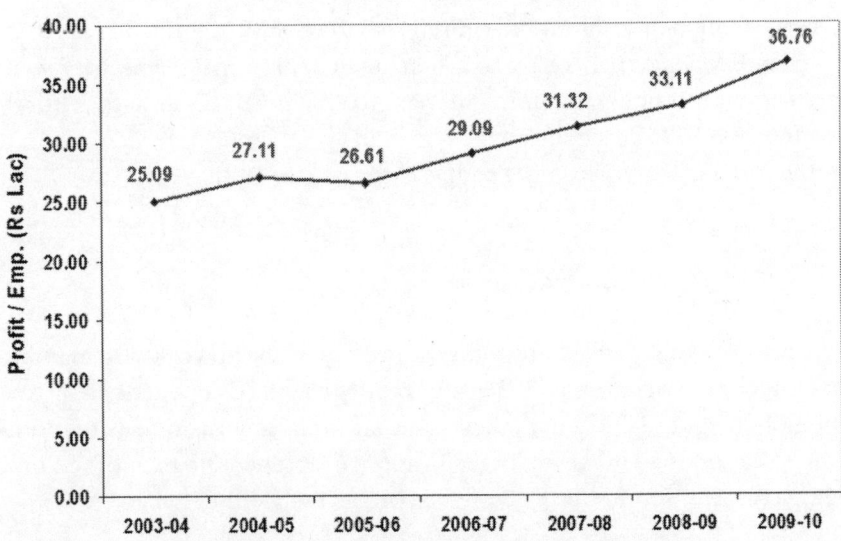

Figure D5: Profit Per Employee (Rs in lakh)

Report On The Role Of Power Management Institute Of NTPC

THE ROLE OF PMI

The working paper submitted on July 20th 2000, had identified areas that corporate Managements have to articulate in operational terms. This step is necessary if training inputs in PMI have to play a critical role in the efforts to prepare NTPC for significant growth and for retaining its leader position in the power sector. This note suggests the role of PMI.

WHAT SHOULD TRAINING ACHIEVE?

The national policy and strategy for the growth of the power sector in India has undergone a change and plans for rapid growth has opened the sector for global inputs. NTPC has taken some steps to respond to the situation. The situation may however, need a more comprehensive plan of action. In this respect, some specific demands on NTPC would be:

  (i) Continuous up gradation of technology.
 (ii) Competitive market strategies and possible diversification.
(iii) System improvement relating to:
    (a) expanded use of IT;
    (b) efficiency in operating and managing tasks;
    (c) being price sensitive, cost control; and
    (d) employing process engineering in administrative and management areas.

(iv) Organisational and people related issues:
    (a) enhanced decentralisation, and review practices;
    (b) responsibility for result at all levels or management; and
    (c) increased cooperation within and between units or activity.
 (v) A change in the way of of thinking about work at all levels, i.e. change in the 'mind-set'.
(vi) Intensive efforts for human resource development. These measures are not comprehensive. They are however, essential for operating in a competitive market situation.

CONTRIBUTION OF TRAINING

Executive Development training is primarily concerned with the following:

 (i)   Knowledge generally at cognitive level;
 (ii) Developing managerial capability to analyse, to diagnose, problem solving, and understanding of managerial processes; and
(iii) Attitude change/value orientation.

The change in (ii) and (iii) aspects have to employ/initiate processes by which the training makes the effort to change. The individual has to be involved in the process of changing his ways of thinking/behaviour. Merely telling him the right and the wrong way of 'doing' and 'thinking' is not likely to bring the desired change. Hence, the effectiveness of the training in these areas depends on the competence and skill of the trainer, teaching methodology and the training material. These inputs for an effective training programme have to be ensured by PMI. In this respect an intensive programme for faculty development is necessary. This is discussed later.

THE NATURE AND TYPE OF PROGRAMMES

The experiences of the western countries which have faced the conditions mentioned in section1 for many years now, suggest the following:

The Duration of Programmes

The training is effective if it has specific and defined goals. Except programmes which primarily provide cognitive knowledge or information, the duration of contact should be long enough for a participant to experiment with what he has learnt. In this sense, goals should be specific and training methodology should provide appropriate conditions for self-experimentation. While the duration of such programmes may vary, they should range between 4–10 days and the schedules must be tight and demanding.

The Programme Coverage

The training schedule of PMI should cover the broad areas of concern as follows:

(i) *Human Processes:* to include programmes which develop deeper understanding of behaviour, ability of managers to predict individual and group behaviour, NTPC's HRD initiatives, policy, etc.

(ii) *Organisational Processes:* to include programmes to examine alternative work designs to achieve harmony between technical and social requirements of the job (socio-technical systems), corporate mission/ objective, problem solving, change and sustaining development, problem relating to efficiency, etc.

(iii) *Organisational Interventions:* to include structured intervention programmes such as TQM, Six Sigma, process engineering, etc.

(iv) *Functional Programmes:* to work with inputs in functional areas such as Finance, Personnel, R&D, etc., in consultation and collaboration with respective departments and divisions.

(v) *Special Programmes on Request:* Functional and operating departments and division may have the need for workshop/training in their areas of concern. Such programmes should be jointly organised by PMI and the concerned unit.

(vi) *Programme to Cover All Managers:* A general management programme designed to cover all levels of managerial employees. The duration of this programme could be 2–3 weeks or more, depending on the level and subject coverage.

Educational Programmes for Junior/Middle Levels

Educational programmes are needed for officers with 8–10 years service in managerial positions and those who have shown exceptional performance between 5–8 years in NTPC. These training programmes could be for a duration of 3–6 months. The difference between a training and an educational programme as pointed out in the report on policy and perspective for management Education submitted in April 2001 by the 18 member committee appointed by the ministry of HRD, Government of India, has drawn the difference between training and education as below:

The educational programme should help students to...enhance their potential to lead and contribute towards organisational effectiveness by applying in decision making relevant concepts, skills and positive human values. (p. 15)

Training invariably has a specific goal having to do with knowledge inputs or skill development. The need for a long-term educational programme is imposed by the change in the business environment. The past experience is no longer a reliable guide to decision making. The changes in the market place are qualitative and not incremental in nature. Invariably a fresh view of the problem and issues is necessary and in this respect conceptual and analytical capabilities are found to be necessary. Organisations in the west have shown that strategic decisions have to be taken at all levels of managerial hierarchy.

The Educational Inputs for Senior Levels

In the USA most organisations have found it necessary to send senior managers for educational programme of one year duration or so. The scheduling of such programmes varies from one institution to another. Large organisations such as GE, McDonalds, Motorola, etc., have set up university like institutions of their own. Many other organisations establish close relations with certain universities which collaborate with concerned institutions to develop and run such programmes for them. NTPC has made certain arrangements in this direction and there may be a need to evaluate the policy in this area. It is conceivable that PMI could develop into an institution to serve this purpose for NTPC and perhaps the power sector as a whole.

Other than Training Activities of PMI

NTPC has gained comprehensive experience in power sector. In the role of an industry- leader, PMI should contribute to the growth of the power sector at the national, the state, and the individual level. PMI has competence which would need sharpening to provide the following:

(i) consulting services;

(ii) training in technical and non-technical areas;

(iii) undertake research in specified areas that can contribute to the improvement of the sector, and provide inputs for policy making at the national and the corporate levels; and

(iv) publication of important findings in India and abroad. PMI undertakes some of these activities. It would however, be necessary to provide training to the faculty in research methods and consulting to undertake these tasks.

MANAGEMENT OF PMI

There are several aspects of the management of PMI that need attention. The task of PMI is vastly different from other units/projects of NTPC. The considerations that need special attention are discussed in the following areas:

1. Autonomy and control relating to PMI
2. Training support system
3. Supervisory responsibilities of unit level training centres
4. Linkages with training and educational institutions in India and abroad
5. The role of the Advisory Council

Autonomy and Control

(i) Autonomy in a position or a unit in an organisation is necessary for achieving the results expected of that position or the unit. Hence, the autonomy for decision making has to be linked to the nature of work and the 'independent' decision making powers necessary to achieve the results. An R&D lab would require greater autonomy than a production line which performs repetitive jobs. The supervison office discharges its responsibility for results by devising 'control measures' that give them relevant date to ensure that the concerned unit is achieving what is desired of it. In this sense 'autonomy' and 'control' systems are linked and have to be devised and exercised simultaneously.

(ii) The 'autonomy' for PMI in specific terms should be related to the task it is required to perform. In general terms, PMI management should be able to take decisions that can enhance the quality of work, i.e. inputs that contribute towards achieving the standard of quality.

Such inputs are faculty and course material development, library, and things relating to training research and consulting. PMI has to establish contacts with educational and training institutions and individuals and obtain their services. The disbursements, accounting and purchases, etc., have to be within the system, because the nature of material, equipment, etc., needed by them is specific to their activities.

The the responsible persons for supervision of PMI should discharge their responsibility by instituting practices such as the following:

(a) Detailed performance budgeting discussion and agreement. The budget should include all the activities such as schedules of work, faculty development, improvement plans, proposed research, publications, etc.

(b) Reporting of the performance on quarterly basis and review.

(c) The detailed study of the audit report.

(d) Appraisal of quality which is important. Quantitative data gives inadequate information in this respect. The supervisory unit should commission an outside agency every two years or so to assess the quality of training. This practice is followed by many teaching institution.

(iii) Keeping in view the necessity of autonomy and control, the following aspects need special consideration:

(a) Agreement on the format of the performance budget ion and review system.

(b) Independent power to undertake faculty development, sending them to seminars, conferences and training within the limits prescribed by NTPC. PMI should also be able to take up assignments from elsewhere. Guidelines should be available for ready use.

(c) Framing of rules and regulations that are suitable for a training institution especially in respect to publications, research and travel.

The Concept of a Profit Centre

In some discussions it was mentioned that PMI should be treated as a profit centre. The concept of profit centre, as it applies to a business unit, should be applied to PMI with caution. The Institute was set up to serve specified needs of NTPC and the power sector in certain essential respects. PMI should concentrate on developing high quality of training, education and research capabilities. Other organisations may also participate in these activities. PMI should endeavour to supplement its budget upto a certain percentage of expenses, say upto 25–30 per cent, but should not chase business to become self- sufficient. It has happened in many teaching institutions that the need to enhance income takes the attention of the management away from training and education to 'income generating activities'.

NTPC should undertake performance budgeting seriously but discourage earnings beyond an agreed percentage of the expenses.

The basic philosophy of a profit centre, viz., it should have control over the inputs that contribute to the results, should apply to PMI as well. Its performance should not however, be measured in terms of the revenue it generates. In fact, PMI's earning activities should be controlled so that it does not get diverted from in basic task, i.e. training, education, research and limited consulting.

These considerations would be different if PMI were to convert itself into a university type institution for power sector education. It is desirable that this question should only be taken up a later stage and in the next two years or so, PMI is provided autonomy to carry out the activities discussed in this report. PMI has to gain greater theoretical depth to convert itself into a university.

Training Support System

(i) The academic support system needs to be strengthened. For example, many teaching institutions have a programme office which handles all administrative tasks relating to programmes. The programme directors have access to the records of earlier programmes on the subject, details relating to scheduling, teaching material used in earlier programmes and other details. The programme directors can concentrate on the academic aspect of the programme. The programme office should also ensure compliance of the copyright regulations in respect to the use of the material in teaching.

(ii) The improvement made by PMI to provide data on training needs is most helpful. However, more intensive efforts are needed to encourage units/project to take the exercise seriously. The operating units should identify their problem areas and projected developments, and discuss the skills and capabilities that would be needed to realise their plans. Personal contact between PMI faculty and units in this area is essential.

Supervisory Responsibility of Unit Level Training Centres

PMI is expected to supervise the work of the 13 unit/project level training centres, and perhaps the new ones that might be set up. In fact, the training centres are within the administrative control of the Management of the unit/project. They are expected to primarily serve the unit/project concerned. In this sense it is appropriate that they are supervised by the local management. The quality of training provided by the concerned training centre depends upon the interest that the unit head takes in training. It also depends on the belief that the unit head and his managers have in training. Hence, the responsibility for proper utilisation of the centre under his/her command, scheduling, quality of manpower, etc., should be placed with the unit head concerned. However, the investment by NTPC in training should not be wasted. While PMI cannot exercise supervisory responsibility, it should undertake the following tasks relating to the centres.

(i) Conduct a six monthly discussion meeting with unit/project heads to demonstrate how training centres can be used by them to achieve and improve the capability of their units. Some case studies of units which have used training well and those that have not, may be useful.

(ii) Conduct an annual training conference of all training heads and personal people to discuss what training methodology has been employed and the results achieved. Some inputs from outside trainers in this discussion may also be useful.

(iii) Conduct training audit once a year to assess how well the training is linked with the job, the quality of training given, the collaboration with operating and training people, etc. At times, outside agencies could be used to conduct the audit. The report should be discussed individually with the concerned unit/project head.

Linkages with Training and Educational Institutions in India and Abroad

PMI faculty must establish close links with training and educational institutions. This is necessary to update training and research programme of PMI. Over time, faculty exchange programmes could also be worked out with training institutions. PMI should also be able to work-out joint training and research programmes with select institutions.

While undertaking this exercise on a planned basis, PMI should be able to assess the quality of the training and educational programmes in different institutions. They could also categorise the institutions for the quality of their programmes. This information should be available to the cell in the head office which nominates managers for external courses. PMI should also have copies of the post training reports that managers may give about the programmes attended by them. This would be useful data for PMI to assess the institutions concerned.

In order to make sure that the same officers are not sent to similar courses run by outside institutions and PMI, it is most desirable that the information about nomination is regularly sent by the unit to the concerned cell in the head office.

The Advisory Council

The meetings of the Advisory Council are infrequent. It is desirable to review the role of the Council. What should it contribute to PMI? Based on this decision, the constitution of the council can be determined. The training institutions could be handicapped by two different kinds of circumstances.

The members of the Advisory Council can comment on areas such as the following:

(i) Do PMI's activities serve industry needs?
(ii) What is the quality assessment of PMI in the market?
(iii) Suggest specific projects to assess the internal capabilities of PMI.
(iv) Are the faculty recruitments, selection and development programme adequate?
(v) Should PMI expand its activities further?
(vi) NTPC should prepare a position in these areas and pose additional questions that need consideration.

The members should have/consist of:

(a) interest in training and some experience of training.

(b) have enough interest in PMI to spend at least three-fourth days in PMI during a year to talk to the faculty and see how the work is carried out. The quality of training cannot be assessed without personal involvement.

(c) teachers drawn from reputable institutions.

The committees cannot contribute if NTPC/PMI were to take casual interest in the council. The success of such committees depends on PMI as it dose on the members.

FACULTY DEVELOPMENT

Company training centres would always need a mix of faculty drawn from within the company and direct recruitment of teachers from academic institutions. Most institutions find it difficult to attract with relevant academic achievements. The reasons for this are many but the following three need special consideration:

(i) The rules and regulations of corporate entities are too restrictive for those who pursue academic careers. They need freedom to interact with peers and more opportunities to do research and publish.

(ii) There has to be a sizeable number of faculty members with academic background to influence the activities of the training centre. A ratio of 75:25 (from the company: academic institutions) may be worth considering.

(iii) The faculty members from an academic background have very few opportunities to progress in the organisation. They should be brought in on deputation from teaching institutions or an opportunity should exist for them to be absorbed in the regular stream they so choose.

Faculty Selection

PMI has a great deal to do in this respect. Faculty selection procedures should be more rigorous than are at present. The motivation of the officer to come to PMI is important. The selection interview should include an academic from outside to offer independent views. The involvement of an outsider for at least two years or so is necessary. Once the system is established the need of an outsider may not exist.

The selection of faculty for direct employment must include an academic from outside.

Induction

The transition from manager to teacher is difficult. The officer would need institutional support to achieve this transition. PMI should hold a week long faculty induction programme for new faculty. The programme should be built around the following concerns.

Helping the new members to:

(i) Think through how to shift concerns from authority and power of the position held in the operating job to that of exercising power of expertise. A teacher gains influence by the degree of help that he provides to a participant in respect to acquiring new knowledge, confidence in use of knowledge and confidence in himself.

(ii) Clarify in their own mind the new demands that the new role would make upon them.

(iii) Think about the teaching technology that would make them more effective as teachers.

(iv) Learn from cases and live experiences of others in respect to change in their role.

(v) Why collaborating with other faculty members is necessary for their own effectiveness as a teacher.

(vi) Acquire the abilities required to be a good researcher.

These are not all inclusive areas. They are however, necessary to help new persons adjust to the mainly unfamiliar requirements of the new role at PMI.

The experiences that managers bring to PMI in faculty position are invaluable. The new position should, however, enable them to reassess the experience and derive relevant learnings from it. As a teacher the experience has to be conceptualised. This is necessary because experience per se cannot be taught. The faculty development programme should emphasise these aspects of broadening their perspective, understanding their own and other people's experiences and develop the capacity to articulate/communicate this knowledge.

Developing Personal Competence

The kind of exposures that help a teacher refine the many aspects of the academic work are the following:

(i) Planned reading
(ii) Contact with a variety of oraganisations
(iii) Research
(iv) Giving seminars on subjects in which the faculty member specialises.
(v) Attending short programmes in institutions that are known for their academic contribution.

PMI should structure exposure of the kind needed for each member of the faculty. In addition, the activities should include the following:

(i) At least one-fourth of the time each member should spend in research, collection of teaching material and specific field assignments.
(ii) Two seminars to be given every year by each faculty which should be open to officers of NTPC and select individuals who are associated with PMI.
(iii) Undertake specific assignments to study developments in Power and other related sectors in India and abroad.
(iv) Publish papers in recognised/referred journals.

PMI should institute awards for recognition of faculty contribution in non-teaching activities. In addition, PMI may consider 2–3 best teacher awards.

SPECIFIC CONTRIBUTIONS TO NTPC AND POWER SECTOR

PMI should contribute to NTPC's growth in two ways:

(i) Undertaking research and consulting work for the corporation and other organisations in power sector. The experience and knowledge gained in this kind of work would help individuals in their teaching. This effort could also enhance the revenue of PMI. The individuals engaged in these activities would also gain as managers when they return to an operating job after their tenure in PMI.
(ii) PMI should arrange atleast four 2–3 hour lecture discussion sessions for top and senior management on new developments in knowledge,

ideas and implications of the emerging scenario, management thought, and new experiments and subjects of concern to corporate decision makers. These seminars may be conducted by invited speakers, members of the top management, academicians, government functionaries, foreign visitors and the like.

FUTURE DIRECTION FOR GROWTH

The committee on policy perspectives for Management Education appointed by Government of India has recommended that educational programmes with sectoral bias would be necessary as the economic/ business activity grows. It is also visualised that some of the existing training institutions with infrastructure for educational programmes, faculty and support system could develop such programmes. Some of these institutions could be granted the status of a 'deemed university' with power to give academic degrees. NTPC may wish to consider whether PMI should develop in this direction over a period of 3–5 years.

References

1. http://books.google.co.in/books?id=2vkxCWv3ChcC&printsec=frontcover &dq=lewis+carroll+through+the+looking+glass+and+what+alice+found +there&hl=en&sa=X&ei=OyCwUt2mN8aJrQex4YCoDA&ved=0CC8Q6A EwAA#v=onepage&q=lewis%20carroll%20through%20the%20looking%20 glass%20and%20what%20alice%20found%20there&f=false

2. Arie De Geus, *The Living Company*, Nicholas Brealey, London, 1997.

3. T.V. Rao, *The HRD Missionary*, New Delhi, Oxford & IBH Publishing Co. Pvt. Ltd., April 1991.

4. *Business Today* issue September 14, 2003 (reference article from page No. 68).

5. Jim Collins, *Good to Great*, Harper Collins, USA, 2001.

6. John Maxwell, *Developing the Leaders Around You,* Thomas Nelson, USA, 1995.

7. Daniel Goleman, in his article 'Leadership that Gets Results', *Harvard Business Review*, March-April 2000.

8. Kalam, A.P.J. Abdul, *India 2020*, Penguin Books (Private) India Ltd., New Delhi, 1998.

9. Marcus Buckingham and Curt Coffman, *First, Break All the Rules*, Pocket Books, 2005.

10. Sumantra Ghoshal et al., *Managing Radical Change*, Penguin Books India, 9 April 2002.

11. Marc Effron and Miriam Ort, *One Page Talent Management: Eliminating Complexity, Adding Value,* The Harward Business Press Publishing, May 2010.